The Mystery of the Last Supper

Apparent inconsistencies in the gospel accounts of Jesus' final week have puzzled Bible scholars for centuries. Matthew, Mark and Luke clearly state that the last supper was a Passover meal, whereas John asserts that it occurred before the festival. The gospel narratives also do not seem to allow enough time for all the events recorded between the last supper and the crucifixion, whilst indicating that Wednesday was a 'missing day' on which Jesus did nothing. Colin Humphreys presents a compelling fresh account of how these inconsistencies can be explained, drawing on evidence from the Dead Sea Scrolls and Egyptian texts and using astronomy to reconstruct ancient calendars. In doing so, Humphreys proposes a new theory – that the last supper took place on a Wednesday, rather than Thursday as traditionally believed – and successfully unifies the supposedly contradictory gospel stories.

Sir Colin J. Humphreys is Professor and Director of Research at the Department of Materials Science and Metallurgy at the University of Cambridge. He is the author of *The Miracles of Exodus* (2003).

The Mystery of the Last Supper

Reconstructing the Final Days of Jesus

Colin J. Humphreys

CAMBRIDGE UNIVERSITY PRESS
Cambridge, New York, Melbourne, Madrid, Cape Town,
Singapore, São Paulo, Delhi, Tokyo, Mexico City

Cambridge University Press
The Edinburgh Building, Cambridge CB2 8RU, UK

Published in the United States of America by Cambridge University Press,
New York

www.cambridge.org
Information on this title: www.cambridge.org/9780521517553

First published 2011
Reprinted 2011

A catalogue record for this publication is available from the British Library

ISBN 978-0-521-51755-3 Hardback
ISBN 978-0-521-73200-0 Paperback

Contents

Illustrations

Foreword

For the past few years I have been following with keen interest and excitement the researches of Colin Humphreys into the last supper narratives in the gospels. Previously he had investigated the exodus of the Israelites from Egypt and the ten unusual happenings recorded as accompanying that event. He also offered a new identification of the 'star of Bethlehem' as a comet that appeared in 5 BC. Finally, he made a fresh attempt to date the crucifixion of Jesus by using astronomical evidence for determining the likely year and also by proposing that Peter's reference in his Pentecost speech to the moon being turned to blood (Acts 2:20) was to a lunar eclipse in AD 33 at which the moon would indeed have had a blood-red appearance.

This new book returns to this last theme and offers a detailed study of the associated puzzles caused by the apparent discrepancy between the gospel of John and the other three gospels on the date of the last supper of Jesus. Colin's solution is a new version of the old theory that different Jewish groups may have used different calendrical systems, together with a proposal that Jesus held his meal not on the Thursday immediately preceding his crucifixion on the Friday but on the Wednesday evening, a view that allows a more adequate period of time for all the recorded events that have to be fitted in between the meal and the crucifixion.

The result is what is sometimes called a *tour de force*, an unusually capable feat of bringing together a vast amount of detailed evidence and showing how there is one complex solution that can account for it all. (Sometimes I have the feeling that people use this phrase when they cannot help admiring the skill and knowledge displayed in the operation but nevertheless find the hypothesis to be 'highly ingenious but ultimately not successful'. That negative implication should not be read into my remarks here.)

The breadth and depth of learning here is quite remarkable in that the author is Professor of Materials Science in Cambridge, and he studies biblical history as a leisure sideline, showing wide-ranging competence in astronomy (aided here by a professional), ancient calendrical studies and biblical scholarship. But difficult subject-matter is treated in a simple and readable manner so that the non-expert can easily follow the argument. The author's enthusiasm carries the reader along almost effortlessly. Frequent summaries help to chart the path that is being followed.

Many people (such as some members of the Jesus Seminar in North America) still hold that the gospel accounts of the life and death of Jesus are implausible and unhistorical to various degrees. But current biblical scholarship is producing a series of lengthy, learned works by professionals who are united in holding that much of the story can be accorded a much higher level of historical reliability when assessed by the appropriate methods. I need only mention the monographs produced by Richard Bauckham, James Dunn, Martin Hengel (and his collaborators), Craig Keener, John P. Meier and Tom Wright, and the symposia edited by Darrell Bock and Robert Webb and by Stanley Porter and Tom Holmen. These are works of technical scholarship each running to very many pages and beyond the reach of the public generally. By contrast Colin Humphreys is writing in much shorter compass and with great clarity for a wider audience.

A very considerable part of what he says in this book would certainly command wide if not total assent among scholars. His demonstration that the last supper and crucifixion must be dated to either AD 30 or AD 33 confirms what experts generally hold, and his preference for the latter date is powerfully argued. His view that there were different calendars side by side at the time of Jesus is not new but is a carefully argued variant based on a new evaluation of the evidence. His redating of the last supper to a Wednesday shows that he is not afraid to challenge traditional opinions that are of questionable validity.

Here, then, is a book that offers a new historical reconstruction of the evidence that must be taken very seriously indeed, and biblical scholars must not assume that because it is written at a more popular level it can be ignored. If I hesitate to say that I agree with every detail of the argument or hold back from saying 'there is no doubt that Colin has solved all the problems', that probably reflects normal scholarly caution.

What if Colin's proposals could be shown to be faulty? Would that verdict force us to doubt the historicity of the last supper? By no means! Scholarship often proceeds by producing fresh hypotheses that may turn out to be falsifiable in whole or in part but act as invitations to come up with something better. This book belongs in that category of bold, imaginative and fresh interpretations of the evidence that take us significantly forward, and I warmly commend it.

I. Howard Marshall
Emeritus Professor of New Testament,
University of Aberdeen

Acknowledgements

It is a pleasure to acknowledge the many people with a wide range of expertise who have helped me. This book is evidence based, and I am indebted to the eminent barrister Andrew Bartlett QC, who used his skills in assessing and analysing evidence to make detailed comments on draft book chapters.

Many leading biblical scholars have read draft chapters and helped me greatly. They include Markus Bockmuehl, Professor of Biblical and Early Christian Studies, University of Oxford; Robert Gordon, Regius Professor of Hebrew, University of Cambridge; Revd Dr David Instone-Brewer, Senior Research Fellow in Rabbinics and the New Testament, Tyndale House, Cambridge; Revd Dr Ernest Lucas, Vice-Principal and Tutor in Biblical Studies, Bristol Baptist College; I. Howard Marshall, Emeritus Professor of New Testament, University of Aberdeen; Alan Millard, Emeritus Professor of Hebrew and Ancient Semitic Languages, University of Liverpool; the late Revd Canon John Sweet, formerly Chaplain and Dean of Chapel, Selwyn College, Cambridge; Dr Peter Williams, Warden, Tyndale House, Cambridge.

Dr Graeme Waddington, an Oxford astrophysicist, has provided invaluable help in using his expert skills in astronomy to provide advice, reconstruct ancient calendars and draw many of the figures in this book. It is a pleasure to thank the biblical chronologist, the late Ormond Edwards of Aberdeen; John Ray, Professor of Egyptology, University of Cambridge; Frederick Van Fleteren, Professor of Philosophy at LaSalle University, Philadelphia, for their expertise and insights.

Anthony Kelly, Emeritus Professor and Distinguished Research Fellow, University of Cambridge, has been a great encouragement and support throughout the writing of this book. Adi Popescu, Fitzwilliam Museum, Cambridge, has provided help in finding ancient coins, which Michael Jones photographed. Matthew Baalham, Tyndale

House, Cambridge, has helped in drawing maps. Finally I would like to thank my two daughters, Kate and Liz, for reading chapters and making many helpful suggestions and my wife Sarah for her support throughout.

The people I have acknowledged above may well not agree with all the contents (and some have probably been too polite to say!). I am extremely grateful to all of them for the time and effort they have spent in helping me to write this book.

1 Four mysteries of the last week of Jesus

On a faraway spring morning, in a remote corner of the Roman empire, soldiers crucified a Galilean Jew known as Jesus of Nazareth. No doubt the ruling authorities believed he would be quickly forgotten, a mere blip in history, one of many hundreds they had crucified. Yet, almost two thousand years later, Jesus is widely recognised as one of the most important persons who has ever lived; many would say *the* most important person.

Arguably the week in which Jesus died is the most momentous week in the history of the world. Probably more has been written about this week ('Passion Week' or 'Holy Week') than about any other week in history. There are probably more paintings of the crucifixion than of any other historical event (for example, see fig. 1.1). However, there is a problem. Our main sources of information about the last week of Jesus, the four gospels, appear to contradict each other. The purpose of this book is to present new information that reveals that the four gospels in fact give a remarkably coherent account of the last days of Jesus. This enables us to reconstruct these days in detail. The new information presented in this book also throws new light upon our understanding of the words and actions of Jesus.

Richard Dawkins, the former Professor for the Public Understanding of Science at Oxford University, writes: 'Although Jesus probably existed, reputable biblical scholars do not in general regard the New Testament (and obviously not the Old Testament) as a reliable record of what actually happened in history ... The only difference between *The Da Vinci Code* and the gospels is that the gospels are ancient fiction while *The Da Vinci Code* is modern fiction ... What I, as a scientist, believe (for example, evolution) I believe not because of reading a holy book but because I have studied

Fig. 1.1 The Three Crosses. Etching by Rembrandt in 1653. The Bible was Rembrandt's most important source of inspiration.

the evidence.'[1] As this book considers the evidence, we will see if it is really true that 'the only difference between *The Da Vinci Code* and the gospels is that the gospels are ancient fiction while *The Da Vinci Code* is modern fiction'.

Let me introduce myself. I am both a scientist and someone who has studied the Bible. In 2009, I gave an invited talk at a major international biblical conference (the Society of Biblical Literature annual meeting in New Orleans), and ten invited talks at international scientific conferences, in locations ranging from Japan to India. I have published in leading biblical journals, such as *Vetus Testamentum*, and leading scientific journals, such as *Nature*. Like Dawkins, I believe in the importance of evidence and this book is evidence-based. I have used a combination of historical and scientific reasoning to see what can be deduced about the last supper and the last days of Jesus by taking into account all the available evidence, not only from the New Testament, but also from the Old Testament, the Dead Sea Scrolls, ancient Egyptian, Babylonian, Roman and Jewish texts and the use of astronomy to reconstruct Jewish calendars. I have consulted widely with leading biblical scholars and an eminent London barrister, who is skilled in assessing evidence.

As Dawkins says, many reputable biblical scholars do not regard the New Testament as a reliable record of what really happened. A major reason is the apparent discrepancies in the gospels concerning the last days of Jesus. If the gospels cannot agree on key events such as the date of the crucifixion and the date and nature of the last supper, then why should we trust them at all? However, if it can be shown that the gospels do, in fact, agree on these issues, this removes an important basis for the scepticism of many scholars.

I am writing this book for both the general public and biblical scholars. The main text is aimed at the general public and assumes no specialist knowledge. The 'Notes' section at the end of the book, in which I dig more deeply into difficult or contentious issues and where I give full references, will be relevant to biblical scholars and theologians. I conclude each chapter with a summary section and the main conclusions of the book are brought together in Chapter 13.

If you read the accounts of the last days of Jesus in the four gospels, you will find that there are a number of places where they appear to contradict each other. For example, Matthew, Mark and Luke claim that the last supper Jesus held with his disciples was a Passover meal, whereas John states that the last supper, and also the trials of Jesus and his crucifixion, all took place *before* the Passover meal. It is because of problems such as this that many biblical scholars believe that the four gospels are full of contradictions and discrepancies.

Could it be, however, that the gospel accounts of the last days of Jesus are *not* filled with discrepancies, but that *we* are failing to understand the gospel writings because of *our* lack of knowledge of life in Israel in the first century AD? Is it *our* ignorance that is preventing us from interpreting some key verses in the gospels in the way the writers intended? These apparent discrepancies lead to some major mysteries surrounding what really happened to Jesus in the days before his crucifixion that have never been solved. So what are these mysteries? Let me outline four of them.

1 The lost day of Jesus

There can be no doubt that the last days of Jesus were of supreme importance to the gospel writers.

Matthew devotes seven chapters (21 to 27; about 25 per cent of his gospel) to describing what Jesus did and said in the week leading to his crucifixion. The same week constitutes over 30 per cent of Mark's gospel, about 20 per cent of Luke and almost 40 per cent of John. Despite this mass of information, when biblical scholars try to reconstruct what happened on each day of this week, many find there is a 'missing day' when nothing seems to have happened at all. This is the Wednesday before the Friday crucifixion. For example, the widely used New International Version (NIV) Study Bible analyses the events on each day of Jesus' last week and writes: 'Day of rest: Wednesday: Not mentioned in the Gospels.'[2]

This is curious. The Jewish day of rest was on the Sabbath, which ran from Friday evening to Saturday evening. Would Jesus really have taken an *additional* day of rest shortly before he died? It is clear from the gospels that he was very busy in the last week before his crucifixion. Even if Jesus had spent all day in prayer on this day, surely at least one of the gospels would have mentioned it. Why then a 'missing day'? So this is the first mystery of the last week of Jesus: what did Jesus do, or what happened to him, on 'lost Wednesday'?

2 The problem of the last supper

The second mystery is the relation between the last supper and the Jewish Passover. The last supper is one of the most famous meals in history. Every week millions of Christians throughout the world commemorate it, calling this special occasion the Lord's Supper, the Mass, the Eucharist, the Breaking of Bread or Holy Communion.

The last supper is described in all four gospels, and the meal plus the words of Jesus at the end occupy as many as 226 gospel verses. Yet there is a problem. Matthew, Mark and Luke explicitly state that the last supper was a Passover meal. On the other hand, the gospel of John equally clearly says that the last supper was held *before* the Passover meal. John Meier, who is the author of the major historical study of the life of Jesus in recent times, writes: 'The Synoptics [Matthew, Mark and Luke] and John are in direct disagreement over the nature of the last supper as a Passover meal and over the date of Jesus' death.'[3] The Passover meal was, and still is, easily the most important meal in the year for Jewish people. It is the occasion which commemorates the exodus of the Israelite slaves from Egypt and the birth of Israel as a nation. At this meal, parts of the book of Exodus are read and the story of the original Passover is recounted and celebrated. For these reasons the Passover meal is much more important for Jews than Christmas dinner is for most Christians. Jewish people would *never* be mistaken about whether a meal was a Passover meal or not.

The first Christians probably started to celebrate the last supper shortly after Jesus died. For example, the apostle Paul, writing in about AD 55 to the church at Corinth, refers to their *existing* commemoration of the last supper and reminds them how it should be celebrated (1 Corinthians 11:17–34). Most scholars believe the gospels were written in their final form in the period AD 60 to AD 100, but from earlier sources. The gospel writers should have known whether the last supper was commemorating a Passover meal. So why do Matthew, Mark, Luke and John apparently disagree? Although the gospels were probably written in their final form after AD 60, we should not forget the words at the start of Luke's gospel: 'Many have undertaken to draw up an account of the things that have been fulfilled among us, just as they were handed down to us by those who from the first were eye-witnesses and servants of the word' (Luke 1:1). Luke is claiming *eye-witness sources*. Eye-witnesses would have known whether the last supper was a Passover meal or not.

The problem of the nature of the last supper has been well known to scholars for centuries. There has been no agreement, so today half of the world's churches use unleavened bread in their commemoration of the last supper, believing it to have been a Passover meal in which unleavened bread was used (Exodus 12:8), whereas the other half use leavened bread because they believe the last supper was held before the

Passover meal. So the second mystery of the last week of Jesus is whether the last supper was a Passover meal or not.

3 No time for the trials of Jesus

The third mystery of the last week of Jesus is that it seems there was not enough time for the trials and all the other events the gospels record between the arrest of Jesus and his crucifixion. The gospel writers differ in the events they record as happening between the last supper and the crucifixion. I have listed them in the table in the *exact* order they occur in each gospel.

Events between the last supper and the crucifixion in the order recorded in each gospel

Matthew	Mark	Luke	John
Last supper	Last supper	Last supper	Last supper
Mount of Olives	Mount of Olives	Mount of Olives	Olive grove
Gethsemane	Gethsemane		
Jesus prayed	Jesus prayed	Jesus prayed	
Disciples fell asleep	Disciples fell asleep	Disciples fell asleep	
Jesus prayed	Jesus prayed		
Disciples fell asleep	Disciples fell asleep		
Jesus prayed	Jesus prayed		
Disciples fell asleep	Disciples fell asleep		
Jesus arrested	Jesus arrested	Jesus arrested	Jesus arrested
			Taken to Annas
			Peter's first denial
			Questioned by Annas
Taken to Caiaphas	Taken to High Priest	Taken to High Priest	Taken to Caiaphas
		Peter denies 3 times	Peter denies twice more
		Cock crows	Cock crows

Trial before Sanhedrin	Trial before Sanhedrin	Trial before Sanhedrin	
Peter denies 3 times	Peter denies 3 times		
Cock crows	Cock crows		
Jesus passed to the guards	Jesus passed to the guards		
Sanhedrin meet	Sanhedrin meet		
Trial before Pilate	Trial before Pilate	Trial before Pilate	Trial before Pilate
		Trial before Herod	
		Trial before Pilate	
Release of Barabbas	Release of Barabbas	Release of Barabbas	Release of Barabbas
Jesus flogged	Jesus flogged		Jesus flogged
Soldiers mock Jesus	Soldiers mock Jesus		Soldiers mock Jesus
			Condemned by Pilate
Simon carries cross	Simon carries cross	Simon carries cross	
Crucifixion	Crucifixion	Crucifixion	Crucifixion

Why do the gospel accounts of the events between the last supper and the crucifixion differ? If you read different newspaper accounts of the same event, for example the tragic September 11, 2001 terrorist attacks in the USA, what you find is that different newspapers tell the same overall story but they give different details. For example, one paper may tell how a New York fireman made a brave rescue from the World Trade Center buildings while another paper may omit this story but tell us the height of the buildings. In order to reconstruct the most complete picture of what happened on September 11, it is necessary to put all the reports together. Similarly, in order to reconstruct what happened in the life of Jesus, we need to put together the information in the different gospels. The four gospels give us four portraits of Jesus. Like four artists painting the same scene, but each from a different position and perspective, each gospel gives us a different view of the life of Jesus.

The table on pages 6–7 shows that the gospels of Matthew and Mark record very similar events. Many scholars believe that Mark is the earliest gospel and that Matthew used Mark as a source (some scholars believe the reverse). Luke's gospel omits some events in Matthew and Mark, and adds some new information. However, Matthew, Mark and Luke are broadly similar and they are often called the synoptic gospels.[4] John's gospel, on the other hand, was probably written last and often differs from the synoptics. He leaves out a great deal of the information in the synoptics, and introduces a significant amount of new material. There is an immediacy in the writings of the synoptic gospels, whereas John is more reflective and theological. However, just because John's gospel is more theological than the synoptics, this does not mean that it is less historically factual.

What I find remarkable about the list of events given in the table is the high measure of agreement between the gospels in the overall order of events, even though different gospels omit different events. The apparent exception to this is Peter's three denials and the associated cock crows (I will return to this in Chapter 12). This means either that each gospel writer must have taken considerable care to get the order of events right, or that each 'inherited' an already well-established order of events which was passed down to him. Either way, the agreement of the four gospels on the order of the events between the last supper and the crucifixion is impressive.

What about apparent minor contradictions in the table? For example, after the last supper, Matthew and Mark describe Jesus' going to the Mount of Olives and then to a place called Gethsemane, but John has Jesus going to an olive grove. These apparent contradictions disappear if you know Aramaic, since the word *Gethsemane* is Aramaic for 'oil press', a place for squeezing the oil from olives. Putting information from the four gospels together, we can deduce that, after the last supper, Jesus and his disciples went to the Mount of Olives (Matthew, Mark and Luke), so-called because of the many olive trees growing on this mountain, as they still do today, and they went to an olive grove there (John), where there was a place for squeezing the oil from the olives (the Gethsemane of Matthew and Mark). So there is no contradiction; rather the gospels are telling us complementary information, which when put together enables us to build up a more complete picture of where Jesus and his disciples went after the last supper.

If we apply the same reasoning and put together all the events listed in the gospels as occurring between the last supper and the crucifixion, then we obtain the following list.

Last supper
Mount of Olives
Gethsemane
Jesus prayed
Disciples fell asleep
Jesus prayed again
Disciples fell asleep again
Jesus prayed a third time
Disciples fell asleep a third time
Jesus arrested
Taken to Annas
Peter's first denial and first cock crow
Interrogation by Annas
Taken to Caiaphas
Peter's second and third denials
Cock crows again
Trial before the Sanhedrin
Jesus handed over to the guards
Jesus before the Sanhedrin again
Trial of Jesus before Pilate
Trial before Herod
Trial before Pilate again
Pilate releases Barabbas
Jesus is flogged
Soldiers mock Jesus
Condemned by Pilate
Simon carries Jesus' cross
Crucifixion of Jesus

Here comes the problem. Biblical scholars and Christians throughout the world believe that the last supper started after sunset on Thursday night and that the crucifixion of Jesus happened the following morning, Friday, at about 9 a.m. (the third hour, Mark 15:25, counting from sunrise). The trials of Jesus before the Sanhedrin,[5] Pilate and Herod all occurred in different parts of Jerusalem. Scholars have literally rushed around Jerusalem with a stop-watch to see how all the events recorded in the gospels could have fitted between Thursday night and Friday morning. Most conclude that it is impossible.

4 The legality of the trials

In order to try to fit in all the events between the last supper on Thursday evening/night and the crucifixion at about 9 a.m. the following morning, scholars are agreed that the main trial of Jesus before the Sanhedrin must have been at night. However, the Jewish rules regarding trials for capital cases do not allow this. They are stated in the Mishnah (a compendium containing regulations attributed to about 150 rabbis who lived from about 50 BC to about AD 200): 'In capital cases they hold the trial during the daytime and the verdict must also be reached during the daytime ... In capital cases a verdict of acquittal may be reached the same day, but a verdict of conviction not until the following day' (*Mishnah Sanhedrin* 4.1).

If these legal rules, written down in about 200 AD but based on earlier practice, applied at the time of the trials of Jesus, then they present a major challenge to the conventional understanding of these trials. As Geza Vermes, Professor Emeritus at Oxford University, states: 'It is hard to imagine in a Jewish setting of the first century AD that a capital case would be tried at night.'[6]

So we have four major problems with the last days of Jesus. First, there is lost Wednesday: a day on which nothing seems to have happened. Second, there is the Passover puzzle: was the last supper a Passover meal or not? Third, there is not enough time between a Thursday evening last supper and the crucifixion at 9 a.m. on Friday to fit in all the events described in the gospels. Fourth, the trials would seem blatantly to flout Jewish legal proceedings, yet although the gospels claim that there were many false witnesses at the trials, not one of the gospels claims that the trials were illegal. The gospels implicitly accept the legality of the trials.

Some readers may feel that knowing the timing of events in the last days of Jesus is unimportant. However, the chronology of the last week of Jesus provides the historical framework of the most momentous week in the history of the world. To understand this week fully we have to get the chronology right. The correct chronology provides key new insights into understanding the words and actions of Jesus in his last week. Chronology is based on calendars, and ancient calendars are based upon astronomy. As we will see, knowledge of ancient calendars turns out to be critical in reconstructing the events of Jesus' last days.

MY APPROACH TO INTERPRETING THE GOSPELS

A large amount has been written about the date, authorship and interpretation of the gospels. The key questions to ask when reading the gospels (or indeed any literature) concern what the writer intended and what his (or her) original audience would have understood him to mean. Often the answer is obvious, but sometimes we can only really understand what the writer meant if we know something about how people lived at the time he was writing. For example, as we saw a few pages ago, it is helpful to know that *Gethsemane* was Aramaic for oil press when reading the gospel accounts of where Jesus went after the last supper.

In this book I will sometimes use the term 'natural interpretation'. What I mean by these words is the interpretation of a biblical text which would have been the most obvious interpretation when the text was written. The natural interpretation of a text is often the same today as it was two thousand years ago, but this is not always the case, of course, because the meaning of words and the background knowledge available to readers can change over time. I believe we should always seek the natural interpretation of the gospels, because it seems reasonable to believe that the writers wanted to communicate as clearly as possible the events in the life of Jesus to their original audience.

My approach to solving the problems addressed in this book has three key elements. The first is that I have tried to take into account all the available evidence. Advances in understanding often result from attention paid to apparently inconsistent evidence. I have therefore treated the contents of the four gospels as data to be taken into account if possible, rather than dismissed on the ground of apparent inconsistency.

The second element is a multidisciplinary approach. This is often the only way of solving complicated problems. For example, the police investigation of a complex murder mystery may require DNA testing and the electron microscopy of hair samples as well as the interrogation of suspects. As we will see, solving the problems of the last days of Jesus involves not only a detailed scrutiny of the gospels but also knowledge of the Old Testament. Perhaps surprisingly, information from ancient Egypt and Babylon and some basic knowledge of astronomy are also needed. Less surprisingly, we need to be familiar with Jewish and Roman writings around the time of Christ. It is only by having a multidisciplinary approach, and synthesising information from these various sources, that we can determine what really happened two thousand years ago in the momentous last week of Jesus.

The third element is that I have used astronomical knowledge to reconstruct ancient calendars. This has been facilitated by the availability of computing power that would have been unthinkable only a few years ago.

A ROAD MAP OF THIS BOOK

As mentioned earlier, this book assumes no specialist knowledge of Jesus or the Bible. We start by building the historical framework surrounding the death of Jesus. Chapter 2 shows that from Roman and Jewish sources we can deduce, beyond reasonable doubt, that Jesus died in the period AD 26–36. We can also show from the gospels that Jesus died on a Friday. The problem of the date and nature of the last supper is investigated in Chapter 3, and we show that Jesus must have died in the Jewish month of Nisan (which corresponds to March/April), on either Nisan 14 or 15. Chapter 4 shows that we can reconstruct the official Jewish calendar at the time of Christ, using modern astronomical calculations.

In Chapter 5, I use this reconstructed Jewish calendar plus biblical information to determine the most probable date of the crucifixion. An entirely different approach is used in Chapter 6, resulting in the same date of the crucifixion, based upon a lunar eclipse on the evening of the crucifixion that is suggested in the New Testament and other ancient documents.

In Chapter 7, I ask whether Jesus could have used the solar calendar of the Qumran community, known from the Dead Sea Scrolls, to celebrate his last supper as a Passover meal, as recently suggested by the Pope. Chapter 8 investigates whether ancient Egypt may hold key clues for solving the problem of the last supper. Chapter 9 discovers a lost calendar of ancient Israel, used in the earlier biblical period. In Chapter 10 I show that this early calendar, which I call the pre-exilic calendar, persisted down to the first century AD and that it was used in Israel at the time of Jesus by several different groups. Chapter 11 discovers 'hidden clues' in the gospels which explain why the account of the last supper as a Passover meal in the synoptic gospels is different from that in John and I determine the day and date of the last supper: a day that many will find surprising. A detailed analysis of the timing of all the events recorded in the gospels between the last supper and the crucifixion is given in Chapter 12. Finally, Chapter 13 brings together all the main conclusions of this book. Some readers may prefer to read at an early stage the new analysis of the gospel accounts of the last days of Jesus given in Chapter 12.

As we have seen, the gospel writers regarded the last week of Jesus as supremely important and they devoted over one thousand verses to describing it. We are about to embark on a real-life detective story to reconstruct the last days of Jesus. In the next chapter we will discover the first key clues.

2 Dating the crucifixion – the first clues

> Christ had been executed in Tiberius' reign by the Governor of Judea, Pontius Pilate.
>
> (Tacitus, *Annals* 15.44)

A small book my father gave to my younger daughter for her tenth birthday remains etched in my memory, and it unintentionally initiated my quest to discover the truth about the momentous last week of Jesus. The book was called *Great Men of History*. Why have I never forgotten this book? Because on the first page it listed every person described in the book and it gave their dates of birth and death, but against Jesus it had: 'Born 4 BC? Died AD 30?' Every other person listed on the front page – Julius Caesar, Alexander the Great, Christopher Columbus, and so on – was given a definite date of birth and death. Jesus was the only person whose dates of birth and of death were followed by question marks.

How strange, I thought. Jesus made a huge mark upon history, much greater than Julius Caesar, Alexander the Great or any of the other 'historical greats' listed. Yet the author of the book did not know the years in which Jesus was born and died. In fact historians and biblical scholars today are still uncertain about these dates. For example, the New International Version (NIV) Study Bible states regarding the life of Christ: 'Exact dates, even year dates, are generally unknown.'[1] The New Testament theologian Josef Blinzler investigated the published statements of about a hundred biblical scholars on the year of Jesus' death: he found that the years AD 26, 27, 28, 29, 30, 31, 32, 33, 34 and 36 had all been suggested. The most popular dates were AD 29 (thirteen scholars), AD 30 (fifty-three scholars) and AD 33 (twenty-four scholars).[2]

There have been many people who have risen to fame from humble origins whose dates of birth are obscure. But not to know the year even of Jesus' death struck me as curious. It somehow left him floating nebulously in the sea of time instead of being anchored in history. However, is it really impossible to know when Jesus died? In this chapter we are going to make a start on sifting through the clues given in the gospels and in other ancient writings to see if we can determine precisely the date of Jesus' death. In addition, it turns out that this date, the date of the crucifixion, is a key date we need to know if we are to reconstruct what happened in the last days of Jesus.

The solution of any longstanding puzzle, whether in history, crime or science, requires the use of both major and minor clues. If only the major clues were needed then the problem would have been solved long ago. The major clues provide the framework for the solution, but it is the detail, the minor clues, that is the key to solving longstanding problems. So it is with reconstructing the date of the crucifixion. In this chapter we are going to find the major clues that provide the historical framework for dating the crucifixion. The first major clue gives us the rough time period for Jesus' death.

THE CLUE OF TIBERIUS

Why is it that scholars agree when Julius Caesar died but not when Jesus Christ died? The main reason is that Julius Caesar was an important official, a supreme Roman ruler, so the precise date of his death was recorded in official papers at the time and by Roman historians shortly afterwards. We know from these records that Julius Caesar died on March 15, 44 BC. Jesus, on the other hand, was poor and held no high position in society. In addition, both Roman and Jewish officials regarded him as a criminal. So no one bothered to record the date of Jesus' death. However, if we can link his death with the lives of important officials whose dates are known, we may be able to estimate the broad time period within which the crucifixion took place. As we will see, the Roman emperor Tiberius provides us with the first key clue for estimating when Jesus died.

A non-Christian source, the Roman historian Tacitus, who lived between about AD 55 and AD 120, gives us an important piece of information which links Christ with Tiberius. Tacitus writes in *Annals*: 'Christ had been executed in Tiberius' reign by the Governor of Judea, Pontius Pilate.' We therefore know from Tacitus that Jesus died in the reign of Tiberius, and, since Tiberius was a Roman emperor, his dates of birth and death were recorded. The Roman writer Suetonius wrote a biography of Tiberius in which he spells out the dates of the major events in his life. The Roman historian Dio Cassius in *Roman History* also gives the same dates, and we can have confidence in them. These historians dated events in the standard Roman way, which was either to write that an event happened 'in the twentieth year of Tiberius' reign', for example, or to name the Roman consul who was in office at the time. Since the consul changed every year, this gave the precise year in which the event occurred.

One of the ways the Romans measured lengths of time was to count years from the foundation of the city of Rome (they called their dating system *ab urbe condita*, AUC for short, which is Latin for 'from the foundation of the city'). Since the year AUC 754 in this Roman calendar corresponds to AD 1 in our calendar, it is easy to transfer dates from one calendar to the other.

UNDERSTANDING ANCIENT CALENDARS

According to both Suetonius and Dio Cassius, Tiberius died on March 16, AD 37. You will find this same date in any school history book, or encyclopaedia, or on the web. However, crucially, these sources usually fail to mention which calendar they are using when they give the date Tiberius died. Yet if we do not know the calendar that is being used, individual dates are meaningless. Understanding calendars turns out to be so important in reconstructing the last week of Jesus that we need to be sure we understand what we mean when we say that Tiberius died on March 16, AD 37.

As is well known, AD stands for *Anno Domini*, which is Latin for 'in the year of the Lord', and BC stands for 'before Christ', so when we use the BC/AD system of dating we are counting years from the birth of

Christ. The AD system was proposed by the Roman scholar and monk Dionysius Exiguus. Whether or not Dionysius was right about the actual date of the birth of Christ (he was probably wrong) does not matter in terms of the mathematics of calendars, because Dionysius *defined* the year AD 1 to be equal to AUC 754, and this definition has been used ever since, up to the present. This means that we can be confident in transferring years from the AUC system used by the ancient Romans to the BC/AD system we use today.

We now understand what is meant when we say that Tiberius died in the year AD 37. What do we mean when we say he died on March 16? Which calendar are we using when we say this? The calendar we use today is called the Gregorian calendar, after Pope Gregory XIII, who, in AD 1582, modified the existing (Julian) calendar, because it was getting out of synchrony with the true solar year, and therefore getting out of step with the seasons. In fact, in AD 1582, the Julian calendar was ten days out of line with the solar year, and this discrepancy was eliminated by jumping straight from October 4 to 15. The ten days were removed from the calendar while still keeping the correct sequence of days of the week (Monday, Tuesday, Wednesday, and so on). Apart from this shift of dates, the Gregorian calendar differs only slightly from the Julian calendar, in the way it calculates leap years.

The Julian calendar was introduced in 45 BC by Julius Caesar, hence its name. When Julius Caesar became the ruler of Rome in 48 BC, the existing lunar calendar used by the Romans was in a state of confusion because it was three months out of step with the seasons (today this would be like celebrating Easter in June). Julius Caesar therefore consulted with the expert Alexandrian astronomer Sosigenes, who devised a totally new calendar based on the sun. Almost everyone in the western world used the Julian calendar from 45 BC right up to AD 1582, after which they gradually changed over to the Gregorian calendar.[3] When we refer to the dates of Tiberius, or Jesus, or anyone else who lived in the period from 45 BC to AD 1582, the accepted convention is to use the Julian calendar. (The accepted convention is also to use the Julian calendar for dates before 45 BC.) All dates I will give in this book, unless I say otherwise, are dates in the Julian calendar. The

Julian calendar was, for example, the calendar the Romans used at the time of Christ, and it makes sense for us to use it for the time of Christ. Incidentally, the day in the Julian calendar runs from midnight to midnight, as does the day we use today.

Interestingly, one place in the world is so wedded to tradition that it still uses the Julian calendar today. This is the island of Foula, named after the Norse words for 'Bird Island', off the coast of Scotland. The *Oceanic*, sister ship to the *Titanic*, was wrecked off Foula in 1914. The fiercely independent forty inhabitants of Foula have never adopted the Gregorian calendar, and they therefore celebrate Christmas on January 6 and New Year's Day on January 13 (because the Julian calendar is now twelve days out of step with the Gregorian calendar). This illustrates the reluctance some groups have to change their traditional calendar, which turns out to be important when we consider the date of the last supper in later chapters.

After this digression on calendars, let us go back to emperor Tiberius. From the evidence given by Suetonius and other Roman writers, most scholars believe that Tiberius began to govern jointly with the existing emperor Augustus (his stepfather) in AD 12, and that the Roman Senate appointed him the new emperor when Augustus died in AD 14.[4] Tiberius ruled the Roman empire until he died on March 16, AD 37.

When Tacitus tells us that Jesus died in Tiberius' reign, is he counting the start of his reign from AD 12, when Tiberius ruled jointly with his stepfather Augustus, or from AD 14, when Augustus died and Tiberius was appointed the new emperor? From the coins issued in Tiberius' reign it is clear that Tiberius himself reckoned the first year of his reign from the death of Augustus in AD 14 (fig. 2.1).[5] In addition, the New Testament scholar John Meier writes: 'As a matter of fact, all the major Roman historians who calculate the years of Tiberius' rule – namely, Tacitus, Suetonius, and Cassius Dio – count from AD 14, the year of Augustus' death.'[6] Since Tacitus tells us that Jesus died in Tiberius' reign, Jesus must therefore have died in the period AD 14–37. We are starting to anchor the death of Jesus in history, but can we narrow down this broad time period using information from the Bible?

Fig. 2.1 Bronze coin from Antioch dated year 1 of Tiberius and year 45 of Actium. The head of Tiberius is on the reverse side. From this double-dated coin we know that Tiberius started to reign in AD 14.

THE CLUE OF CAIAPHAS

The gospels record that Jesus was crucified when Caiaphas was the high priest. For example, Matthew 26:57 states: 'Those who had arrested Jesus took him to Caiaphas, the high priest.' John's gospel confirms this (John 11:49). The Jewish historian Josephus in *Jewish Antiquities* refers to Caiaphas many times, and from the details given by Josephus nearly all scholars deduce that Caiaphas was the high priest from about AD 18 to 36, these dates being correct to within a year or so.[7] So Jesus died in the reign of Tiberius (AD 14–37) and when Caiaphas was high priest (about AD 18–36).

THE CLUE OF PILATE

As we have seen, Tacitus states in *Annals*: 'Christ had been executed in Tiberius' reign by the governor of Judea, Pontius Pilate.' So Jesus died not only when Tiberius ruled, but also when Pontius Pilate was the Roman governor (called the Prefect) of Judea. Not only Tacitus, but also all four gospels say the crucifixion occurred when Pontius Pilate was the governor of Judea. When was this? From information in Josephus' *Jewish Antiquities* we can date his governorship to the period from AD 26 to sometime before Passover in AD 37.[8]

Roman and Jewish leaders ruling when Jesus died

Roman and Jewish leader	Date of rule
Tiberius: the Roman emperor	AD 14 – March 16, AD 37
Caiaphas: the Jewish high priest	c. AD 18 – c. AD 36
Pilate: the Roman governor of Judea	AD 26 – before Passover AD 37

Let me summarise our findings so far. Jesus died when Tiberius was the Roman emperor, Caiaphas was the high priest and Pilate was the governor of Judea. Since Jesus died when Tiberius, Caiaphas and Pilate were all ruling, the earliest possible date for his death is AD 26 (see table). The latest possible date is AD 36, since Caiaphas was high priest to about AD 36, Pilate governed to some time before Passover in AD 37 and Jesus died at Passover time, as we saw in the last chapter. The crucifixion must therefore have been in the period AD 26–36. Most biblical scholars agree with this, so what I have written so far is not new. But I have analysed the evidence afresh and I believe we can indeed say, beyond reasonable doubt, that Jesus died in the period AD 26–36.

It may be worth noting that the evidence we have assembled so far for when Christ died, that it was when Tiberius, Caiaphas and Pilate were all ruling in their different ways, tells a consistent story. In addition, the historical evidence from the gospels agrees with the historical evidence from both Roman and Jewish historians. We have started to root the time of the death of Jesus in history.

THE CLUE OF THE DAY JESUS DIED

We have just deduced the rough time period in which Jesus died. Another key piece of information is the day of the week on which he died. All four gospels agree that Jesus died the day before the Jewish Sabbath. For example, Mark states the crucifixion occurred on 'Preparation Day (that is, the day before the Sabbath)' (Mark 15:42). Which day is meant by 'Preparation Day' and 'the day before the Sabbath'? From the earliest times, except for the Sabbath, the days of the Jewish week were numbered not named. They were, and still are, called the first day, the second day, the third day, and so on to the seventh, which differs by being named and is called the Sabbath. The first day of the Jewish week is our Sunday, so the seventh day, the Sabbath, is our Saturday. The sixth day (our Friday) was called 'the eve of the Sabbath', or 'the day of preparation', both in the New Testament and by the Jewish historian Josephus. The gospels agree that Jesus died the day before the Sabbath, hence Jesus died on a Friday.

When does the Jewish day start? It is well known that it starts in the evening, at sunset, and ends twenty-four hours later at the next sunset. How curious! Why would anyone choose to *start* their day when the light from the sun was *ending*? As we will see in later chapters, it turns out to be important to understand why the Jewish day starts at sunset.

The ancient Jews were not alone in starting their day in the evening. A number of other ancient civilisations did this, for example the ancient Babylonians, Persians and Assyrians. All the ancient civilisations that started their day in the evening had one thing in common: they all used a lunar calendar in which the first day of the month was the day on which the new moon was first visible.

Having found this out, I decided I needed some expert help in astronomy, so I went to see Graeme Waddington, an astrophysicist who is very knowledgeable about both ancient and modern astronomy. He explained that the crescent of the new moon is first visible in the sky shortly after sunset. The first day of the month in lunar calendars was determined by when the new lunar crescent was first seen, and this was in the evening. That is why all ancient civilisations which used this type of lunar calendar started their day in the evening.

We now have a clear and convincing reason for why the Jewish day starts in the evening, at sunset. It is because of the astronomical fact that the new moon is first visible in the night sky, shortly after sunset. So the new light from the new moon signifies a new month: a nice piece of symbolism. Today the Jewish lunar calendar is a calculated one, but in the first century AD, when Jesus lived, the first day of the lunar month was determined by observing the new lunar crescent.

The Jewish Sabbath therefore runs from Friday evening to Saturday evening, and Preparation Day, the day before the Sabbath, runs from Thursday evening to Friday evening. Let me now mention a further possible source of confusion. Although the Jews started their *day* at sunset, they measured their hours of *daylight* from sunrise. It is rather like using both a twenty-four-hour and a twelve-hour clock. At Passover time (our March or April), sunrise in Jerusalem occurs at about 6 a.m. So midday is the sixth hour. Matthew's gospel tells us that Jesus died at 'about the ninth hour' (Matthew 27:46). We can therefore deduce from the Bible that Jesus died at about 3 p.m. We now have both the day (Friday) and the time (3 p.m.) of the death of Jesus, and this is the second key clue to finding the exact date of the crucifixion.

THE TIME BETWEEN THE CRUCIFIXION AND THE RESURRECTION

I am now going to look at information that some people believe is inconsistent with a Friday crucifixion. This is the time interval given in the Bible between the crucifixion and the resurrection. In order to solve this problem we are going to have to look at how the Jews counted days.

A large number of biblical references say that Jesus rose on the third day after his crucifixion (for example, Matthew 27:64, Luke 24:7, Acts 10:40, 1 Corinthians 15:4). All four gospels state that the resurrection occurred on the first day of the Jewish week, which, as we have seen, ran from Saturday evening to Sunday evening. The gospels do not give the exact time of the resurrection, except that Jesus was already risen when Mary Magdalene, Mary his mother and Salome came to anoint his body with spices just after sunrise on Sunday morning (Mark 16:2). Hence Jesus died at 3 p.m. on Friday and the gospels have the resurrection occurring at or before sunrise on the following Sunday. Is this time period consistent with Jesus rising 'on the third day'?

How did the ancient Jews count days? We can deduce from various passages in the Old Testament that part of a day was counted as a whole day.[9] Was this same inclusive method of counting days, in which part of a day counted as a whole day, used in the first century AD, when Jesus lived and the gospels were written?

A famous Jewish scholar, Rabbi Eleazar ben Azariah, who lived around AD 100 and was descended from the Old Testament priest Ezra, spells out how days were counted: 'A day and a night are an Onah [a portion of time] and the portion of an Onah is as the whole of it.'[10] The Rabbi is saying that, in counting days, a portion of a twenty-four-hour period of a day and a night counts as a whole day and a night (an Onah). Applying this to the gospels, when Jesus died at 3 p.m. on Friday this therefore counts as the first Jewish day (Thursday sunset to Friday sunset), the body of Jesus was in the tomb on the second Jewish day (Friday sunset to Saturday sunset) and he rose from the dead on the third Jewish day (Saturday sunset to Sunday sunset). When the Bible says that Jesus rose from the dead on the third day, this is therefore consistent with a Friday crucifixion and a Sunday resurrection.

How does the Bible count days? Example: Jesus rose on the third day	
From death at 3 p.m. Friday to sunset Friday	The first day
Sunset Friday to sunset Saturday	The second day
Sunset Saturday to the resurrection before sunrise on Sunday	The third day

All the evidence from the Bible and from early Christian literature agrees with this, with the possible exception of just one verse in the Bible. A number of Christian sects believe this verse indicates a Wednesday or Thursday crucifixion, as do some more mainstream biblical scholars.[11] So what is this verse that causes some to doubt that the crucifixion was on a Friday? It is the words of Jesus recorded in Matthew 12:40: 'For as Jonah was three days and three nights in the belly of a huge fish, so the Son of Man will be three days and three nights in the heart of the earth.'

If Jesus were speaking these words today, counting back three days and three nights from a Sunday would indeed lead to a Wednesday or Thursday crucifixion, depending on how one counted, and a Friday crucifixion would be ruled out. But we have to realise that Jesus spoke these words in the first century AD and, as we have seen, at this time people did not necessarily count days as we do today. We also have to remember that there are *many* biblical verses and also *many* passages in early Christian literature that *clearly* indicate Jesus died on a Friday. So how are we to interpret the 'three days and three nights' of Matthew 12:40?

According to Rabbi Eleazar ben Azariah, a portion of a day and a night counts as a whole day and night (an Onah). When Jesus died at 3 p.m. on Friday this therefore counts as a whole day and night (Thursday sunset to Friday sunset). The body of Jesus was in the tomb on the second day and night (Friday sunset to Saturday sunset), and, according to the gospels, he rose from the dead on the third day and night (Saturday sunset to Sunday sunset). Counting in the way Jewish people counted in the first century AD, a Friday crucifixion and Sunday resurrection are therefore consistent with Jesus being dead for three Onahs, that is, for 'three days and three nights'. Although this *inclusive* method of counting days and nights seems strange to us today, I do not think it would have seemed strange at all to Jewish people living in the first century AD, because this was the way they would have been brought up to count. In addition, Matthew would hardly have included the 'three days and three nights' words of Jesus in his gospel if he felt they contradicted the Friday crucifixion and Sunday resurrection he clearly indicated later.

We can therefore say that all four gospels (even Matthew 12:40) and all early Christian writings agree that Jesus died on a Friday. We can now put together the first two pieces of the jigsaw and say with confidence that Jesus died on a Friday sometime in the period AD 26 to 36. We have made a start on constructing the jigsaw. Many others have also of course put these two jigsaw pieces together. However, can we narrow the date range further? Finding the third piece of the jigsaw that enables this is a real challenge. But as we will see, it can be done, and we are going to do this in the next chapter, where we look at the date and nature of the last supper. The biblical scholar F. F. Bruce was not wrong when he called the date and nature of the last supper 'the thorniest problem in the New Testament'.

When did Jesus die?	
Time	About 3 p.m.
Day	Friday
Year	AD 26–36

SUMMARY

Let me briefly summarise what we have found in this chapter. First, from the known dates when Tiberius was the Roman emperor, Caiaphas was the high priest and Pontius Pilate was the governor of Judea, we can say, beyond reasonable doubt, that the crucifixion was some time in the period AD 26–36. Second, all the biblical evidence gives Friday as the day of Jesus' death. Third, the gospels state that Jesus died at about 3 p.m. We can therefore deduce that Jesus died at about 3 p.m. on a Friday in the period AD 26–36. This information provides us with the framework for dating the crucifixion, which is itself a key marker date in reconstructing the last week of Jesus. In the next three chapters we will see if we can home in on the exact date when Jesus died.

3 The problem of the last supper

> And he [Jesus] said to them [his disciples at the last supper], 'I have eagerly desired to eat this Passover with you before I suffer' . . . Then seizing him, they [the temple guard] led him away and took him into the house of the high priest [Caiaphas].
>
> (Luke 22:15, 54)
>
> Then the Jews led Jesus from Caiaphas to the palace of the Roman governor. By now it was early morning, and to avoid ceremonial uncleanness the Jews did not enter the palace; they wanted to be able to eat the Passover.
>
> (John 18:28)

These passages from Luke and John strikingly illustrate the problem of the time and nature of the last supper. The verse from John seems to follow on from the verses from Luke, except that the Feast of Passover has been shifted from *before* the arrest and trials of Jesus to *after* these events. If Jesus had already eaten the Passover with his disciples before his arrest and trials (Luke, and also Matthew and Mark), how was it that the Jews were still waiting to eat the Passover after his arrest and trials (John)? This looks like a straight contradiction and, as I have written earlier, it has puzzled biblical scholars for centuries. In this chapter we will examine some of the solutions that have been proposed. First, I want to explore in detail the apparent disagreement between the gospels about the last supper.

THE LAST SUPPER IN JOHN

John appears to say that the last supper, the trials of Jesus and the crucifixion were *all* before the Passover meal. Concerning the last supper, John writes: 'It was just before the Passover Feast ... The evening meal was being served' (John 13:1, 2). This 'evening meal' is the last meal John records Jesus having before his crucifixion. The description John gives of events at this meal makes it clear that the meal is the same occasion as the last supper described by the synoptic gospels. For example, both John and the synoptics describe Jesus dipping a piece of bread in a dish and then giving this to the traitor Judas. In addition, in all four gospels the meal was held at night, whereas a normal evening meal was held in the late afternoon. However, John explicitly states that this meal was 'just before the Passover Feast'.

Following the last supper, Jesus was arrested and John makes the statement quoted at the start of this chapter (John 18:28). It is clear from this verse that, according to John, the trials of Jesus before the high priest, Caiaphas, and the Roman governor, Pilate, occurred before the Jews who had arrested him had eaten their Passover meal. In addition, at the end of the trial by Pilate, John states: 'It was the day of Preparation for the Passover' (John 19:14). Thus John says that the last supper *and* the trials of Jesus were before the Passover.

After Jesus had been crucified, John writes: 'Now it was the day of Preparation, and the next day was to be a special Sabbath. Because the Jews did not want the bodies left on the crosses during the Sabbath, they asked Pilate to have the legs broken and the bodies taken down' (John 19:31). What is meant by 'special Sabbath'? The Old Testament book of Leviticus tells us that on the fifteenth day of the first month of the Jewish religious year, Nisan (corresponding to March/April), the Israelites were to 'hold a sacred assembly and do no regular work' (Leviticus 23:7). The Passover meal was eaten after sunset, at the start of Nisan 15,[1] so Leviticus indicates that this day was a day of rest which came to be called the Sabbath of the Passover. Nisan 15 could fall on any day of the week (just as April 15, say, can fall on any day of the week), but when it happened to fall on the normal weekly Sabbath, it was called a special Sabbath.[2] Such a conjunction of weekly Sabbath and annual Passover still occurs in the Jewish calendar. John calls the day after the crucifixion a special Sabbath because in the year of the crucifixion the regular Sabbath, from Friday evening to Saturday evening, happened to coincide with the Passover Sabbath, on Nisan 15. Hence, according to John, the crucifixion was on Nisan 14, the day before the Passover meal.

In summary, John consistently says that the last supper (John 13:1, 2), the trials of Jesus (John 18:28 and 19:14) and the crucifixion (John 19:31) were all *before* the Passover meal. The natural interpretation of John is that the crucifixion occurred on Nisan 14, and the Passover meal followed at the evening start of the next Jewish day, on Nisan 15.

THE LAST SUPPER IN THE SYNOPTIC GOSPELS

Matthew, Mark and Luke appear to tell a very different story from John. According to Mark 14:12, 'On the first day of the Feast of Unleavened Bread, when it was customary to sacrifice the Passover lamb, Jesus' disciples asked him, "Where do you want us to go and make preparations for you to eat the Passover?"' The disciples then prepared the Passover meal (Mark 14:16) and that evening Jesus ate this last supper with his disciples (Mark 14:17–18). Matthew and Luke tell a similar story to Mark, and Luke records Jesus poignantly saying as he eats the meal: 'I have eagerly desired to eat this Passover with you before I suffer' (Luke 22:15). Notice that, according to the synoptics, *both* the disciples of Jesus and Jesus himself call the last supper the Passover.

The time of the Passover meal in the year of the crucifixion	
After the last supper	John
After the trials of Jesus	John
After the crucifixion	John
At the time of the last supper	Synoptic gospels

An obvious interpretation of the synoptic gospels is that the last supper really was a Passover meal, eaten at Passover meal time in the evening at the start of Nisan 15, with the crucifixion occurring later that Jewish day (i.e. still on Nisan 15, since the Jewish day runs from sunset to sunset). This disagrees with the Nisan 14 date of the crucifixion indicated by John. Thus the synoptics and John appear to disagree directly on whether the last supper was a Passover meal *and* over the date of the crucifixion.

Jesus' inner circle of twelve disciples were all present at the last supper. Afterwards, they might have forgotten minor details but surely they would have remembered if it was a Passover meal or not. Hence there were a significant number of reliable eye-witnesses to the nature of the last supper. This is what makes the apparent disagreement among the gospels so surprising. However, is it possible that, as I suggested in the first chapter, the synoptics and John are actually in agreement, and that I, and others, have misunderstood what they were trying to say? Indeed, are there clues in the gospels themselves as to why they apparently disagree? Clues that would have been understood by their original audience, so that all four gospels would have been consistent, but which, two thousand years later, we no longer understand? I believe there are, and we will find these 'hidden clues', and their meaning, in later chapters.

For now, let us consider the core problem: the real or apparent disagreement between the synoptics and John over the date and nature of the last supper. Was it a Passover meal or not? Biblical scholars have wrestled with this for centuries and they hold a wide range of views. I will summarise the main interpretations below.

POSSIBLE INTERPRETATIONS OF THE LAST SUPPER

There are four main interpretations of the last supper given by biblical scholars:[3]

1 The synoptics are right and John is wrong

On this interpretation the last supper was a Passover meal held in the evening at the start of Nisan 15, and the crucifixion occurred later that Jewish day, on Nisan 15. In a classic book, *The Eucharistic Words of Jesus*, the New Testament scholar Joachim Jeremias has argued particularly powerfully that the last supper was a Passover meal,[4] and his views have strong support. I have consulted a large number of biblical commentaries on the gospels. Very many scholars believe the synoptics are right and that John is mistaken about the date and nature of the last supper.

Scholars who believe that John is wrong about the date and nature of the last supper argue that he was motivated more by theological than by historical considerations. For example, C. K. Barrett writes: 'John's interests were theological rather than chronological ... He did not hesitate to repress, revise, rewrite, or rearrange.'[5] In particular, such scholars suggest it was important theologically for John that Jesus died at the time the Passover lambs were being slain, since John's gospel earlier portrays Jesus as being the Lamb of God (John 1:29). These scholars argue that John therefore placed the crucifixion on Nisan 14, the day the Passover lambs were slain, for the sake of theological symbolism rather than historical fact.

2 John can be interpreted to fit the synoptics

Many scholars believe that the synoptics are right in identifying the last supper as a Passover meal and that John has not distorted history but, correctly interpreted, agrees with the synoptics. For example, Don Carson argues that when John writes 'It was just before the Passover Feast ... the evening meal was being served' (John 13:1, 2), we have to remember that at this meal Jesus washed his disciples' feet (John 13:3–12). Carson argues that the foot washing would have occurred just before the meal started, so John is really saying that just before the Passover Feast Jesus washed his disciples' feet and then he sat down to eat the Passover with them.[6]

How do such scholars interpret John 18:28, which says that for reasons of ceremonial uncleanness, the Jews at the trials of Jesus did not enter Pontius Pilate's palace since they wanted to be able to eat the Passover? Carson writes: 'It is tempting here to understand *to eat the Passover* to refer, not to the Passover meal itself, but to the continuing Feast of Unleavened Bread, which continued for seven days. There is ample evidence that "the Passover" could refer to the combined feast of the paschal meal itself plus the ensuing Feast of Unleavened Bread.'[7] So Carson argues that 'to eat the Passover' refers not to the Passover meal itself but to a later and less important meal in Passover week.

Concerning John 19:31, that Jesus was crucified the day before a special Sabbath, Carson and others (for example Craig Blomberg) argue that the term 'a special Sabbath' simply meant that the regular weekly Sabbath fell in Passover week and not that the weekly Sabbath coincided with the special Passover day of rest on Nisan 15.[8]

In summary, many scholars believe that the synoptics are right that the last supper was a Passover meal, and that John can be interpreted to agree with them. According to this theory, as with interpretation 1 above, the last supper was held in the evening at the start of Nisan 15, and the crucifixion occurred later that Jewish day, still Nisan 15.

3 The last supper was a Passover-like meal

Some scholars have proposed that the last supper described by the synoptics was not a strict Passover meal, but it was a Passover-like meal. For example, John Meier writes: 'Sensing or suspecting that his enemies were closing in for an imminent, final attack, and therefore taking into account that he might not be able to celebrate the coming Passover meal with his disciples, Jesus instead arranged a solemn farewell meal just before Passover ... The supper, though not a Passover meal ... would naturally be both solemn and religious, accompanied by all the formalities that Jeremias uses to prove the Passover nature of the supper.'[9] Similarly, Tom Wright, the Anglican Bishop of Durham, UK, calls the last supper a 'quasi-Passover'.[10] These scholars, and others, suggest that Jesus, knowing of, or suspecting, his imminent arrest, held a Passover-like meal on the evening before the official Passover. Supporters of this theory interpret Luke 22:15, 'I have eagerly desired to eat this Passover with you before I suffer', to refer to the specially brought-forward Passover-like meal that they were about to have. Scholars who favour this interpretation note that the Passover lamb is the centrepiece of a real Passover meal, yet the synoptics make no mention of a Passover lamb being slain, roasted and eaten at the last supper. This interpretation of the synoptics is in broad agreement with John's gospel in which the last supper is explicitly stated to have occurred before the Feast of Passover (John 13:1). The timing also agrees, so on this theory all four gospels have the last supper on the evening at the start of Nisan 14, with the crucifixion later that Jewish day. A significant minority of biblical scholars support this interpretation.

4 The different calendar theory

The official Jewish calendar at the time of Jesus in the first century AD is described by the Jewish historian Josephus.[11] In this calendar, Passover time was specified precisely; Josephus records that the slaughtering of the lambs for the Passover meal occurred at the temple in Jerusalem between the ninth and eleventh hours (that is between 3 p.m. and 5 p.m.) on the fourteenth day of Nisan. The Passover meal commenced after sunset that evening, that is, at the start of Nisan 15, since the Jewish day runs from evening to evening. There is a striking scene in the play version of *Fiddler on the Roof* in which a Jewish family goes to the Jerusalem temple and their Passover lamb is slaughtered. They return home, stand on the flat top of their house and watch the sun go down. They turn around, watch the full Passover moon rise, then go down from the roof and joyfully eat their Passover meal. The fifteenth day of the month is at full moon time, since the first day of the month is the day of the new crescent moon, and a lunar month is either twenty-nine or thirty days long.

In addition to the official Jewish calendar, we know from the Dead Sea Scrolls, found in caves by Qumran close to the Dead Sea and then sold (see Fig. 3.1), that the Jewish community at Qumran used a solar calendar in which the year had 364 days. This year was divided into four quarters of 91 days each, and each quarter had three months of length 30, 30 and 31 days. In 1957, a French scholar, Annie Jaubert, ingeniously proposed that Jesus held the last supper at Passover time according to this calendar.[12] A clever feature of the calendar is that their year of 364 days divides exactly into fifty-two weeks of seven days each. This means that a given *date*, for example, Nisan 14, always fell on the same *day* of the week each year, which was very convenient. (Think how convenient it would be for us if December 25 fell on the same day of the week every year.) Also, the Qumran community day ran from sunrise to sunrise, because they used a solar calendar. We

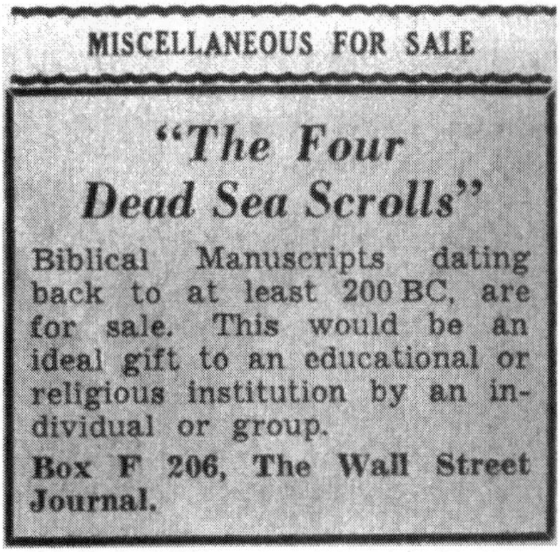

MISCELLANEOUS FOR SALE

"The Four Dead Sea Scrolls"

Biblical Manuscripts dating back to at least 200 BC, are for sale. This would be an ideal gift to an educational or religious institution by an individual or group.

Box F 206, The Wall Street Journal.

Fig. 3.1 Advertisement in the June 1, 1954, *Wall Street Journal* in which some Dead Sea Scrolls went up for sale.

know from the Dead Sea Scrolls that the Qumran community had their annual Passover meal on Nisan 14, which for them was always a *Tuesday* evening.

Jaubert proposed that Jesus held the last supper with his disciples on Tuesday evening, according to the Qumran calendar, and he was crucified a few days later on Friday. She suggested that the synoptic gospels used the Qumran calendar, so they correctly described the last supper as a real, not a quasi, Passover meal held at Passover time (in the Qumran calendar). John, on the other hand, used the official Jewish calendar and so he correctly described the last supper as occurring before the official Passover. According to this theory, all four gospels give Nisan 14, in the official calendar, as the crucifixion date.

Other 'different calendar' theories exist, summarised by Howard Marshall[13] and Harold Hoehner.[14] However, most biblical scholars are not convinced by any of the different calendar theories proposed so far, including that of Jaubert, and only a small minority of scholars support a different calendar theory (although the Pope has recently spoken in favour of the different calendar theory of Jaubert. I will consider his words in Chapter 7).

The table summarises the main interpretations of the gospels concerning the last supper and the date of the crucifixion.

Main interpretations of the gospel accounts of the last supper and the date of the crucifixion

	Interpretation		Implied date of crucifixion
1	Synoptics correct	John wrong	Nisan 15
2	Synoptics correct	John can be interpreted to agree	Nisan 15
3	John correct	Synoptics correct if last supper was a Passover-like meal	Nisan 14
4	John correct	Synoptics correct if a different calendar was used	Nisan 14

A PRELIMINARY ASSESSMENT

When I first thought about the problem of the last supper, I was unhappy with all of the solutions proposed above. Interpretation 1 requires John to have grossly distorted historical facts for the sake of theological symbolism. As we have seen, John states that the Passover was not only after the last supper, it was also after the trials of Jesus and after his crucifixion. This positioning of the Passover is like a thread running through the fabric of John's account. If this thread is removed then the fabric is in danger of falling apart. John clearly had theological motives in writing his gospel; in particular he wrote it so that people would believe that Jesus is the Son of God (John 20:31). However, is it likely he would have distorted so much the order of events surrounding the crucifixion for the sake of these motives? In addition, portraying Jesus as a Passover lamb is not a major theme of John's gospel.[15]

The problem with interpretation 2 is that it is not the natural interpretation of John's gospel. For example, when John writes that the evening meal (the last supper) was just before the Passover Feast (John 13:1), this looks to me like a *deliberate* time statement by John. He follows this statement by referring to the evening meal being served (John 13:2) and *then* to the foot washing (John 13:3–12). It therefore seems that John is saying that *both* the meal and the foot washing occurred before the Passover Feast. As John Meier writes: 'John pointedly places the meal just before Passover (John 13:1).'[16] When John says the Jews at the trial of Jesus by Pilate wanted to be able to eat the Passover (John 18:28) the Greek phrase John uses for 'to eat the Passover', *phagein to pascha*, is identical to the one used by the synoptics to describe what was to happen at the last supper (Matthew 26:17, Mark 14:12, Luke 22:8, 15). In addition, John is explicit that at the end of the trial by Pilate: 'It was the day of preparation of Passover' (John 19:14). In both cases it would therefore seem that the main Passover meal held at the start of Passover week was intended and not some lesser meal later in the week.

The problem with interpretation 3 is that Matthew, Mark and Luke describe the last supper as a *real* Passover meal, not a Passover-like meal or a quasi-Passover meal. The synoptics record *Jesus himself* calling this meal the Passover. Surely they would not have done this unless they were convinced that the last supper really was a Passover meal. The objection that they do not mention a Passover lamb is not as strong as it might seem. Everyone knew there was a lamb at the Passover meal, hence it was not necessary to mention it: it could be assumed.

The difficulty with interpretation 4 is that only one 'different calendar' theory has been proposed in detail and has received any support from biblical scholars: that of Annie Jaubert. However, she assumes that the Passover of the Qumran community was *before* that in the official Jewish calendar, whereas I will show it to have been *after* the official Passover (see Chapter 7). This totally rules out Jaubert's theory. Thus there are no 'different calendar' theories that are convincing.

Hence the main interpretations of the last supper so far proposed all have serious drawbacks, as recognised by many biblical scholars.

For example, R. T. France writes: 'But in what sense was this [the last supper] a Passover meal? The debate occasioned by the differing statements of John and the Synoptics has been extremely complex, and the issue remains unresolved.'[17] This book will propose a new solution to this problem.

THE LAST SUPPER AND THE DATE OF THE CRUCIFIXION

As we have seen, biblical scholars are totally divided on which interpretation of the last supper they support. These interpretations give rise to two options for the date of the crucifixion, Nisan 14 or 15, and scholars do not know with any certainty which is right. We also have a wide range of years to choose from, AD 26–36, as we deduced in Chapter 2. Can we narrow down the options? If we can reduce the options on possible dates for the crucifixion we may also be able to eliminate one or more proposed interpretations of the last supper.

To help us think about this problem, let me use a more modern-day analogy. Let us suppose that police find a skeleton of a man murdered in the last century. They call in forensic scientists who indicate the man was killed sometime in the period 1926–36. Various papers are found saying the man died on a Friday. Then some conflicting evidence emerges, some of which suggests that he died on April 14, but other evidence says April 15. How can we narrow down the possible dates for his death?

The simplest way, which I have just done, is to go to a computer search engine like *Google* and type in 'calendar'. The first website that appeared gave the calendar for any year since 1900. By typing in '1926', I found that April 14 in 1926 was on a Wednesday and April 15 was a Thursday, so if the man died on Friday, 1926 could not have been the year of the murder. In fact there are only three possibilities: April 14 fell on a Friday in 1933 and April 15 fell on a Friday in 1927 and 1932. The past calendars show that these are the only dates that are possible for the murder. If our imaginary police detectives were to persevere they might find other evidence that enables them to say that, for example, 1927 was too early and 1933 too late for the man's death, leaving

Friday, April 15, 1932 as the only possible date for the murder. This is the approach I will use in the next chapter to narrow down the possible dates of the crucifixion. First, we take the three key clues we have discovered in this chapter and the previous one, to find the possible dates for the crucifixion. These are that Jesus died in the period AD 26–36, it was on a Friday and it was either Nisan 14 or 15. Putting these clues together enables us to ask the following question:

In which of the years AD 26–36 did Nisan 14 or 15 fall on a Friday?

To answer this question we need to find Jewish calendars for the years AD 26–36. Now comes the problem. Unfortunately there are no records of the Jewish calendar in Jerusalem for these years. It therefore seems impossible to make further progress on finding the date when Jesus died.

As I first thought about this problem, way back in 1981, I wondered if astronomy could help. Scientists use the equations of motion of the moon and the earth to calculate the dates of ancient eclipses. Can we similarly use astronomy to reconstruct the Jewish calendar in the first century AD, since we know that the first day in each month was determined by observing the first appearance of the new moon? Can we calculate when these new moons would have been seen?

This is what we are going to do in the next chapter. We will in fact be following in the footsteps of one of the greatest scientists of all time, Sir Isaac Newton, who used astronomy to try to find the date of the crucifixion. However, we will use more accurate equations and methods than were available to him. We will also answer the questions of many biblical scholars who doubt that astronomy can be used with confidence in this way. Their doubts are justified for previous calendar reconstructions, but not for the new reconstructions given in the next chapter.

SUMMARY

Before we do this, let me summarise what we have found in this chapter and the last. First, from the known dates when Tiberius was the Roman emperor, Caiaphas was the high priest and Pilate was the governor of Judea we can say, beyond reasonable doubt, that the crucifixion was some time in the period AD 26–36. Second, all the biblical evidence either explicitly states, or is consistent with, Friday as the day of Jesus' death. Finally, John appears to disagree with the synoptics on whether or not the last supper was a Passover meal. Four possible interpretations of the last supper have been given which yield that Jesus died on either Nisan 14 or 15 (Nisan was the first month of the Jewish year, corresponding to March/April in our calendar). In order to determine the date of the crucifixion, and also throw light on the nature of the last supper, we therefore have to find in which year Nisan 14 or 15 fell on a Friday in the period AD 26–36.

The date of the crucifixion	
Day of week	Friday
Jewish day	Nisan 14 or 15
Period of time	AD 26–36

4 Can we reconstruct the Jewish calendar at the time of Christ?

> Some of Judaism's most profound truths are to be found, not in texts but in time, in the Jewish calendar itself.
>
> (Jonathan Sacks, the Chief Rabbi of Britain and the Commonwealth)[1]

The Jewish calendar must have been at least as central to the lives of Jewish people at the time of Christ as our calendar is to us today. For example, on Nisan 1, in the spring of each year, Jews would have marked the start of their religious year (their civil year, used for official purposes, started in the autumn). In the first two weeks of Nisan, Jewish people would have travelled from many countries to Jerusalem to celebrate the great Feast of Passover. On Nisan 10 they would have selected a Passover lamb for sacrifice at the temple in Jerusalem on Nisan 14, as instructed in the book of Exodus. On Nisan 15 they would have eaten their Passover meal and remembered the events of the Exodus. On Nisan 16 they might have watched the barley being harvested in the fields, after seeing the priests waving the first sheaves of barley in the temple earlier that day, as specified in the book of Leviticus,[2] and so on.

The Jewish calendar must have been so central to the lives of Jewish people in the first century AD, for both religious and agricultural reasons, that to my mind it is simply not credible that the traditions handed down by eye-witnesses to the gospel writers were confused about whether Jesus died on Nisan 14 or 15, particularly because these two days, when the Passover lambs were slain, roasted and eaten, were the most important days in the whole year in the Jewish calendar. *We* may be confused about these dates, two thousand years later, but surely not the gospel writers. Yet, as we saw in the last chapter, John and the synoptic gospels appear to contradict each other over whether the crucifixion occurred before or after the Passover meal. Is John's account true, or that of the synoptics, or neither, or both? Is the truth about this confusion to be found, to quote Jonathan Sacks, 'in the Jewish calendar itself'? I believe that it is, and in order to discover the truth about the last week of Jesus we will have to understand the Jewish calendar at the time of Christ.

In the last chapter I suggested that by using astronomy it may be possible to travel backwards in time, reverse the centuries, and reconstruct the actual calendar Jewish people in Jerusalem would have used at the time of Jesus. In this chapter I will describe how this can be done. I will also answer the questions of many leading biblical scholars who doubt that astronomy can really be used to calculate the Jewish calendar at the time of Christ because of the problems of a cloudy sky preventing seeing the new moon and of 'leap' months added by the priests: I will show how both of these can be taken into account. In the next chapter we will see if there are sufficient clues in the gospels to use with our reconstructed calendar to enable us to determine the *exact* date on which Christ died.

ASTRONOMY AND THE JEWISH CALENDAR

In the first century AD the Jewish calendar was an observational one: each month began with the evening when the new crescent moon was first visible, shortly after sunset. The moon was the Jewish calendar in the sky (see fig. 4.1). The priests of the temple in Jerusalem had a team of men who, each month, looked for the new crescent moon. When at least two of these trustworthy witnesses agreed they had seen it, the priests would question them, and if the priests agreed that the sighting was genuine, then trumpets were blown to tell all Jerusalem that it was a new moon and a new month. Fires were lit on hills and messengers were sent to spread the news throughout the land.

Before going further it is useful to understand why a new crescent moon is only visible for a short period of time after sunset, before disappearing. The new crescent moon seen from Jerusalem typically starts to be visible about fifteen minutes after sunset, remains visible for about thirty minutes and then disappears for the rest of the

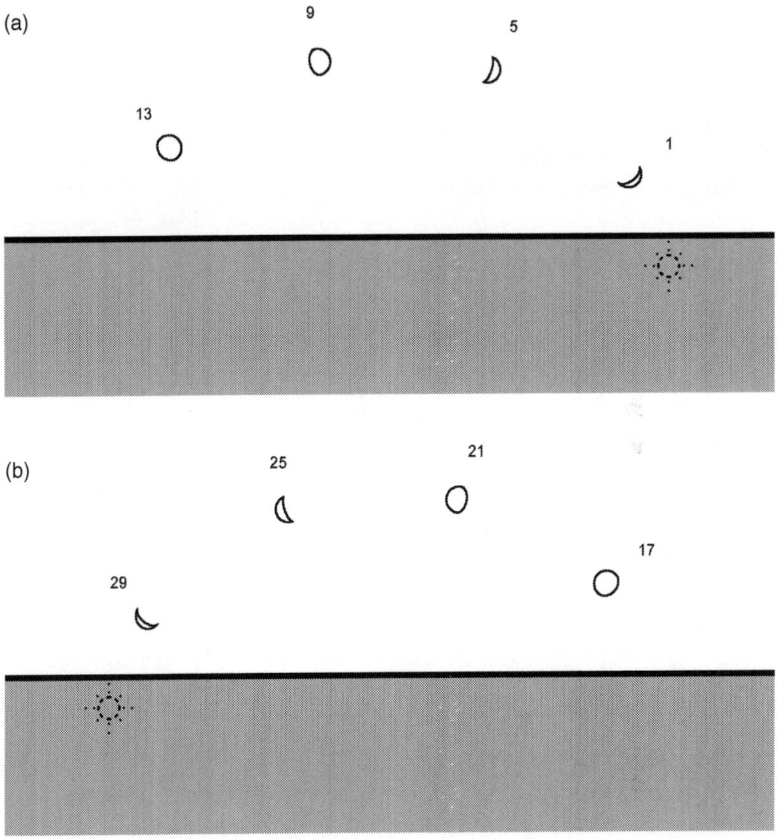

Fig. 4.1 The appearance of the moon throughout the lunar month. The numbers refer to the day in the lunar month. (a) The waxing moon (increasing in size). (b) The waning moon (decreasing in size). A skilful observer can tell the day of the month, to within a day, from the shape of the moon.

night. Why does the new moon behave in such an apparently curious way?

As everyone knows, we see the sun rising in the east each day and setting in the west. Hence, just before sunset, if we look to the west we see the sun slightly above the horizon. At new moon time, just before sunset, the moon is slightly above the sun in the western sky (fig. 4.2a). The moon is then invisible because it is too close to the sun (it is 'lost'

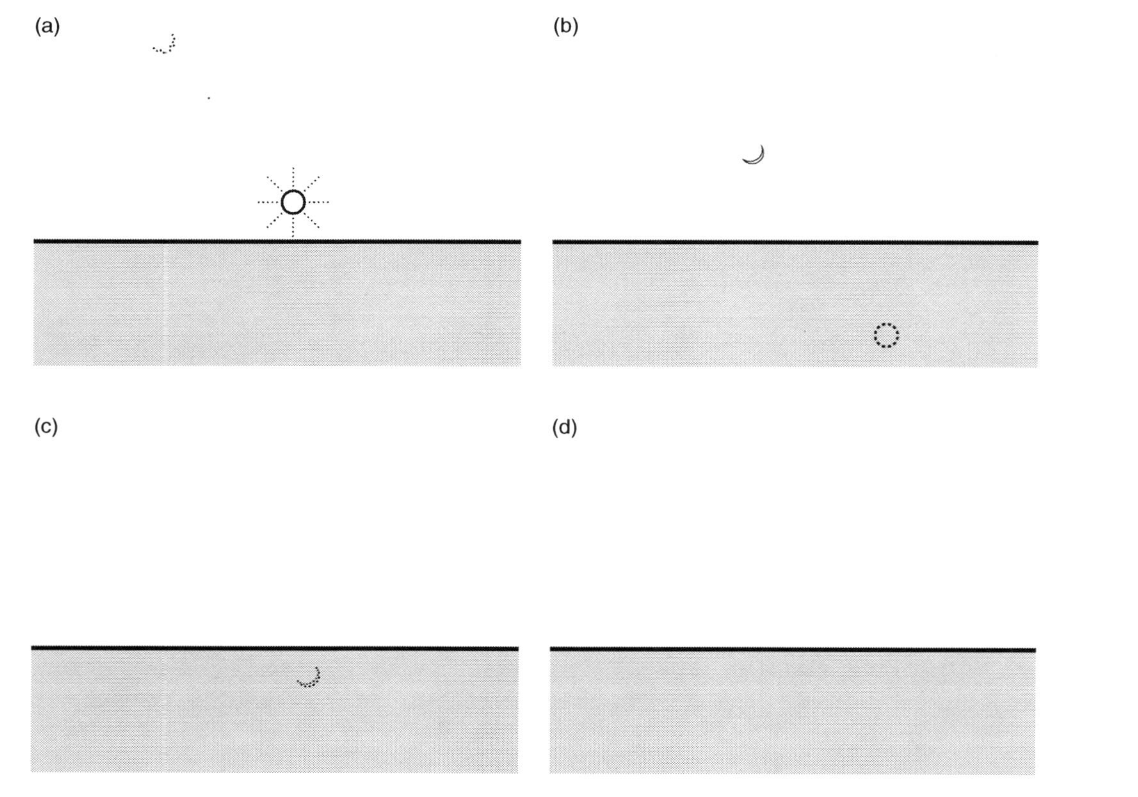

Fig. 4.2 Observing the new crescent moon (in the evening sky). (a) Just before sunset: the moon and the sun are both above the horizon; the moon is lost in the glare from the sun and is not yet visible. (b) Half an hour after (a), the sun has set and the moon is now visible above the horizon. (c) One hour after (a), the moon has now also set and being below the horizon is no longer visible. (d) Midnight: both the sun and the moon are below the horizon and cannot be seen.

in the glare from the sun).[3] The sun then sets, because it moves below the horizon, the sky darkens and the thin crescent of the new moon becomes visible (typically about fifteen minutes after sunset) because the moon is no longer lost in the glare from the sun (fig. 4.2b). However, the moon moves around the earth in the same direction as the sun, and it also sets in the western sky. (I am writing from an observer's viewpoint. The effect is, of course, due to the earth rotating on its axis once every twenty-four hours.) The new moon remains visible for typically thirty minutes before it, too, sets below the horizon (fig. 4.2c), and cannot be seen again that night because it is below the horizon for the rest of the night (fig. 4.2d).

When the new crescent moon is visible

Time	Visibility
Daytime	Invisible
Immediately after sunset	Invisible
From about 15 minutes to about 45 minutes after sunset	Visible
For the rest of the night	Invisible

Very understandably, some eminent scholars who lack knowledge about astronomy can make mistakes about ancient calendars. For example, the Assyriologist Professor Mark Cohen, in his book devoted to ancient calendars, *The Cultic Calendars of the Ancient Near East*, writes: 'This situation [determining the start of the lunar month] must have been particularly acute if the sighting of the first crescent of the new moon occurred towards morning.'[4] As we have seen, it is an astronomical impossibility for the first crescent of the new moon to be seen towards morning, because the new moon is *below* the horizon at this time (see fig. 4.3a).[5] Somewhat similarly, Nikos Kokkinos writes: 'It is still not impossible that the new moon was detected after sunrise of the following day (in the Julian calendar), some twelve hours later.'[6] In fact it *is* impossible to see the new moon just after sunrise since it is below the horizon at this time and hence invisible

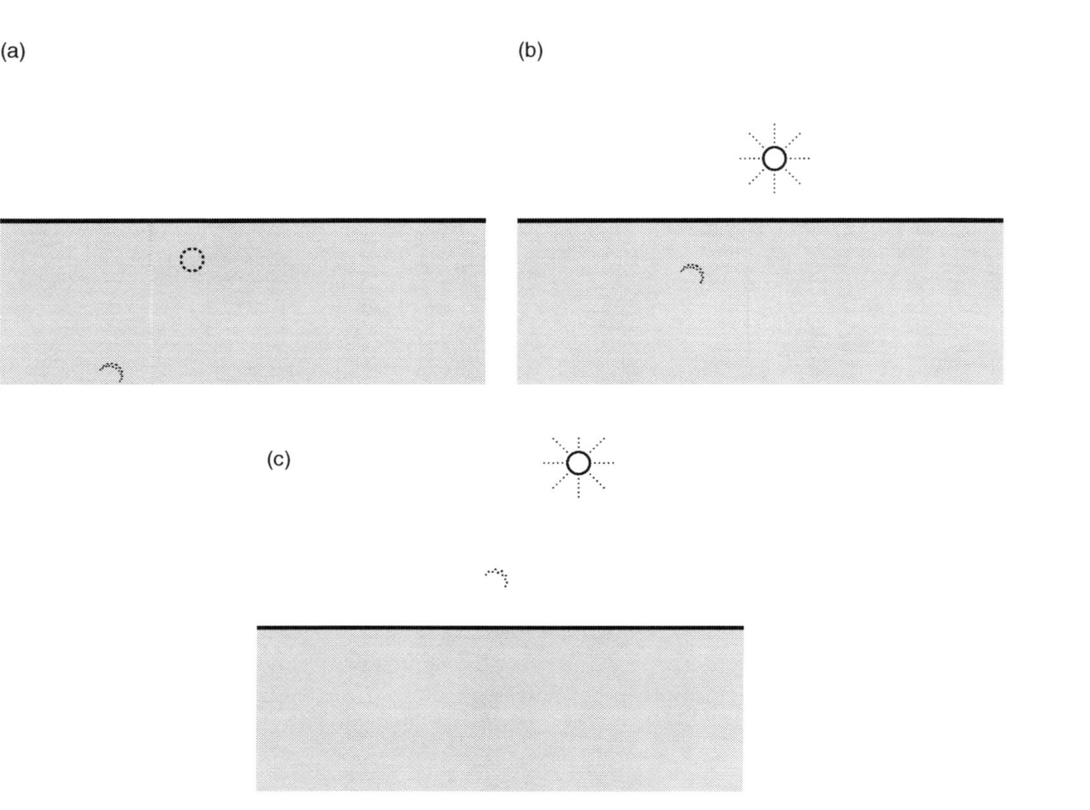

Fig. 4.3 The invisibility of the new crescent moon in the morning sky. (a) Just before sunrise, both the sun and the moon are below the horizon and hence invisible. (b) Just after sunrise, the moon is still below the horizon and so remains invisible. (c) After sunrise, both the sun and the moon are now above the horizon, but the moon remains invisible, being lost in the sun's glare in the bright sky.

(see fig. 4.3b). It is also impossible to see the new moon when it has risen above the horizon because it is lost in the sun's glare in the bright sky (fig. 4.3c). At noon, both the sun and the new moon are higher in the sky than in fig. 4.2c, but the new moon is still invisible, because it is lost in the sun's glare in the bright sky. I make these points because, fascinatingly, they turn out to be important when we consider the solution to the problems of the last week of Jesus.

RECONSTRUCTING THE FIRST-CENTURY AD JEWISH CALENDAR

When I started to investigate, back in 1981, the use of astronomy to reconstruct the first-century AD Jewish calendar, I soon found that I was not the first person to have had this idea. A number of people had attempted this previously, including the great seventeenth-century scientist Sir Isaac Newton. Newton's work was built upon by a number of lesser-known scientists, and then, in 1934, the eminent Oxford historian and astronomer Dr J. K. Fotheringham produced an improved calendar reconstruction that is still referenced by biblical scholars today.

However, there is a problem. Reconstructing the first-century AD Jewish calendar is not straightforward; in particular it is not simply a matter of winding backwards in time the equations of motion of the moon and the earth. To understand this, and how the problems can be solved, we need to return to the astronomy outlined at the start of this chapter. First, let me recap what we already know. In the first century AD, the official Jewish calendar was a lunar calendar in which the month began with the first sighting of the new lunar crescent. This crescent is first visible in the western sky in the evening, shortly after sunset. The first day of the month then naturally begins that evening.

It is important to understand that the new moon itself is invisible to the human eye, because it is lost in the glare from the sun. At new moon time, the moon, in its orbit around the earth, is between the earth and the sun (fig. 4.4a). Astronomers call the moment when the

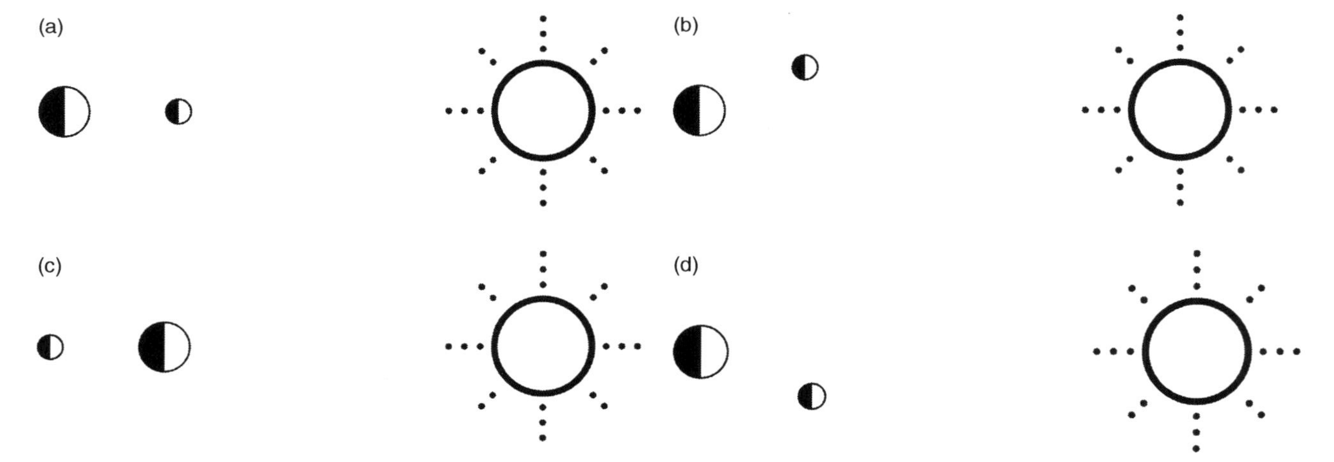

Fig. 4.4 (a) Conjunction: the moon (in the middle) is between the sun (on the right) and the earth (on the left). The moon cannot be seen from the earth because it is lost in the glare from the sun. (b) First visibility of the new crescent moon. A day or so after conjunction the moon can be seen as a thin crescent in the evening sky following sunset. (c) Full moon occurs two weeks after conjunction, when the moon is opposite the sun in the sky. (d) Last visibility of the old crescent moon. As the moon approaches conjunction once again, it is visible in the morning sky before sunrise as a thin crescent.

moon, sun and earth are in a line 'conjunction'. At the time of conjunction the moon is completely invisible to the unaided eye, because the dark portion of the moon faces the earth.[7] It is only after a certain length of time following conjunction, typically about thirty hours, that the first faintly glowing lunar crescent becomes visible (fig. 4.4b). Two weeks after conjunction we have the full moon, when the moon is opposite the sun in the sky, rising at sunset and setting at sunrise (fig. 4.4c). As the moon approaches conjunction, it is last seen, typically about thirty hours before conjunction, as a thin crescent in the morning sky (fig. 4.4d). This is why there are two or three nights every lunar month when no moon can be seen at all between the disappearance of the 'old moon' in the morning sky and the reappearance of the 'new moon' in the evening sky. Many ancient civilisations (for example, Egypt) believed that the moon had died and was in the underworld during this period. It was then conceived on the day of conjunction and, one or two days later, the crescent of the new moon signalled its visible rebirth every month.

The visibility of the moon each lunar month	
Conjunction (moon, sun, earth in line)	Moon invisible
About 30 hours later	New crescent moon first visible
About 14 days later	Full moon
About 14 days later	Old crescent moon last visible
About 30 hours later: conjunction	Moon invisible

It is relatively straightforward for astronomers to wind back in time the equations of motion of the moon around the earth and the earth around the sun and calculate the times of conjunction in the first century AD. It is much more difficult to calculate when the thin crescent of the new moon would first have been seen following conjunction. For this reason, most scientists from the time of Newton up to about 1930 did not attempt to calculate when the lunar crescent would first be visible, but instead calculated the time of conjunction and then added typically thirty hours to take them to when they thought the lunar crescent would first be visible.

However, it is known that this thirty-hour criterion is only an average figure. The actual time which must elapse after conjunction for the first crescent of the new moon to be visible from Jerusalem varies from a minimum of seventeen hours to a maximum of forty-two. Hence these early astronomical reconstructions, up to about 1930, of the first-century AD Jewish calendar sometimes gave the wrong day for the first day of the month. Biblical scholars were therefore cautious about using astronomy to calculate the ancient Jewish calendar, and rightly so.

FOTHERINGHAM'S CALCULATIONS

In 1934, J.K. Fotheringham published his influential paper, 'The Evidence of Astronomy and Technical Chronology for the Date of the Crucifixion.'[8] Fotheringham used a more realistic criterion for when the crescent of the new moon would first be seen than the thirty-hour one that had been used previously, and his calculations correctly predicted many observations of new moons.

Many biblical scholars were initially enthusiastic about these calculations until it was realised that several new moons had been recently observed which should not have been seen, according to Fotheringham's calculations. The enthusiasm of scholars then understandably waned, because the calculations were clearly not totally reliable (they were correct about 90 per cent of the time). For example, the eminent biblical scholar Joachim Jeremias wrote: 'Later both Schoch [another Oxford astronomer] and Fotheringham, on the basis of a new light [that is, light from the new crescent moon] observation made by many people in Kubebe, were compelled to admit that their formula was not accurate ... Astronomical chronology leads unfortunately to no certain result.'[9]

WADDINGTON'S COMPUTATIONS

In 1981 I was at Oxford University, and thinking in my spare time about the problems of dating the crucifixion. Almost fifty years had elapsed since Fotheringham, working at the same university, had published his 1934 paper. I knew that astronomy had made major advances in those fifty years; for example we could land a man on the moon with pinpoint precision, and I wondered if it was possible to improve on Fotheringham's calculations. I needed expert astronomical advice on this, so I approached the Oxford astrophysicist, Graeme Waddington. 'Graeme,' I said, 'would you be interested in seeing if it is possible to improve upon the calculations made in 1934 by Fotheringham? Surely astronomy must have advanced a lot since 1934.'

Waddington rose to the challenge and wrote a superb set of computer programs using a totally different approach from Fotheringham. Briefly, whether the crescent moon is visible or not depends on a number of factors including how dark the sky is after sunset, which depends upon the position of the sun below the horizon, the position of the moon in the sky at and after sunset, the brightness of the thin lunar crescent, how this is degraded by the atmosphere, etc. Waddington calculated all these effects and even took into account how the unevenness of the moon's surface affected its brightness. Further details are given in a paper we published in the leading scientific journal *Nature*.[10]

Incidentally, papers submitted to *Nature* are published only after extensive refereeing by experts. Normally there are two referees, who are anonymous. However, because of the high public profile our paper was likely to have if it was published, our paper had four referees. Unusually, because the referees were extremely positive, we were told their identity. We had an expert on astronomy, an authority on ancient calendars, a biblical scholar and a bishop with expertise in the life of Christ. I was particularly keen to have our calculations given the stamp of approval by both scientific and theological experts, which is why the paper was submitted to *Nature* rather than to a theological journal. The important point here is that leading experts agreed that our calculations were significantly more accurate than those of Fotheringham, and hence our paper merited publication in *Nature*.

In addition, Waddington checked the predictions of his calculations against 1,282 recorded observations of new moons and they gave the correct answer *every* time, including the occasions on which Fotheringham's calculations failed to give the right answer. We can therefore have confidence in them. Waddington's calculations of the date of Nisan 14, based on the earliest possible sighting of the crescent moon (which gives the date of Nisan 1) for the period AD 26–36 are given in the table.

The date of Nisan 14 in Jerusalem, AD 26–36, in the Jewish calendar

Year (AD)	Day	Date of Nisan 14
26	Sunday	April 21
27	Thursday	April 10*
28	Tuesday	March 30
29	Monday	April 18+
30	Friday	April 7+
31	Tuesday	March 27
32	Sunday	April 13*
33	Friday	April 3
34	Wednesday	March 24
35	Tuesday	April 12
36	Saturday	March 31

The date of Nisan 14 given is the Julian day (from midnight to midnight), starting at 6th hour Nisan 14 and ending at 6th hour Nisan 15.

* Nisan 14 AD 27 and AD 32 could have been on the following day if the new moon was not detected owing to poor atmospheric transparency.

+ In each of these cases it is not impossible, but highly improbable, that Nisan 14 would have occurred on the preceding day.

Let me say a few words about the use of the table and its footnotes. We can have considerable confidence in all the dates given, apart from the following dates when Waddington's calculations show the new crescent moon was very faint, and hence it is marginal whether the light from the new moon would have first been seen that day or the next. In particular, Nisan 14 in AD 27 and AD 32 could have been on the following day if the new moon was not detected owing to what scientists call 'poor atmospheric transparency', that is, a not very clear sky. On the other hand, Nisan 14 in AD 29 and 30 could have been on the preceding day if the night sky was exceptionally clear. It is interesting to note that Graeme Waddington's figures in the table agree substantially with the earlier calculations of Fotheringham. Minor differences will be pointed out in the next chapter.

It is important to realise that the calculations themselves reveal that on some occasions it is marginal whether the new moon will be seen on one night or the next. However, in these cases I will include *both* possibilities in the analysis to be performed in the next chapter. Thus this table, if used correctly, can cover *all* possibilities. In particular, it can be used to answer the key question we posed in the last chapter: in the period AD 26–36 when did Nisan 14 or 15 fall on a Friday?

TRANSFERRING DATES FROM THE JEWISH TO THE JULIAN CALENDAR

The date of Nisan 14 in the table (Sunday, April 21, AD 26, and so on) is the calculated date in the Julian calendar. As explained in Chapter 2, this is the standard convention used by historians and biblical scholars for referring to all dates before the Gregorian calendar reform in AD 1582, and the Julian calendar is named after the person who introduced it, Julius Caesar. However, there is a small difficulty in transferring dates between the Jewish lunar calendar and the Julian solar calendar, because the Jewish day runs from sunset to sunset and the Julian day (which was the day used by the ancient Romans and which we still use today) runs from midnight to midnight.

How do we transfer dates from the Jewish calendar to the Julian calendar when the days in each calendar start at different times? This is a frequent source of confusion, even among scholars, but there is a standard convention historians use which I will use throughout this book. The convention is that the (midnight-to-midnight) day in the Julian calendar transfers to the (sunset-to-sunset) day in the Jewish calendar that started six hours earlier. For example, let us take the first date in the table. What do we mean when we say that in AD 26, Sunday April 21 (in the Julian calendar) was Nisan 14 (in the Jewish calendar)? We mean that Sunday April 21 corresponds to most of Nisan 14, from midnight through to 6 p.m., plus part of Nisan 15, from 6 p.m. to midnight.

Example of transferring dates from the Julian calendar to the Jewish calendar

Date in Julian calendar	Date in Jewish calendar
April 21, AD 26, midnight-to-midnight day	Midnight-to-sunset, Nisan 14 plus sunset-to-midnight, Nisan 15

I am deliberately spelling out in detail how we transfer dates between the Jewish and the Julian calendars because most historians and biblical scholars do not explain this. As I keep repeating, understanding ancient calendars is so important in reconstructing the last week of Jesus that we need to be as clear as possible about them.

THE SCEPTICISM OF BIBLICAL SCHOLARS

How have biblical scholars reacted to the improved calculations of the date of Nisan 14 in AD 26–36, which Waddington and I published in *Nature* (reproduced in the table on p. 50)? As we have seen, scholars have been familiar with previous astronomical calculations of the Jewish calendar by Fotheringham and scientists before him, and they have been sceptical about them, for the good reason that they have not been totally accurate. Many biblical scholars now appear to accept the improved accuracy of the calculations in my 1983 *Nature* paper with Waddington, and this paper is referenced in many biblical commentaries and related books (for example, in the 1998 revised edition of Jack Finegan's *Handbook of Biblical Chronology*, in John Meier's *A Marginal Jew: Rethinking the Historical Jesus*, published in 1991, and so on). However, most scholars remain extremely cautious about the use of these calculations, a typical comment being that of Meier: 'The tentative nature of all these calculations must therefore be stressed.'[11]

Why are Meier, and most other biblical scholars, so sceptical of the astronomical reconstruction of the Jewish calendar given by Waddington and myself, when we have demonstrated that the mathematical methods used accurately predict the observations of 1,282 new moons in both recent and earlier times, and we have found not a single occasion on which these calculations fail? The answer is that scholars have changed the focus of their criticisms. Although they now seem to accept the *accuracy* of our modern calculations, unlike those of Fotheringham and his predecessors, they question their *relevance* to the Jewish calendar for two reasons which need to be taken seriously. I will quote from Meier since he articulates his doubts particularly clearly. Meier writes: 'At first glance, the use of science to solve this problem of biblical chronology (the date of the crucifixion) looks very promising; but there is more than one obstacle to a clear scientific solution'.[12] Meier specifies two 'obstacles to a clear scientific solution'. First, the possibility of a cloudy sky obscuring the new moon and second, the possibility of a leap year.

THE PROBLEM OF A CLOUDY SKY

Concerning the problem of a cloudy sky, Meier writes: 'The declaration [of two witnesses that they had seen the new light of the new moon] therefore depended not on whether the new light actually existed, but on whether human beings had *seen* it [my italics].

Clouds, rain, dust and other atmospheric disturbances of which we cannot now be sure could have delayed the sighting of the new moon.'[13]

The point Meier makes about the problem of a cloudy sky is a good one, and it has not been satisfactorily answered previously by, for example, Fotheringham, or in the 1983 *Nature* paper by Waddington and myself. Jerusalem has a Mediterranean, rather than a desert, climate, and clouds and rain in March and April are not uncommon. So although rainfall in Jerusalem is typically nil from June to September, it is 64 mm (2.5") in March and 28 mm (1.1") in April.[14] However, average daily hours of sunshine in these months are high, because most of the rain falls at night or in short, sharp, daytime bursts. As a rough estimate, the chance of clouds preventing the new moon being seen from Jerusalem in these months is probably about 10 per cent. Was the climate in Jerusalem the same two thousand years ago as it is today? Most scholars agree that the best estimate is to assume that it was much the same then as now. For example, olive trees still thrive on the Mount of Olives today, just as they did two thousand years ago.

Only five miles to the east of Jerusalem the climate and soil change to that of a desert and the rainfall is less than half that in Jerusalem. As John Wilkinson says: 'Clouds regularly disappear as they pass over the Mount of Olives [which is to the east of Jerusalem].'[15] It is not unreasonable to suppose that the priests of the temple might have placed some witnesses of the new moon five miles to the east of Jerusalem, where cloud cover would have been much less, thus maximising the opportunity of seeing the new moon. These witnesses would then have rushed back to Jerusalem on their camels and declared whether or not the new moon was visible. They had to report before the end of twilight (when the first stars became visible) which is typically ninety minutes after sunset in Jerusalem in March/April. Since the new crescent moon is first visible about fifteen minutes after sunset they would have had time to get back. However, the problem remains of what happened to the calendar on those occasions when the sky was cloudy, or there was a dust storm. The time from one new moon to the next is 29.53 days. So on average the new moon will be seen approximately every 29.5 days. Since a month is a whole number of days, some lunar months last for twenty-nine days and others for thirty days. A lunar month cannot last for twenty-eight or thirty-one days.

What happened if the evening of the twenty-ninth day was cloudy so that witnesses were unable to see whether or not there was a new moon? Unfortunately, we have no Jewish literature that answers this question. However, it is likely that the *observation* of the moon was paramount and then the start of the month would indeed have been delayed by a day because of a cloudy sky.[16] However, if a cloudy sky delayed the start of the month by a day, we can *fully* take this into account in the table above by adding one day to each day in the table. For example, the date of Nisan 14 in AD 26 becomes Monday, April 22, not Sunday, April 21. The table gives the dates of Nisan 14 for the period AD 26–36 if clouds delayed the start of the month by one day.

The effect of a cloudy sky delaying the date of Nisan 14 in Jerusalem, AD 26–36

Year (AD)	Day	Date of Nisan 14
26	Monday	April 22
27	Friday	April 11
28	Wednesday	March 31
29	Tuesday	April 19
30	Saturday	April 8
31	Wednesday	March 28
32	Monday	April 14
33	Saturday	April 4
34	Thursday	March 25
35	Wednesday	April 13
36	Sunday	April 1

From the table, we can see that in the period AD 26–36, if the month of Nisan was delayed by a day because of a cloudy sky, Nisan 14 would fall on a Friday in AD 27 (April 11) and Nisan 15 would fall on a

Friday in AD 34 (March 26). I will take these possibilities into account in the next chapter, when we answer the question of when Nisan 14 or 15 fell on a Friday.

We should also ask whether two successive cloudy evenings might have delayed the start of the month by two days? In particular, since lunar months had to be either twenty-nine or thirty days long, if it was cloudy on the evenings of *both* the twenty-ninth and the thirtieth days of the month, then what would happen? The commonsense solution is that if the night was cloudy on both the twenty-ninth and the thirtieth day of the month then the Jewish priests would proclaim a new month anyway, because they knew a lunar month could not last for thirty-one days. In this case we do have textual evidence that this was indeed what happened. The Tannaitic Commentary *Sifra Emor* 10 (paragraph 229.1) explicitly states that the month was declared to be thirty days long if the moon was not seen on the twenty-ninth. So the *maximum* delay in the start of a month due to a cloudy sky was one day. Using the tables in this chapter we can therefore *fully* take into account not only if the sky was clear but also if it was cloudy at new moon time. This is the first time that such calculations have taken into account the possibility of a cloudy sky.[17]

THE PROBLEM OF LEAP YEARS

Meier, and other scholars, then raise a second difficulty: the problem of leap years. Meier writes: 'To adjust the lunar calendar to the actual solar year, every now and then a leap year would have to be added to the Jewish calendar. There was probably no regular cycle of leap years in the early 1st century AD; they were added whenever the authorities decided from concrete observation (especially of agriculture) that they were needed. We cannot be sure whether a leap year fell between AD 29 and 34. Any calculations must therefore remain tentative.'[18]

Meier is correct in pointing out the problem of a leap year, but he is incorrect in stating that 'Any calculations must therefore remain tentative', because we can *fully* take into account leap years in our calculations. Indeed, we did this in our original *Nature* paper. To answer this second criticism of Meier we need to understand about leap years. We all know about leap years in our calendar today, but how were leap years determined in the Jewish calendar in the first century AD?

As we have seen, some lunar months last for twenty-nine days and others for thirty days. Twelve lunar months, of twenty-nine and thirty days each, total 354 days. But a solar year contains approximately 365 days. Thus a lunar year contains about eleven days less than a solar year. For agricultural and religious festival reasons, the Jews needed to keep lunar months in step with the seasons, and hence in approximately the same place in the solar year, and they did this by adding an additional lunar month, sometimes called an intercalary month or a 'leap month', when necessary at the end of their lunar year (just before the month of Nisan). In a similar way we keep our Gregorian calendar in step with the true solar year by adding a 'leap day' when necessary at the end of February. The Jews needed to keep their lunar calendar in step with the solar year because, for example, on Nisan 14 the Passover lambs were sacrificed, and they needed to be ready, and on Nisan 16 the first sheaves of barley were waved in the temple by the priests. If the barley wasn't ready, there was nothing to wave at this festival, called a first-fruits festival. On the other hand, if the barley was over-ripe then the crops would be lost because harvesting could not commence until the first-fruits had been waved in the temple. So it was essential that the Jewish lunar calendar kept in step with the solar year.

We know from Jewish records that different methods of adding leap months were used at different periods of Jewish history, but in the first century AD the addition of a leap month was regulated annually by the Sanhedrin (a Jewish council chaired by the high priest) according to certain criteria. The most important of these, known as the rule of the equinox, was that Passover must fall after the spring equinox (this is the day in the spring when the length of the day equals the length of the night, hence the name equinox). For example, Anatolius, Bishop of Laodicea in Syria, wrote as follows in *Canons of the Passover* in about AD 270: 'This [the rule of the equinox] is not our own reckoning, but it was known to the Jews long ago even before Christ and it was carefully observed by them. One can learn it from what is said by Philo, Josephus and Musaeus ... when these writers explain questions concerning the Exodus, they say it is necessary that all alike sacrifice the Passover after the vernal equinox, in the middle of the month.' (Interestingly, in AD 325 the Council of Nicaea issued the Easter Rule: that Easter Sunday should be after the vernal (spring) equinox, and this rule is still used today.) If, towards the end of a Jewish year, it was estimated that Passover would fall before the equinox then the addition of an extra month before Nisan was decreed. The tables giving the dates of Nisan 14 in this chapter have been constructed on this basis.

However, a leap month could also be decreed before Nisan if the crops had been delayed by exceptionally bad weather (since the first-fruits of barley had to be ready for presentation in the temple on Nisan 16), or if the lambs were too young. Think of the power this gave the Sanhedrin. I have many times wished for the ability to decree an extra month as I approached a deadline. However, there is no power without responsibility, and think of the criticism that would be heaped on the Sanhedrin if they decreed an extra month unnecessarily so that the barley was then over-ripe, and the harvest was lost. (There would then have been a scarcity of animal feed, since barley was mainly used for feeding animals.)

Unfortunately we possess no historical records of the proclamation of leap months in the period AD 26–36. It is therefore possible that in some years Nisan was one month later than given in the tables in this chapter because of exceptionally severe weather. Waddington has repeated his series of calculations assuming that a leap month was proclaimed in *each* year in the period AD 26–36 because of bad weather. The calculations, given in our *Nature* paper, show that in the period AD 26–36, if Nisan was one month later, Nisan 14 would not fall on a Friday in any year, and Nisan 15 would only fall on a Friday in AD 34 (April 23). Thus we have *fully* taken into account in our calculations the possibility of leap years. We have now answered the concerns of Meier and other biblical scholars about the reliability and use of our reconstructed calendar. I believe we can use it with confidence.

SUMMARY

We reached some important conclusions in this chapter. In the first century AD, each month in the Jewish calendar began with the evening when the new crescent moon was first visible. We showed that it is possible to reconstruct this ancient calendar using modern astronomical calculations. These calculations agree with over one thousand recorded observations of new moons, and give the correct answer every time. We can therefore have considerable confidence in them. The calculated date of Nisan 14 in Jerusalem in the period AD 26–36 is given in a table in this chapter.

Many biblical scholars accept the accuracy of these modern scientific calculations, but they are cautious about using them for two reasons: first, the possibility of a cloudy sky obscuring the new moon, and second, the possibility of there being a leap year. Concerning the problem of a cloudy sky, I have shown that the most a month could be delayed by is one day. The date of Nisan 14 in the period AD 26–36 if a cloudy sky delayed the start of the month is given in another table in this chapter. Using this table and the previous one, we can say when Nisan 14 or 15 fell on a Friday, whether or not the month was delayed because of a cloudy sky.

Concerning the possibility of priests proclaiming a leap year, which involved inserting an extra month before Nisan into the Jewish calendar, we can take this into account in our calculations. It is then found that in the period AD 26–36, if there was such a leap year, then Nisan 14 would not fall on a Friday in any year and Nisan 15 fell on a Friday on April 23, AD 34. We can therefore fully answer the two reservations biblical scholars have about the use of modern astronomy to reconstruct the first-century AD Jewish calendar. Hence I believe we can have considerable confidence in this calculated calendar. It provides us with the key framework we require to reconstruct the last days of Jesus.

In the next chapter we will use this calendar, and a variety of biblical clues, to determine the *exact* date on which Jesus died. We will also find that, perhaps surprisingly, we can use our reconstructed calendar to throw light upon the nature of the last supper, and rule out two of the most popular interpretations of biblical scholars. In this next chapter we are going to fit together some really key pieces of the jigsaw of the last week of Jesus.

5 The date of the crucifixion

> For Christ, our Passover lamb, has been sacrificed.
>
> (1 Corinthians 5:7)

> But Christ has indeed been raised from the dead, the first-fruits of those who have fallen asleep.
>
> (1 Corinthians 15:20)

In the last chapter I argued that we can use astronomy to reconstruct the first-century AD Jewish calendar. In this chapter we will see if it is possible to use our reconstructed calendar, together with biblical and historical clues, to determine not only the year but also the precise day and month on which Christ died. If we know this date, this enables us to start to answer the question of whether or not the last supper was a Passover meal. In particular, in Chapter 3 we gave four possible interpretations of the gospels concerning the date and nature of the last supper. In this chapter we will show that we can reject two of these interpretations. As we will see, both biblical and non-biblical clues fit together in a most remarkable way.

DETERMINING THE DATE OF THE CRUCIFIXION

Let us start by reminding ourselves about what we already know. In Chapters 2 and 3, I showed that the crucifixion was in the period AD 26–36, it was on a Friday and it was on either Nisan 14 or 15 in the official Jewish calendar, depending on the correct interpretation of John's gospel and the synoptics. Virtually all biblical scholars agree with these three statements, and I believe they are correct, beyond reasonable doubt.

In Chapter 4 I used astronomy to reconstruct the official Jewish calendar in Jerusalem, and I presented tables giving the dates of Nisan 14 in the period AD 26–36, which took into account the possibility of a cloudy sky delaying the sighting of the new moon. I also took into account the possibility that the Jewish priests had inserted an extra 'leap month' into the calendar at the end of the Jewish year because the winter had been exceptionally cold. Using the tables in the last chapter we can specify the possible dates of the crucifixion, which are when Nisan 14 or 15 fell on a Friday in the period AD 26–36. These dates are given in the table.

Possible dates for the crucifixion

Jewish day	Gospel interpretation	Date (Julian calendar)
Nisan 14	John correct. Synoptics correct either if the last supper was a Passover-like meal, or if they used a different calendar.	Friday, April 11, AD 27 Friday, April 7, AD 30 Friday, April 3, AD 33
Nisan 15	Synoptics correct. John either wrong, or can be interpreted to agree with the synoptics.	Friday, April 11, AD 27 Friday, March 26, AD 34 Friday, April 23, AD 34

Friday, April 11, AD 27 in the table occurs against both Nisan 14 and 15. This is because the calculations of Waddington show that Friday, April 11, AD 27 could have fallen on either Nisan 14 or 15, depending on the atmospheric conditions at the start of that month, because the day on which the new lunar crescent could have been first detected is very marginal, as I explained in the last chapter. In addition, if the month of Nisan was delayed by a day because of a cloudy sky, Nisan 15 would fall on a Friday on March 26, AD 34, and if it was delayed by a month because of an exceptionally severe winter, Nisan 15 would fall on a Friday on April 23, AD 34. To cover all options I have included all possibilities.

It is interesting to note that the dates in the table above are identical to the possible dates for the crucifixion given earlier by Fotheringham,[1] except that Waddington's more accurate calculations show that April 11, AD 27 could have fallen on either Nisan 14 or 15, and that March 26, AD 34 and April 23, AD 34 are also possibilities. The computations of astronomers can land a man on the moon, or a robot on Mars, with pinpoint precision. We really can have considerable confidence in the dates in the above table, calculated using modern astronomical methods. These dates are the *only* possible dates for the crucifixion.

From this table we can see that the only possible years for the crucifixion are AD 27, 30, 33 and 34. All other years are impossible. Several modern scholars have suggested that the crucifixion occurred in AD 36.[2] From our table we can say that this is impossible. So we are starting to see how the use of astronomy to reconstruct ancient calendars can help to solve historical biblical problems and rule out the ideas of some scholars. But can we narrow down further the possible dates for the crucifixion? To do that we need to find some more clues from the Bible and other ancient literature.

THE CLUE OF JOHN THE BAPTIST

Luke provides us with another piece of the jigsaw by specifying when John the Baptist started his ministry. This is relevant to finding the date of the crucifixion because after John the Baptist started preaching Jesus came to him to be baptised, so the date of the crucifixion must be after John the Baptist started his ministry.

There can be no doubt that Luke intended to pinpoint the year in which John the Baptist started preaching and to root this in history. He writes: 'In the fifteenth year of the reign of Tiberius Caesar – when Pontius Pilate was Governor of Judea, Herod tetrarch of Galilee, his brother Philip tetrarch of Iturea and Traconitis, and Lysanias tetrarch of Abilene – during the high priesthood of Annas and Caiaphas, the word of God came to John son of Zechariah in the desert. He went into all the country around the Jordan, preaching a baptism of repentance for the forgiveness of sins' (Luke 3:1–3).

Luke not only specifies the precise year when John the Baptist started his ministry, in the fifteenth year of the Roman emperor

Tiberius, he also sets the scene politically, by telling us who was ruling some of the Roman provinces at the time: Pontius Pilate was governor of Judea, Herod tetrarch of Galilee, and so on (incidentally, this Herod is not Herod the Great, who was alive when Jesus was born, but his son, Herod Antipas).

What year was the fifteenth year of the reign of Tiberius? As we saw in Chapter 2, Tiberius began to govern jointly with the existing emperor Augustus, his stepfather, in AD 12. Augustus died on August 19, AD 14 and the Roman Senate appointed Tiberius as the new emperor less than one month later, on September 17, AD 14. When Luke says that John the Baptist started his ministry in the fifteenth year of Tiberius, was he counting the fifteen years from AD 12 or AD 14?

Luke tells us that he wrote his gospel for a person called Theophilus (Luke 1:4), and from the way that Luke addresses him he was probably a Roman official.[3] The style in which Luke writes, 'In the fifteenth year of the reign of . . .', is typical of the style of Roman and Greek historians of the time. So how did Roman historians of the time count the years of Tiberius? As we saw in Chapter 2, John Meier states: 'All the major Roman historians who calculate the years of Tiberius' rule – namely, Tacitus, Suetonius and Cassius Dio – count from AD 14, the year of Augustus' death.'[4]

Nearly all modern scholars agree that the 'fifteen years' of Luke 3:1–2 should be counted from AD 14. However, a few scholars, for example Rainer Riesner, argue that the fifteen years should be counted from Tiberius' joint rule with Augustus.[5] There is no evidence to support this and Meier somewhat scathingly states: 'Presumably, Luke, who is intent on trying to follow the conventions of Greco-Roman historiography, would not have chosen an unheard-of means of reckoning Tiberius' years over a generally accepted one.'[6] In addition, it is clear from the coin evidence that Tiberius started to reign in AD 14 (see Chapter 2, fig. 2.1).

It is therefore clear that the fifteenth year of the reign of Tiberius should be counted from his appointment as the new emperor by the Roman Senate on September 17, AD 14. If we were counting the years of his reign today we would say that the first year was September 17, AD 14 to September 17, AD 15, so that the fifteenth year of his reign was from September 17, AD 28 to September 17, AD 29. However, once again we must remind ourselves that the way we count today is not necessarily the same as the way people counted in the first century AD.

Since Luke was writing to the Roman Theophilus, and since Luke 3:1–2 is written about the Roman emperor Tiberius, using a Roman style of writing, Luke is probably using the standard Roman method of counting regnal years when he refers to the fifteenth year of Tiberius. It is known that Roman historians of the time, such as Tacitus, dated the first year of a ruler's reign from January 1 of the year following the ruler's appointment.[7] So Roman historians counted the first year of the reign of Tiberius as January 1 to December 31, AD 15 (and the last year of the reign of the previous emperor, Augustus, as January 1 to December 31, AD 14), since the Roman year, using the Julian calendar, started on January 1. Thus Luke probably meant by the 'fifteenth year of the reign of Tiberius' the period January 1 to December 31, AD 29.

However, we cannot be certain that Luke used the standard Roman method of counting the years of rulers, and he may have used a Jewish calendar. If he was using the Jewish religious calendar that began in the spring, then, as Finegan shows, the fifteenth year of Tiberius was spring AD 29 to spring AD 30. If he was using the Jewish civil calendar that began in the previous autumn then the fifteenth year was autumn AD 28 to autumn AD 29.

The fifteenth year of the reign of Tiberius	
Using Roman Julian calendar	January 1 to December 31, AD 29
Using Jewish religious calendar	Spring AD 29 to spring AD 30
Using Jewish civil calendar	Autumn AD 28 to autumn AD 29

Thus the earliest possible date for John the Baptist to have started his ministry is autumn AD 28 and so the crucifixion of Jesus could not have occurred as early as AD 27. So in our table of possible dates for the crucifixion we can cross out AD 27. This is consistent with what we know about the life of Pilate. As we have seen, Pilate became the governor of Judea in AD 26. Most scholars believe that Pilate had been governor for some time before the crucifixion (see Luke 13:1 and 23:12). Thus on these grounds alone an AD 27 crucifixion is highly unlikely.

THE CLUE OF THE APOSTLE PAUL

Having ruled out AD 27 as being too early for the crucifixion, we can now eliminate AD 34 as being too late, since it would conflict with the date of Paul's conversion. We can date the later events in Paul's life with reasonable confidence. Working back from these, and using time intervals given by Paul himself (for example, three years and fourteen years, see Galatians 1:18 and 2:1), leads many scholars to infer that Paul's dramatic conversion on the road to Damascus was in AD 34.[8] Some other scholars date the conversion of Paul to AD 31 or 32,[9] in part because they believe the crucifixion was in AD 30. If the three years of Galatians 1:18 and the fourteen years of Galatians 2:1 are taken to run consecutively, which is the natural interpretation since Paul writes, 'Then after three years I went up to Jerusalem ... Fourteen years later I went up again to Jerusalem' (Galatians 1:18–2:1), then Robert Jewett's careful analysis shows that the date of Paul's conversion cannot have been later than AD 34.[10]

There are strong early traditions, dating back to the second century AD, that Paul's conversion occurred eighteen months after the crucifixion.[11] This time interval is consistent with the many events known to have happened between the crucifixion of Jesus and the conversion of Paul.[12] Hence the crucifixion cannot have been as late as spring, AD 34. There is no positive evidence in favour of AD 34 and I will therefore rule it out.[13]

JOHN'S CRUCIFIXION CHRONOLOGY IS CORRECT

Having eliminated AD 27 and 34 from the table in this chapter as possible years for the crucifixion, this leaves only two possible crucifixion dates: Friday, April 7, AD 30 and Friday, April 3, AD 33. Both of these dates are on Nisan 14 in the official Jewish calendar and this is a really important conclusion. The first point to note is that this conclusion rules out two of the four possible interpretations of the last supper that I gave in Chapter 3. In particular it rules out the interpretation 'Synoptics correct. John wrong. Crucifixion on Nisan 15', and the interpretation 'Synoptics correct. John can be interpreted to agree. Crucifixion on Nisan 15.' These are in fact the interpretations of the last supper favoured by the majority of biblical scholars. What I have shown, I believe beyond reasonable doubt, is that these interpretations cannot be correct. Thus the last supper cannot have been a Passover meal held on the appointed day, Nisan 15, in the official Jewish calendar. John is therefore correct in placing the crucifixion on Nisan 14. The belief of many scholars that John locates the crucifixion on Nisan 14 for the sake of theological symbolism at the expense of historical fact is hence incorrect.

Biblically and calendrically possible dates for the crucifixion

Jewish day	Gospel interpretation	Date (Julian calendar)
Nisan 14	John correct. Synoptics correct either if the last supper was a Passover-like meal, or if a different calendar was used.	Friday, April 7, AD 30 Friday, April 3, AD 33

Some scholars maintain that astronomical calculations do not totally exclude the possibility of the crucifixion being on Nisan 15. For example, Jeremias states, based on his understanding of Fotheringham's calculations, 'It [astronomical chronology] establishes the probability that Friday, April 7, 30 and Friday, April 3, 33, fell on Nisan 14, which would correspond to the Johannine chronology. But it does not completely exclude the possibility that Friday April 27, 31 (or, as a considerably weaker possibility, Friday, April 7, 30), fell on Nisan 15, which would agree with the Synoptic chronology.'[14] I would like to emphasise that the accurate calculations of Waddington make it absolutely clear that neither Friday, April 27, AD 31 nor Friday, April 7, AD 30 fell on Nisan 15. The calculations completely exclude these possibilities. Since it is so important, let me repeat that the crucifixion was on Nisan 14, in agreement with John, either Friday, April 7, AD 30 or Friday, April 3, AD 33.

THE SYMBOLIC SIGNIFICANCE OF JESUS DYING ON NISAN 14 AND RISING ON NISAN 16

Josephus (*War* 6.423) tells us that in the first century AD the Passover lambs were slain between 3 p.m. and 5 p.m. on Nisan 14, in the Jerusalem temple. We have just deduced that Jesus died on the same day, Nisan 14, and the gospels tell us that he died at the ninth hour (Matthew 27:45–50, Mark 15:33–37, Luke 23:44–46), that is at 3 p.m., at the time the first Passover lambs were being sacrificed. This striking symbolism of Jesus as the Passover lamb is used by the apostle Paul. For example: 'Christ, our Passover lamb, has been sacrificed' (1 Corinthians 5:7).

We can see how precise Paul was in his use of symbolism by considering a later part of the same letter to the Corinthians in which Paul writes: 'Christ has been raised from the dead, the first-fruits of those who have fallen asleep' (1 Corinthians 15:20). Here Paul is referring to Christ's resurrection, which he believed, in accordance with the very earliest Christian traditions, occurred on the third day after the crucifixion (1 Corinthians 15:4), that is, on the Sunday after the Friday.[15] What does Paul mean by using the word 'first-fruits' to refer to Christ? His first-century AD audience would have been in no doubt. The Old Testament book of Leviticus describes what the Jewish people called a first-fruits festival, which celebrated the barley harvest. 'Bring to the priest a sheaf of the first grain you harvest. He is to wave the sheaf before the Lord so that it will be accepted on your behalf; the priest is to wave it on the day after the Sabbath' (Leviticus 23:10–11).

What day is meant by 'the day after the Sabbath'? Segal argues that the view of the Sadducees on the date of the sheaf waving may have prevailed at one period of Jewish history, and the view of the Pharisees at another.[16] So which view prevailed at the time of Christ? Biblical scholars disagree on this, but the clear statements of the Jewish writers Philo and Josephus seem decisive. Philo (*c*.20 BC to AD 45) states in *De specialibus legibus* (2.144–75) that the first sheaf of barley was presented in the temple on the second day of the feast, that is on Nisan 16. Josephus agrees and writes: 'On the second day of unleavened bread, that is to say the sixteenth . . . they offer to Him the first-fruits of the barley . . . Thereafter all are permitted, publicly or individually, to begin harvest' (*Antiquities* 3.250–1). I therefore believe it is clear that at the time of Christ the first-fruits festival of barley was on Nisan 16.

Feasts and festivals around Passover in the Jewish calendar at the time of Christ

Nisan 1	Start of Jewish religious year
Nisan 10	Passover lambs selected
Nisan 14	Passover lambs slain from about 3 p.m. to 5 p.m.
Nisan 15	Passover meal eaten: first day of Feast of Unleavened Bread
Nisan 16	First-fruits festival to inaugurate the barley harvest

An interesting description of how the barley was collected and waved in the temple is given in the Mishnah, a rabbinic commentary compiled in about 200 AD, which states: 'On the eve after the first day of Passover, messengers from the court used to go to one of the barley fields near Jerusalem and in a festive ceremony would harvest a handful of barley which they then waved over the altar . . . The ceremony on the 16th of Nisan permitted the people to eat from the fresh harvest of that year' (Mishnah Menahot 10.3 and 10.6).

Paul cleverly uses the symbolism of this first-fruits festival to refer to the resurrection. What Paul is saying is that just as waving the first sheaf of barley in the temple inaugurated and enabled all of the barley to be gathered in, so the resurrection of Christ inaugurates and enables all those who have died ('fallen asleep') to be resurrected and gathered in. The chronology underlying the symbolism Paul uses is *exact*. We have just shown that the crucifixion was on Friday, Nisan 14. The resurrection on the following Sunday was therefore on Nisan 16, precisely the day the priests waved the first-fruits of the barley in the temple.

This dual symbolism of Christ both as the Passover lamb and as the first-fruits of those who rise from the dead is particularly striking. In using this symbolism Paul is acknowledging that the crucifixion was on Nisan 14 and that the resurrection was on Nisan 16, otherwise the basis of the symbolism is destroyed. It seems improbable that Paul would have used the *dual* symbolism of Christ as the Passover lamb and as the first-fruits of those who rise from the dead if *both* events were one day out. Paul has chosen this pair of symbols *because* of the dates. So Paul's implied chronology of the crucifixion events, recorded in one of the earliest New Testament documents, 1 Corinthians, written in about AD 55, is identical to that of John, which many scholars believe was the last gospel to be written, probably in about AD 90. Both are consistent with the chronology of the synoptic gospels, probably written between AD 60 and AD 90, provided the last supper was not a Passover meal held on the day specified in the official Jewish calendar.

Jack Finegan reflects a widespread belief among biblical scholars when he writes: 'The date of Nisan 14 for the death of Jesus depends largely upon the Gospel according to John.'[17] However, even if John's gospel did not exist, it is implicit in Paul's writings that Jesus died on Nisan 14. Many scholars suggest that the chronology of the crucifixion in the synoptics is likely to be more accurate than that in John, because the synoptics were written earlier. However, the crucifixion chronology given by Paul was probably written earlier still, in about AD 55, and Paul agrees with John. The synoptics also agree if the last supper was not a real Passover meal, or if it was a real Passover, but held using a different calendar from the official one.

Incidentally, if we accept that the crucifixion was on Friday, Nisan 14, and the resurrection on Sunday, Nisan 16, then in the year of the crucifixion Nisan 16 happened to coincide with the day after the normal weekly Sabbath that fell in Passover week. Hence in that year, both the Pharisees and the Sadducees would have been happy that the barley first-fruits festival was held on Nisan 16. Thus the chronology of the symbolism used by Paul would have been exact for both of these Jewish groups.

Are there any references in early non-biblical literature to whether or not Jesus died on Nisan 14 or 15? I am aware of only two.

The apocryphal *Gospel According to Peter* (verse 3) states explicitly that Jesus' death was on the eve of Passover, that is on Nisan 14. A Jewish source, the Babylonian Talmud (*Sanhedrin* 43a), records that 'On the eve of Passover they hanged Yeshu', earlier referred to as 'Yeshu the Nazarene' ('Jesus' is the Greek equivalent of the Semitic 'Yeshu'). Thus there is remarkable unanimity from all sources that the crucifixion was on Nisan 14, and consequently the only two plausible dates for the crucifixion are Friday, April 7, AD 30 and Friday, April 3, AD 33. Do we have any biblical clues that will enable us to say which of these two dates is correct?

CAN WE PINPOINT THE DATE OF THE CRUCIFIXION?

I believe there is a simple, straightforward argument that enables us to determine uniquely the date of the crucifixion, and it is this. The ministry of Jesus started after that of John the Baptist, whose role was to prepare the way for Jesus. Luke specifies that John the Baptist started his ministry in the fifteenth year of the reign of Tiberius, and I have shown that the earliest possible date for this was autumn AD 28. John records three different Passovers occurring during the ministry of Jesus (including the one at the crucifixion), so the earliest possible date for the first Passover of Jesus' ministry is spring AD 29, for the second Passover is spring AD 30, and for the third Passover is spring AD 31. Hence the crucifixion could not have been in AD 30, leaving April 3, AD 33 as the only possible year for the crucifixion. To my mind this argument is simple and conclusive.

The above argument uses the earliest possible dates for the ministry of John the Baptist and of Jesus. Let us now look at the most probable dates. As we saw earlier in this chapter, Luke was probably reckoning the fifteenth year of the reign of Tiberius using the Roman calendar, in which case he is saying that John the Baptist started his ministry sometime in the year January 1 to December 31, AD 29. It is clear from the gospels that John the Baptist had been preaching and baptising for some time before he baptised Jesus. Hence the first Passover of Jesus' ministry is most unlikely to have been in spring

AD 29 and much more likely to have been in spring AD 30 or even 31. Many scholars believe that in addition to the three Passovers in the ministry of Jesus mentioned explicitly by John, there was an additional Passover that John does not mention, but that can be deduced from various 'time notes' in his gospel.[18] If this is the case, then the ministry of Jesus lasted for three years, and the first Passover of his ministry was in AD 30, with the crucifixion in AD 33. On the other hand, if there were only three Passovers in Jesus' ministry, then it lasted for two years, the first Passover was in AD 31 and the crucifixion was in AD 33. Either way, what I believe is conclusive is that we can rule out AD 30 as the year of the crucifixion, leaving April 3, AD 33 as the only possible date.[19]

HOW OLD WAS JESUS WHEN HE STARTED HIS MINISTRY?

The Bible gives only two references to the age of Jesus. Luke tells us that 'Jesus himself was about thirty years old when he began his ministry' (Luke 3:23). On the other hand, John reports the Jews saying to Jesus during the course of his ministry: 'You are not yet fifty years old and yet you have seen Abraham' (John 8:57). Both figures are round numbers. As Hoehner points out, in John 8:57 the Jews were emphasising Jesus' youth in contrast to his claim that he existed before Abraham, hence we should not take the 'fifty years' statement too literally.[20]

Returning to Luke, it is interesting to contrast the precision with which he states that John the Baptist started his ministry 'In the fifteenth year of the reign of Tiberius' (Luke 3:1) with the imprecision regarding the start of Jesus' ministry: he was 'about thirty' (Luke 3:23). It would seem that Luke did not know the precise year of Jesus' birth, hence he can give only an approximate age for him. Hoehner asks: 'How much latitude can one allow for "about" thirty years of age? It seems that no more than two or three years on either side of thirty is feasible.'[21] Paul Maier argues that 'Luke's "about thirty" could well serve for any actual age ranging from 26 to 34.'[22]

I have argued elsewhere that Jesus was born in April, 5 BC.[23] Jesus' public ministry may have started some months before the first

Passover of his ministry, in, say, autumn AD 29, so that his ministry was for about three and a half years. If Jesus was born in April, 5 BC then he would have been 33 when he commenced his ministry (remembering that there is no year zero in the calendar which goes from 1 BC to AD 1). This is consistent with Luke 3:23, that he was 'about thirty' at this time. If 'about' permits four years' variation rather than three years, then the first Passover of Jesus' ministry could have been in AD 31 (with his ministry lasting for about two and a half years). Either way, Jesus was around his thirty-seventh birthday when he died on April 3, AD 33.

'IT HAS TAKEN FORTY-SIX YEARS TO BUILD THIS TEMPLE'

There is one further clue that is relevant to the date of the crucifixion, which is a fascinating one known as 'the temple reference'. At the first Passover of Jesus' ministry, John 2:20 records that the Jews said to Jesus as he was standing in the temple court in Jerusalem: 'It has taken forty-six years to build this temple.' What did the Jews mean by this? If they were referring to the original construction of the temple by Solomon in about 966 BC then their words clearly made no sense. However, Josephus tells us that the temple was reconstructed by Herod: 'It was at this time, in the eighteenth year of his reign, after the events mentioned above, that Herod undertook an extraordinary work, the reconstruction of the temple of God at his own expense, enlarging its precincts and raising it to a more imposing height' (*Antiquities* 15.380). (Incidentally, this Herod is Herod the Great, who was alive when Jesus was born (Matthew 2:1), not his son, Herod Antipas.)

Josephus writes that Herod reconstructed the temple 'in the eighteenth year of his reign'. Fortunately we know when this was, because slightly earlier in *Antiquities*, in section 15.354, Josephus writes: 'And when Herod had completed the seventeenth year of his reign, Caesar [Augustus] came to Syria.' The Roman historian Dio Cassius tells us in *Roman History* precisely when Caesar Augustus came to Syria, it was in the spring of 20 BC. So that marked the end of Herod's seventeenth year (we know that the Jewish historian Josephus reckoned the years of

Herod's reign as beginning on Nisan 1, the start of the Jewish religious year). Hence Herod's eighteenth year, in which he began to reconstruct the temple, was the year from Nisan 1, 20 BC to Nisan 1, 19 BC.[24]

Returning to John 2:20, what did the Jews mean when they said to Jesus: 'It has taken forty-six years to build this temple'? There are two Greek words the gospels, Josephus, etc., use for 'temple', and it is important to understand the difference between them. The first word, *hieron*, refers to the whole temple area, a large building complex that included the inner temple, three enclosed courtyards, storerooms, etc. *Hieron* is the word used for 'temple' in John 2:14, 15, for example ('In the temple courts he [Jesus] found men selling cattle . . . So he made a whip out of cords, and drove all from the temple area'). The second Greek word, *naos*, refers specifically to the inner sanctuary (comprising the vestibule, the holy place and the holy of holies). It was the *naos*, rather than the *hieron* as a whole, that was regarded as the dwelling-place of God.[25]

The Greek word used in John 2:20 is *naos*. It is therefore clear that this verse refers to the sacred inner sanctuary, and not to the whole temple complex. Shortly after writing that Herod began to reconstruct the whole temple complex in his eighteenth year, Josephus tells us about the huge preparations required before the building work could start. Josephus states that Herod 'prepared a thousand wagons to carry the stones, selected ten thousand of the most skilled workmen, purchased priestly robes for a thousand priests, and trained some as masons, others as carpenters, *and began the construction only after all these preparations had diligently been made*' (*Antiquities* 35.390). Josephus then writes: 'But the temple itself (*naos*) was built by the priests in a year and six months' (*Antiquities* 15.421). The work on the temple complex was not completed until 64 AD, six years before its destruction by the Romans. A key question is how long the preparatory work took before the eighteen months of building work started. If it took about six months and if Herod started the reconstruction of the temple in his eighteenth year, which we have seen was in the Nisan-to-Nisan year 20/19 BC, then Josephus is telling us that Herod completed building the inner temple, the *naos*, about two years later, which takes us to the year Nisan 1, 18 BC to Nisan 1, 17 BC. Many scholars agree with this.[26]

Returning again to the words of the Jews in John 2:20, 'It has taken forty-six years to build this temple (*naos*)', we can see that there is something odd about this verse. This NIV translation (and many others) implies that the work of building the inner temple was still going on forty-six years later, whereas, as we have seen, Josephus tells us that the inner temple took only eighteen months to build: it was the work on the other temple buildings which was still going on. As Finegan, Hoehner and others point out, the Greek word the NIV translates as 'to build' in John 2:20 is in the *past* tense, and therefore the real meaning of this verse is: 'this inner temple (*naos*) was built forty-six years ago'. Adding forty-six years to the Nisan-to-Nisan year 18/17 BC, when the inner temple (*naos*) was completed according to Josephus, and remembering that historical years go from 1 BC to AD 1 with no year zero, brings us to the Nisan-to-Nisan year AD 29/30. This means that Jesus' first Passover was in the spring of AD 30, and that the Jews were telling Jesus that the inner temple had stood for forty-six years at this time.

The temple reference is therefore consistent with a three-year ministry of Jesus, with the first Passover of his ministry being in AD 30 and the crucifixion in AD 33. Those scholars who support an AD 30 crucifixion offer alternative interpretations of John 2:20 – for example, that John may have confused the events that occurred at different Passovers, particularly the incident of the cleansing of the temple, so that the 'temple reference' occurred at the last Passover of Jesus and not the first, and this would then be consistent with an AD 30 crucifixion. However, the question of the number and timings of temple cleansings is a different matter from the forty-six years temple reference (I discuss the temple cleansings below). The interpretation of the 'temple reference' I have given above, that it occurred in AD 30 at the first Passover of Jesus' ministry, has strong support from scholars such as Finegan and Hoehner, and it is the natural interpretation of John 2:20.

A few scholars, for example Ormond Edwards in *The Time of Christ*,[27] maintain that the 'temple reference' takes us to AD 31, and not AD 30, for the first Passover of Jesus' ministry. They note the large amount of preparatory work described by Josephus before the reconstruction of the temple began. They argue that this preparatory work must have taken one year or eighteen months, which should be added to the time for rebuilding the inner temple given by Josephus. If this interpretation is correct, then the ministry of Jesus lasted for two years, with the crucifixion being in AD 33. Without more information we cannot be certain whether the ministry of Jesus was for two or three years, so I give both possibilities in the table. However, either way, an AD 30 crucifixion is ruled out and the only possibility is AD 33.

Key dates in the ministry of John the Baptist and Jesus

Event	Date
John the Baptist started his ministry	January 1 to December 31, AD 29
First Passover in the ministry of Jesus	Spring AD 30 or 31
The crucifixion	April 3, AD 33

THE CLEANSING OF THE TEMPLE

According to John 2:13–17, Jesus dramatically drove the money-changers out of the temple in the *first year* of his ministry, near Passover time (see fig. 5.1). However, according to the synoptics, the cleansing of the temple occurred in the *last week* of Jesus. Clearly, either John is right, or the synoptics are right, or Jesus made a protest in the temple at least twice, once near the start and again near the end of his ministry.

Most scholars believe the synoptics are correct in placing the temple cleansing in the last week of Jesus. For example, R. T. France writes: 'It is likely that among the many factors leading to Jesus' death the one which most united all elements of the Jewish people against him was that he was perceived as an opponent of the temple . . . If this understanding of the significance of the event is correct, it supports the general consensus that the incident took place on Jesus' final visit to Jerusalem, rather than at the outset of his ministry where John has placed it. Such a climactic challenge to the temple and its authorities could not be ignored.'[28]

Did Jesus cleanse the temple *both* in the first and in the last year of his ministry? Most scholars are scathing that such an event

Fig. 5.1 Christ Driving the Money Changers from the Temple. Etching by Rembrandt in 1635. The etching shows Christ driving out the money changers using a 'whip made out of cords' (John 2:15).

happened twice. For example, France states: 'The suggestion that it happened twice is about as probable as that the Normandy landings took place both at the beginning and the end of the Second World War.'[29] I am not so sure. If Jesus had cleared the temple of money-lenders, etc., in the first year of his ministry, presumably they would have moved back in again. So when Jesus visited the temple in his last week he would have seen them there again. It seems not at all unlikely that he would have driven them out again. Indeed, one could argue that it would have been inconsistent for him not to have done so.

I am grateful to the barrister Andrew Bartlett QC for the following comments: 'One might reasonably suppose that each time Jesus visited Jerusalem he was moved to protest in one way or another at what he saw as misuse of the temple. In addition to the issue of chronology, the two accounts are different in their details. As might be expected, comparison of the two shows Jesus ratcheting up his critique, from the first occasion ("How dare you turn my Father's house into a market" John 2:16) to the second ("You have made it a 'den of robbers'" Mark 11:17, Luke 19:46, Matthew 21:13). The impact on the authorities would have been very different. On the first occasion he would have been seen as an overheated pilgrim accompanied by some friends. A verbal rebuke was sufficient (John 2:18–20). On the final occasion he came as a well-known prophet with a large following, issuing an unmistakable challenge which the authorities could not immediately deal with and which they decided to meet with a permanent solution (Mark 11:18, Luke 19:47–48, Matthew 21:8–11, 21:46, 26:3–4).'

THE CURIOUS BEHAVIOUR OF PILATE AT THE CRUCIFIXION

Knowing that the crucifixion was in AD 33 and not in AD 30 helps us to understand the attitude of Pilate at the trials of Jesus. It has puzzled many theologians that at these trials the gospels depict Pilate as a weak character, subject to pressure from the Jews, whereas Philo, Josephus, and also Luke 13:1, 'The Galileans whose blood Pilate had mixed with their sacrifices', depict him as a ruthless ruler who was also strongly anti-Jewish. Pilate was appointed procurator of Judea in AD 26 by Sejanus, who was a well-known anti-Semite; in fact the historian Philo records that Sejanus wanted to exterminate the Jewish race (Philo, *Legatio ad Gaium*, 159–61). However, Philo then records that the Roman emperor Tiberius executed Sejanus for sedition on October 18, AD 31 and subsequently ordered all governors throughout the Roman empire not to mistreat the Jews. Hence the gospels' portrayal of Pilate, at Jesus' trials, as weak and keen to please the Jews is consistent with the crucifixion occurring after October AD 31.

SUMMARY

All the evidence for the date of the crucifixion supports Jesus dying at 3 p.m. on Friday, April 3, AD 33.[30] This date corresponds to Nisan 14 in the Jewish calendar. The apostle Paul uses this date as the basis of his symbolic reference to Christ as our Passover lamb, since the Passover lambs were sacrificed from 3 p.m. to 5 p.m. on Nisan 14, and of his image of the resurrected Christ being the first-fruits of those who rise from the dead, by analogy with the first-fruits festival of barley on Nisan 16. This chronology is also consistent with Jesus cleansing the temple in the first year of his ministry, as described by John. Jesus may have cleansed the temple again in the final year of his ministry (synoptics).

In this chapter we have deduced the date Jesus died using a wide range of biblical and non-biblical evidence, together with our reconstructed Jewish calendar for the first century AD. In the next chapter I will describe a novel method of dating the crucifixion using an entirely different approach which does not depend upon our reconstructed calendar. The key question is, does it give the same date as we have deduced in this chapter: April 3, AD 33?

6 The moon will be turned to blood

When the day of Pentecost came, they [the apostles] were all together in one place. Suddenly a sound like the blowing of a violent wind came from heaven ... All of them were filled with the Holy Spirit and began to speak in other tongues as the Spirit enabled them.

Then Peter stood up with the Eleven, raised his voice and addressed the crowd: 'Fellow Jews and all of you who live in Jerusalem, let me explain this to you; listen carefully to what I say. These men are not drunk, as you suppose. It's only nine in the morning! No, this is what was spoken by the prophet Joel: "In the last days, God says, I will pour out my spirit on all people ... I will show wonders in the heaven above and signs on the earth below, blood and fire and billows of smoke. The sun will be turned to darkness and the moon to blood before the coming of the great and glorious day of the Lord. And everyone who calls on the name of the Lord will be saved."'

(Acts 2:1–2, 4, 14–17, 19–21)

Picture the dramatic scene. Peter spoke the above words on the day of Pentecost, to the crowds who had gathered in Jerusalem to celebrate this feast, the second of the three great Jewish feasts. Just over seven weeks earlier Jesus had been crucified, at the time the lambs were slain for the Feast of Passover, the first of the three great Jewish feasts. All Jerusalem would have been buzzing with rumours that Jesus had risen from the dead and that he had spoken and even eaten with some of his followers.

In the period between the crucifixion and the day of Pentecost, Jesus' disciples had been inward looking, holding meetings together in an 'upper room' in Jerusalem (Acts 1:13), behind locked doors for fear of the Jews (John 21:19 and 26), and talking amongst themselves about the momentous events they had witnessed (Acts 1:15–26). But on the day of Pentecost the fearful disciples were transformed. Acts reports that they were 'filled with the Holy Spirit' (Acts 2:4), left their upper room and proclaimed the story of Jesus to the crowds who had gathered in Jerusalem to celebrate the Feast of Pentecost. Their words flowed with such fervour and enthusiasm that they were accused of being drunk (Acts 2:13).

Then Peter stood up and addressed the crowd. The first thing he told them was that the disciples were not drunk because it was only nine in the morning. If he had been speaking today he might have added that the pubs, clubs and wine bars were not yet open! No, he said, what the crowds were witnessing was no less than the fulfilment of the apocalyptic predictions of the prophet Joel.

Think of the electrifying atmosphere in the crowd as Peter said these words. Some of them would have witnessed the crucifixion, just over seven weeks earlier. Many of them would have heard rumours about the resurrection. All of them had just seen the transformed disciples of Jesus speaking with amazing power and conviction. Peter was saying to the crowd that they were living at a turning point in history, at a time when a major prophecy was being fulfilled, God was pouring out his Spirit as never before, and everyone who called upon the name of the Lord would be saved. I imagine there were tingles running down the spines of some of the audience as Peter said these powerful words, and huge hostility from some of the others.

HOW SHOULD WE INTERPRET PETER'S PENTECOST SPEECH?

What *precisely* did Peter mean when he said, 'This is what was spoken by the prophet Joel', and what would his audience have understood him to mean? Most scholars argue that although Peter was claiming that *some* of the Joel prophecy had recently been fulfilled, in particular the outpouring of the Spirit, much of the rest of the prophecy was yet to be fulfilled. For example, C. K. Barrett states that 'the great and glorious day of the Lord' (Acts 2:20) is 'the last day ... the day of judgement ... the day on which the Lord Jesus Christ descends from heaven to consummate the story of the people of God'. Barrett then states that the celestial portents, the wonders in the heavens above, 'have not yet appeared but will form the immediate prelude to the coming of Christ'.[1]

The interpretation of Barrett, and many other biblical scholars, that Peter intended most of his quotation from Joel to refer to the future, is clearly a possibility. However, I suggest it is not the *natural* interpretation of Peter's words. Peter prefaced his quotation from Joel 2:28–32 with the words: 'Let me explain this to you . . . This is what was spoken by the prophet Joel.' Peter was therefore claiming that recent events were the fulfilment of the prophecy he was about to quote. If the last part of the prophecy referred not to recent events but to future events, then why didn't Peter stop his quotation from Joel at a suitable point and omit quoting the futuristic parts? Or why didn't Luke, the writer of Acts, do the same?

There is therefore another possible interpretation of Peter's words, which is that Peter was claiming that recent events were the fulfilment of *all* the prophecy that he quoted. This is the interpretation I am going to explore in this chapter, because it may give us another way of dating the crucifixion.[2]

The idea that Peter regarded all of Joel's prophecy as fulfilled in the year of the crucifixion receives support from the distinguished biblical scholar F. F. Bruce. Bruce writes concerning Acts 2: 'The "last days" began with Christ's appearance on earth and will be consummated by his reappearance; they are the days during which the age to come overlays the present age. Hence the assurance with which Peter could quote the prophet's words and declare "This is it".'[3] Bruce then specifically refers to Acts 2:19–21: 'I will show wonders in the heaven above and signs on the earth below . . . The sun will be turned to darkness and the moon to blood.' Bruce writes: 'The wonders and signs to be revealed in the world of nature may have more relevance in their immediate setting than is sometimes realised . . . More particularly, little more than seven weeks earlier the people of Jerusalem had indeed seen the darkening of the sun, during the early afternoon of Good Friday; and later in that same afternoon the paschal full moon may well have risen blood red in the sky in consequence of that preternatural gloom. These phenomena are now interpreted as harbingers of the day of the Lord – a day of judgement, to be sure, but more immediately the day of God's salvation to all who invoked his name.'[4]

The event which was understood as the outpouring of the spirit occurred on the day of Pentecost. It may be worth noting, as we saw in Chapter 5, that just as the first-fruits festival of barley occurred in Passover week, on Nisan 16, so Pentecost was another first-fruits festival, this time of the wheat harvest (Leviticus 23:15). This first-fruits festival was held precisely seven weeks after Nisan 16 (fifty days counting inclusively as the Jews did, but forty-nine days (seven weeks of seven days) counting as we do today).[5]

William Neil writes that Peter regarded the resurrection as fulfilling the promises about the last days: 'Peter quotes Joel 2:28–32, where the prophet, in an apocalyptic passage, speaks of the signs of the messianic age, including a great outpouring of the Spirit of God, together with various natural portents. Peter regards the Pentecostal experience of the disciples and the miraculous events in Jesus' ministry, above all the Resurrection, as generally fulfilling the promise made by God through his prophet and heralding the beginning of the "last days".'[6]

THE SUN WILL BE TURNED TO DARKNESS

Let us continue with our interpretation of Peter's quotation from Joel, that Peter is claiming that all this prophecy has recently been fulfilled. If this is the case, then 'the sun will be turned to darkness' (Acts 2:20) is an obvious reference to the three hours of darkness at the crucifixion (Luke 24:44), and Peter's audience would surely have seen it as such. As Bruce states: 'Little more than seven weeks earlier the people of Jerusalem had indeed seen the darkening of the sun, during the early afternoon of Good Friday.'[7]

Is there a physical mechanism for what might have caused this darkness? Luke describes the darkness as follows: 'It was now about the sixth hour [noon], and darkness came over the whole land until the ninth hour [3 p.m.], for the sun stopped shining' (Luke 24:44). Some people have suggested that an eclipse of the sun might have been responsible for this darkness, but a solar eclipse is only possible at new moon time, and the crucifixion occurred on Nisan 14, in the middle of the Jewish month, which was full moon time. In addition, a solar eclipse lasts for minutes not hours. However, a number of scholars suggest that the sun may have been darkened by a khamsin dust storm. I describe in my book *The Miracles of Exodus* a sandstorm I witnessed in Kuwait, which totally blotted out the light from the sun for several hours, so that I had to turn the light on in my hotel room, although it was midday.[8] Sandstorms called khamsins (also known as siroccos) are common in the Middle East in the spring (*khamsin* is derived from the Arabic word for 'fifty' because the season for dust storms lasts about fifty days from mid-March each year). Support for the theory that it was a sandstorm which was responsible for the darkness at the crucifixion may come from the apocryphal Sibylline Oracles. These state in a section about the Messiah: 'And straightway dust is carried from heaven to earth, and all the brightness of the sun fails at midday from the heavens.'[9] In addition, the Greek word translated 'fails' in 'all the brightness of the sun fails at midday' in the Oracles is identical to the Greek word used by Luke and translated in the NIV as 'stopped shining' in 'for the sun stopped shining' (Luke 24:44). I therefore suggest that the words, 'The sun will be turned to darkness' (Acts 2:20), in Peter's Pentecost speech refer to the three hours of darkness at the crucifixion, which may have been due to a sandstorm or dust-storm.

Sir Robert Hanbury Brown gives a fascinating eye-witness description of a dust-storm in the Sudan: 'On 26th June we had the most extraordinary dust-storm that had ever been seen by the inhabitants . . . There was no wind, and the sun was as bright as usual in this cloudless sky, when suddenly a gloom was cast over all; a dull yellow glow pervaded the atmosphere. I saw approaching a solid range of immense brown mountains [of sand], high in the air. So rapid was the passage of this extraordinary phenomenon that in a few minutes we were in actual pitch darkness . . . So intense was the darkness that we tried to distinguish our hands placed close before our eyes. Not even an outline could be seen.'[10]

THE MOON WILL BE TURNED TO BLOOD

Since the darkened sun occurred at the crucifixion, I would like to explore the possibility that 'the moon was turned to blood' also occurred at the crucifixion, because these events are coupled in Acts 2:20, 'The sun will be turned to darkness and the moon to blood', and both events are stated to occur 'before the coming of the great and glorious day of the Lord', which I have identified with the resurrection. Apart from Peter's Pentecost speech, there is some other textual material that on the evening of the day of the crucifixion the moon turned to blood. The apocryphal 'Report of Pilate' states, 'Jesus was delivered to him by Herod, Archelaus, Philip, Annas, Caiaphas, and all the people. At his crucifixion the sun was darkened; the stars appeared and in all the world people lighted lamps from the sixth hour till evening; the moon appeared like blood.'[11]

Much apocryphal writing consists of highly theatrical literature, which cannot be used as historical evidence. Tertullian twice records that Pilate wrote a report of all the events surrounding the crucifixion and sent this to the emperor Tiberius.[12] The manuscript fragments we have of the Report of Pilate are all of later date, and scholars are divided on whether they are partly based on this very early lost document, if it existed, or whether the report is a Christian 'forgery' that used Acts as a source. Most scholars believe the report to be a Christian forgery because it is so favourable to Jesus. If the report we possess is based on the original Report of Pilate, then it provides independent evidence that the moon appeared like blood following the crucifixion. On the other hand, if the report is a Christian forgery, probably made up on the basis of Acts, as seems likely, then this suggests there was a tradition that at the crucifixion the moon appeared like blood.

Is there any further information suggesting that the moon appeared like blood following the crucifixion? There is, and it comes from a theologian and scholar who vigorously opposed unorthodox beliefs, Bishop Cyril of Alexandria. Cyril was a monk and a priest who lived in the Egyptian city of Alexandria from about AD 378 to 444 and who became the Bishop and Patriarch of Alexandria. Some of his extensive theological writings have survived, and in one of these, after stating there was darkness at the crucifixion, he adds, 'Something unusual occurred about the circular rotation of the moon so that it even seemed to be turned into blood', and he notes that the prophet Joel foretold such signs.[13] Hence Cyril of Alexandria interpreted the portents in the passage of Joel that Peter quoted on the day of Pentecost to refer to the time of the crucifixion.

We therefore have three documents that suggest the moon appeared like blood on the evening of the crucifixion: the Acts of the Apostles, the Report of Pilate and the writings of Bishop Cyril of Alexandria. As I first thought about this, back in 1981, I realised the evidence was tentative. Let me summarise this evidence. A possible interpretation of Peter's Pentecost speech, which I believe is the intended interpretation, is that at the crucifixion the moon appeared like blood. The Report of Pilate, probably a Christian forgery based on the Acts, explicitly states this, which suggests it may have been a tradition among some Christians. Bishop Cyril of Alexandria, also explicitly states this and says it fulfilled the prophecy made by Joel. I suggest that the 'Report of Pilate' and the words of Cyril may be used tentatively as secondary supporting evidence to Peter's Pentecost speech, that the moon appeared like blood on the evening of the crucifixion.

THE MEANING OF THE MOON WAS TURNED TO BLOOD

I have in front of me, as I write this, a copy of *The Times* dated January 10, 2001. On the front page there is a stunning colour photograph of an eclipsed moon, and the caption underneath reads: 'The blood-red moon over the Welsh borders last night.' The first paragraph under the moon photograph reads: 'Thousands of people who braved freezing temperatures to watch last night's total lunar eclipse were rewarded with a stunning view of one of nature's marvels: the Moon turned blood-red.' Why does an eclipsed moon look blood red? There is a good scientific reason (fig. 6.1).[14] Notice the similarity of the words of *The Times* newspaper and those of Peter speaking two thousand years earlier.

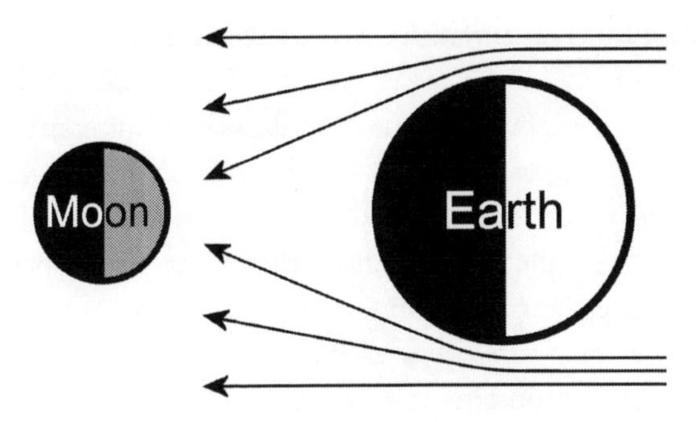

Fig. 6.1 Why the moon can appear blood red. During a lunar eclipse, the moon is in the earth's shadow and hence should appear black. However, light rays from the sun are bent (refracted) into the earth's shadow by the earth's atmosphere. During their passage through the earth's atmosphere the light rays undergo scattering by the air molecules they encounter. This preferentially removes the shorter (blue/green) wavelengths of light from the rays and so the light reaching the moon is red. The eclipsed moon reflects this red light back to the earth and so it appears red.

Peter said: 'The sun will be turned to darkness and the moon to blood.' *The Times* writes: 'The Moon turned blood red.' It is therefore very suggestive that when Peter spoke of the moon being turned to blood he was referring to the natural marvel of a lunar eclipse, just as *The Times* newspaper was. To investigate the likelihood of this we need to know whether people living around the first century AD popularly referred to lunar eclipses as the 'moon being turned to blood'.

'THE MOON TURNED TO BLOOD' IN ANCIENT TEXTS

There are many references in ancient literature to the moon appearing like blood and here is a fascinating small selection of those that can be dated historically. The earliest dateable reference I have found is from the Roman historian Quintus Curtius Rufus, who writes that two days after Alexander the Great crossed the River Tigris, the moon was 'suffused with the colour of blood' (*History of Alexander* 4.10.2). Two days after Alexander the Great crossed the Tigris was September 20, 331 BC, and astronomical calculations show that there was an eclipse of the moon that night. Hence we can say, beyond reasonable doubt, that the blood-coloured moon Quintus Curtius described was due to a lunar eclipse.

The Roman historian Dio Cassius describes the great confusion that existed in the camp of Vitellius before the second battle of Cremona because the moon 'appeared both blood coloured and black' (*Roman History* 65.11). Calculations show that there was a partial lunar eclipse at just the right time, on October 18, AD 69. A different partial lunar eclipse at moon rise on March 2, AD 462 was described in the *Hydatius Lemicus Chronicon* as follows: 'On March 2 with the crowing of cocks after the setting of the sun the full moon was turned to blood.' Again, astronomical calculations show there was an eclipse at precisely the right time.

We see from the above quotations (and there are many others I could have given) that over a long period of time, from 300 BC to AD 400, and indeed up to *The Times* writing in the present day, the phrase 'the moon was turned to blood' appears to be a standard description of a lunar eclipse. It is therefore reasonable to suppose that when Peter, the 'Report of Pilate' and Cyril of Alexandria refer to the moon turning to blood, they may have been describing a lunar eclipse. Biblical commentators do not appear to have made this deduction before, although, as we have seen, F. F. Bruce almost reaches this conclusion: 'Little more than seven weeks earlier the people of Jerusalem had indeed seen the darkening of the sun, during the early afternoon of Good Friday; and later in that same afternoon the paschal full moon may well have risen blood-red in the sky in consequence of that preternatural gloom.'[15]

The gospels do not mention an eclipse on the evening following the crucifixion. However, it must be remembered that the Romans and all of Israel's neighbours worshipped celestial bodies, and that the ancient world did not distinguish between astronomy and astrology. Apart from Jews and Christians, everyone believed that, in the words of Plato, 'The stars were made for signs.' Jews and Christians were different; they had one God and were expressly forbidden to worship the sun, moon and stars. Jews and Christians were brought up to believe that the sun, moon and stars were *not* made for signs.

Only one gospel (Matthew) reports the star that accompanied the birth of Jesus, and Matthew points out that it was the pagan Magi, not the Jews, who appreciated its significance (Matthew 2:1–2). The gospel writers inevitably had to be selective in deciding what to record out of the many events that must have accompanied the crucifixion. To these writers, events such as the rending of the curtain of the temple at the crucifixion would have seemed of much greater theological significance than a lunar eclipse, and indeed three gospel writers report on the temple curtain being torn in two (Matthew 27:51, Mark 15:38 and Luke 23:45). I therefore believe we should not be surprised that the gospels do not refer to a lunar eclipse at the crucifixion.

LUNAR ECLIPSES VISIBLE FROM JERUSALEM IN AD 26–36

I have suggested above that the natural interpretation of Peter's Pentecost speech, the 'Report of Pilate' and the words of Cyril of Alexandria is that there was a lunar eclipse on the evening of the crucifixion. We can test this hypothesis by calculating whether or not there was a lunar eclipse visible from Jerusalem at Passover time in the period AD 26–36, the possible date span for the crucifixion (Chapter 2). I am not the first person to think of this approach. In 1872, J. R. Hind published a paper in *Nature* on historical eclipses, and he noted that the 'moon was eclipsed on the generally received date of the Crucifixion, AD 33, April 3'. However, the calculations of Hind showed that this eclipse was not visible from Jerusalem and so it was considered to be irrelevant to the date of the crucifixion and was forgotten. This may be why modern biblical scholars, such as Bruce, have not made the connection between a blood-red moon and a lunar eclipse at the crucifixion.

The eclipse calculations of Hind in 1872 were inaccurate, however, because he did not take into account the effects of long-term changes in the earth's rate of rotation.[16] It is only recently that we have been able to do this.[17] Eclipses of the moon and the sun are very precise astronomical events, in which the moon, sun and earth have to be exactly in line. Because of the accuracy needed, calculations of the times of ancient eclipses have to be even more precise than the computations required to reconstruct ancient calendars, and considerable astronomical expertise is required. Back in 1981, I therefore once again asked the Oxford astrophysicist Graeme Waddington if he could calculate all lunar eclipses visible from Jerusalem at Passover time in the period AD 26–36.

Waddington used modern astronomical techniques, taking into account factors such as the varying rate of rotation of the earth as we go back in time, to calculate all lunar eclipses (total and partial) visible from Jerusalem at Passover time in the period AD 26–36. Was any eclipse visible? There was one, and only one. When did it occur? It was on Friday, April 3, AD 33. It is only since 1980 that it has been possible to state with confidence that there was a lunar eclipse visible from Jerusalem on Friday, April 3, AD 33, which, for the reasons given in the previous chapter, is the most probable date of the crucifixion. Modern science has made this knowledge available for our generation.

Waddington and I first published the lunar eclipse interpretation of Peter's Pentecost speech in our 1983 *Nature* paper,[18] and subsequently in *Chronos, Kairos, Christos*.[19] Waddington has recently updated his calculations, using the latest information on how the rate of rotation of the earth has varied with time, and I will give the results of his calculations below. These computations of eclipse times two thousand years ago are correct to about three minutes.

THE LUNAR ECLIPSE ON APRIL 3, AD 33

As we have just seen, we have only one possible answer to the question of whether there was a lunar eclipse visible from Jerusalem at Passover time in the period AD 26–36. The date, Friday, April 3, AD 33, agrees with the most probable date for the crucifixion we determined in the previous chapter. I would like to emphasise that the two methods I have used to determine the date of the crucifixion are independent. For example, the eclipse dating has nothing to do with when John the Baptist or Jesus started their ministries, nor when the inner court of the temple in Jerusalem was completed. This remarkable agreement on the date of the crucifixion using these very different approaches suggests to me that the tentative interpretation of Acts 2 we have been exploring in this chapter is probably correct.

Is there more we can say about this eclipse on the night following the crucifixion? Most lunar eclipses occur when we are asleep and so we do not see them. However, Waddington's calculations show that the eclipse on April 3, AD 33, was visible from Jerusalem at moon rise. In fact the Passover moon when it rose that evening was eclipsed. Many people in Jerusalem, watching for the Passover moon to rise so they could start their Passover meal, would have seen it. The timing was perfect for the maximum number of people in Jerusalem to have seen this eclipse.

We can use astronomy to reconstruct in detail the appearance of this eclipsed moon. The start of the eclipse was invisible from Jerusalem since the moon was then below the horizon. The eclipsed moon actually rose over the Mount of Olives, viewed from Jerusalem, at about 6.20 p.m. This signalled the start of the Jewish Sabbath, from Friday evening to Saturday evening, and also the start of Passover day, Nisan 15, in AD 33. The eclipse was a partial eclipse. The eclipsed part of the moon was positioned near to the top. Hence as the moon rose, initially most of it would have been seen 'in eclipse'. When the moon had half risen above the Mount of Olives, its calculated appearance is shown in Fig. 6.2. The moon would have appeared red, the colour being shaded from deeper to lighter going from top left to bottom right. Picture the scene. Jesus dies at about 3 p.m. on Friday, April 3, AD 33, as the Passover lambs are being slain. The crowds watching the crucifixion depart and go home. The body of Jesus is taken down from the cross and hastily put in a tomb before the Sabbath started (John 19:31–42). All Jerusalem looks for the Passover moon to rise, to signal the start of the Passover Feast. Instead of seeing the expected full yellow paschal moon rising, the moon they see is suffused with the colour of blood. The effect would have been dramatic. Calculations show that the eclipse ended at about 7.11 p.m. The crowd on the day of Pentecost would surely have understood Peter's words about the moon turning to blood as referring to this striking eclipse that many of them had seen so recently.

Fig. 6.2 The eclipsed moon rising over the Mount of Olives on Friday April 3, AD 33. This calculated image shows the moon half-risen above the Mount of Olives. The moon would have appeared red, the colour being shaded from deeper to lighter going from top left to bottom right.

Could the khamsin dust-storm itself have caused the moon to have appeared blood-red (as Bruce may be implying), without the need for a lunar eclipse? According to Luke, the darkness lasted from the sixth hour (noon) to the ninth hour (3 p.m.) (Luke 24:44). As we have seen, the moon rose at 6.20 p.m., so the dust-storm had subsided three hours earlier. We can therefore rule out the khamsin dust-storm as causing the moon to appear blood-red: there would not have been enough sand left in the atmosphere for this. However, the remnants of the dust-storm could well have further reddened the eclipsed moon. Since we can rule out the dust-storm as being the prime cause of the red moon, this leaves the eclipse as the only plausible explanation. This leads to April 3, AD 33 as the date of the crucifixion.

Lunar eclipses visible from Jerusalem at Passover time in AD 26–36	
Time	Date
6.20 p.m. (moon rise) to 7.11 p.m.	Friday, April 3, AD 33

SUMMARY

Speaking on the day of Pentecost, about seven weeks after the crucifixion, Peter said that the predictions of the prophet Joel had been fulfilled, not only the outpouring of the Spirit, but also the sun being turned to darkness and the moon being turned to blood. The natural interpretation of Peter's words is that recent events had fulfilled this prophecy. The event which was understood as the outpouring of the spirit clearly occurred on the day of Pentecost. The sun being turned to darkness is an obvious reference to the three hours of darkness at the crucifixion, probably due to a khamsin sandstorm.

Concerning the moon being turned to blood, in addition to Peter's Pentecost speech, there are two other texts that refer to the moon turning to blood around the time of the crucifixion: the apocryphal Report of Pilate and the writings of Cyril of Alexandria. Both report that it was on the evening of the crucifixion that the moon appeared like blood.

'The moon turning to blood' is a graphic description of a lunar eclipse, in which the moon appears blood-red. There are many references in ancient texts to the moon turning to blood. Some of those can be dated historically, astronomical calculations can be performed, and it can be shown that there was a lunar eclipse at precisely the right time. It is therefore reasonable to suppose that when Peter, the 'Report of Pilate' and Cyril of Alexandria refer to the moon turning to blood on the evening of the crucifixion, they were describing a lunar eclipse.

Detailed astronomical calculations show that at Passover time in the period AD 26–36 there was one, and only one, lunar eclipse visible from Jerusalem. This was on Friday, April 3, AD 33. The rising moon that evening would have been seen blood-red. This date, Friday,

April 3, AD 33 agrees with the most probable date for the crucifixion that we determined in the previous chapter, using a totally different method. Two independent methods therefore yield the same date for the crucifixion: April 3, AD 33.

We have now reached some significant conclusions. We have shown that John's gospel is correct in saying that the last supper was before the official Passover meal, and it is correct in placing the crucifixion on Nisan 14 in the official Jewish calendar, Jesus dying at the time the first Passover lambs were sacrificed. We will now assess whether the synoptic gospels are also correct. In particular, did they use a different calendar from the official calendar when they described the last supper as a Passover meal? In the next chapter we consider the best-known different calendar theory, that Jesus used the Qumran solar calendar to celebrate his last supper as a Passover meal.

7 Did Jesus use the solar calendar of Qumran for his last supper Passover?

> He [Jesus] celebrated Passover with his disciples probably according to the calendar of Qumran, that is to say, at least one day earlier [than Passover in the official Jewish calendar].
>
> (Pope Benedict XVI's Holy Thursday Homily,[1] Vatican City, April 6, 2007)

On Easter Thursday, 2007, Pope Benedict XVI made the controversial statement quoted above. I write 'controversial' because, as we have seen in Chapter 3, only a small minority of biblical scholars support a different calendar solution of the synoptics/John last supper controversy. However, now that Pope Benedict, who is a fine scholar, has come out in favour of a different calendar, the Qumran solar calendar, I will give this calendar particular attention. By the end of this chapter we will know, I believe beyond reasonable doubt, whether Jesus used the Qumran solar calendar for his last Passover.

The significance of the Pope's statement should not be underestimated. It was highlighted in many newspapers around the world. For example, the UK national daily paper the *Daily Telegraph* stated on April 7, 2007: 'The Pope has sought to resolve a 2000-year-old dispute about the Last Supper. Theologians have long argued over whether the meal that Jesus had with his disciples was the traditional Passover menu of roast lamb. The gospel of St John states that Jesus was crucified on the day of preparation for the Passover, the day before. St Mark says that Jesus requested a room to "eat the Passover with my disciples". The Pope explained that Jesus could have celebrated the meal not according to the [official] lunar calendar, but according to the solar calendar which is outlined in the Dead Sea Scrolls. "He probably ate with his disciples according to the Qumran calendar, which is to say at least a day before, and he would have celebrated it without roast lamb, in the same way as the Essene community at Qumran." The *Telegraph* ended its report by stating: 'The Pope's explanation was hailed as radical by theologians, who added that it reinforced the possibility that Jesus was an Essene.'[2]

Today, most people take the calendar they use, normally the Gregorian calendar, for granted. But even today there are exceptions to this. For example, members of Orthodox churches still cling to their tradition of celebrating Christmas and Easter according to the Julian, not the Gregorian, calendar. The Chinese students in my research group in Cambridge, England, celebrate New Year's Day not on January 1, but on the first day of the first month of the Chinese lunar calendar. By using a different calendar for their festivals, Orthodox Christians and Chinese students are identifying themselves with their community and its traditions.

Before considering the Qumran calendar, I will return to Pope Benedict XVI's Holy Thursday Homily of 2007, because much of what he said agrees closely with the evidence I have presented in this book. The Pope has clearly thought deeply about the problem of the last supper. In his Holy Thursday Homily he stated: 'In the narration of the Evangelists, there is an apparent contradiction between the Gospel of John, on the one hand, and what, on the other hand, Matthew, Mark and Luke tell us. According to John, Jesus died on the cross precisely at the moment at which, in the temple, the Passover lambs were being sacrificed. His death and the sacrifice of the lambs coincided.'

The Pope continued: 'This means that he died on the eve of Passover, and that, therefore, he could not have personally celebrated the paschal supper; at least this is what it would seem. On the contrary, according to the three synoptic Evangelists, the last supper of Jesus was a paschal supper, in its traditional form. He introduced the innovation of the gift of his body and blood. This contradiction, until a few years ago, seemed impossible to resolve.' This is indeed the puzzle I described earlier in this book.

He then continued: 'The majority of the exegetes thought that John did not want to communicate with us the true historical date of the death of Jesus, but had opted for a symbolic date to make the deeper truth more evident: Jesus is the new and true lamb that spilled his blood for us all. The discovery of the manuscripts of Qumran has led us to a convincing possible solution that, while not accepted by all, is highly probable. We can now say that what John referred to is historically correct. Jesus truly spilled his blood on the eve of Passover at the hour of the sacrifice of the lambs.'

The Pope has affirmed strongly what I have deduced earlier: that the account in John is historically correct, and that the symbolism in John is not at the expense of historicity, but is based on historical fact. All the evidence from the Bible, calendars and astronomy fits this interpretation. The words of the Pope and the conclusions of this book so far are in close agreement. However, could Jesus have used the Qumran solar calendar to celebrate his last supper as a Passover meal? Later in this chapter I will answer this question, but first let me describe this fascinating calendar.

THE QUMRAN SOLAR CALENDAR

We know from the Dead Sea Scrolls found in caves at Qumran (fig. 7.1), close to the Dead Sea, that the Qumran community used a solar calendar with a sunrise-to-sunrise day. This different calendar isolated them from Jews who used the official calendar. For example, Shemaryahu Talmon, the Professor Emeritus of Bible Studies at the Hebrew University of Jerusalem, writes: 'A difference of calendation [between Jews] was at times considered a weightier cause of socio-religious dissent than basic tenets of faith ... Someone who does not observe the festivals in accord with the schedule to which the community in whose midst he lives adheres, will be considered an outsider, even a heretic.'[3]

The Damascus Document [4] and many of the Dead Sea Scrolls, for example the well-known Temple Scroll,[5] make it clear that the solar calendar described in both Jubilees[6] and 1 Enoch[7] was the main calendar used by the Qumran community. Many copies and fragments of Jubilees and 1 Enoch have been found in the caves of

Fig. 7.1 Qumran caves. In these and other caves the Dead Sea Scrolls were found.

Qumran. In fact, it seems likely that the book of Jubilees was so central to the life of the Qumran community that it was viewed as Scripture, and 1 Enoch is regarded as Scripture by the Ethiopian Orthodox Church today.[8] Most scholars date Jubilees to about 100 BC, or possibly earlier.[9]

Chapters 72–82 of 1 Enoch are most relevant to the Qumran calendar and they form a fascinating treatise on astronomy, sometimes called 'The Astronomical Book' or 'The Book of Heavenly Luminaries (Lights)'.[10] Scholars date this astronomical section of 1 Enoch as pre 100 BC.[11] Although there is some uncertainty about the dates of Jubilees and 1 Enoch, scholars are agreed that both books are pre-Christian and that the Qumran community based its calendar upon them.

It is clear from the Dead Sea Scrolls that the Qumran solar calendar had a year of twelve months totalling 364 days. The lengths of the three spring months were 30, 30 and 31 days, and similarly the three summer months were 30, 30 and 31 days long, and so on for the three autumn and the three winter months. Although Jubilees and 1 Enoch claim that this solar calendar was the calendar instituted by Moses, there is no other evidence for this and it seems that it may have had its origin in a 364-day calendar that existed in ancient Mesopotamia from the seventh century BC onwards.[12] The Qumran calendar has the attractive property that its year of 364 days is exactly divisible by seven, so that a given *date* always falls on the same *day*. For example, New Year's Day (the first day of the first month of the year) in this calendar is always a Wednesday. Since this calendar has a sunrise-to-sunrise-day, New Year's Day is the twenty-four-hour period from sunrise on Wednesday to sunrise on Thursday.

Why does the new year in the Qumran calendar always start on a Wednesday? The reason is fascinating. The creation story in Genesis chapters 1 and 2 describes God creating the world in six days, and on the seventh day he rested. The seventh day therefore became the Jewish day of rest, the Sabbath, Saturday. This means that the first day of creation must have been on a Sunday. However, God created the 'two great lights', the sun and the moon, not on the first day but on the fourth day (Genesis 1:19). If the story is taken literally, the first day of creation was Sunday, and the fourth day of creation was Wednesday.[13] Since you cannot have a solar calendar without the sun, the Qumran community (following Jubilees and 1 Enoch) started each new year on a Wednesday, when the sun was created, and not on a Sunday, when God commenced his creation according to this reading of Genesis. Hence Nisan 1, the first day of the first month of the year, in the solar calendar of Qumran was always on a Wednesday (the twenty-four-hour period from Wednesday sunrise to Thursday sunrise), and Nisan 14 was always on a Tuesday (the twenty-four-hour period from sunrise on Tuesday to sunrise on Wednesday). The Qumran community held their Passover meal on Nisan 14, as instructed by Moses in Exodus 12 (see Chapter 9) and not on Nisan 15, as in the official calendar. The Qumran Passover meal was therefore always eaten on a Tuesday evening. The Qumran Community believed that no sacrifices could take place on a Sabbath except Sabbath sacrifices. Their solar calendar ensured this was the case.

DID JESUS USE THE QUMRAN SOLAR CALENDAR FOR HIS LAST PASSOVER?

Annie Jaubert was, I believe, the first to suggest that Jesus held his last supper at Passover time according to the Qumran solar calendar. Her book, *La date de la cène*[14] (*The Date of the Last Supper*), is a brilliant piece of detective work. She argued that Jesus held his last supper as a real Passover meal on Tuesday evening, Nisan 14 in the Qumran calendar. He was then crucified on Friday, Nisan 14 in the official calendar, dying on Friday afternoon when the Passover lambs were slain. Pope Benedict XVI built on this work of Jaubert in his Holy Thursday Homily of 2007, saying: 'He [Jesus] celebrated Passover with his disciples probably according to the calendar of Qumran, that is to say, at least one day earlier [than Passover in the official calendar].'

There are two problems with the theory that Jesus used the Qumran solar calendar to hold his last supper as a Passover meal. The first problem is the length of time between a last supper on Tuesday evening and the crucifixion on Friday. When we analyse the events recorded in the gospels between the last supper and the crucifixion (see Chapter 12) we find that a last supper on Tuesday evening gives too great a time interval before the crucifixion on Friday. Perhaps the Pope realises this, and that is why he said that Jesus celebrated Passover 'at least one day earlier' than the official Passover. However in the Qumran calendar theory of Jaubert, Jesus held his last supper Passover on Tuesday evening, *three days* before the official Passover meal on Friday evening.

The second, and most critical, problem with the Qumran solar calendar theory is that Jaubert, and other supporters of this theory, including Pope Benedict, assume that Passover in the Qumran calendar fell before, and in the same week as, Passover in the official calendar. Only then could Jesus have held his last supper as a Passover meal before the official Passover. We will therefore now ask the key question, did Passover in the Qumran calendar fall *before* or *after* Passover in the official calendar? The answer to this question determines whether it was possible for Jesus to have used the Qumran calendar to celebrate his last supper as a Passover meal.

THE QUMRAN SOLAR CALENDAR REVISITED

As we have seen, the length of the year in the Qumran solar calendar was 364 days. However, the length of the true solar year is 365¼ days, to a good approximation. This means that every year the Qumran calendar became out of step with the true solar calendar by 1¼ days. So in four years the Qumran calendar would be five days out of step with the true solar year. Our solar calendar of 365 days also slowly becomes out of step with the true solar year, but we prevent this by adding an extra 'leap day' every four years, at the end of February, to keep our solar calendar in step with the true solar year of 365¼ days. Adding 'leap days' is known as intercalation. As we have seen, in the official Jewish lunar calendar, an extra lunar month was added (intercalated) about once every three years to keep this calendar in step with the true solar year.

The problem we have with the Qumran calendar is that we have not yet found any ancient documents that tell us whether the Qumran community added extra 'leap days' to keep in step with the true solar year or not. As the Qumran calendar expert Shemaryahu Talmon states: 'The intercalation system of the Qumran [calendar] with the true solar year still escapes our knowledge.'[15]

There are two possibilities: either extra days were added to the Qumran calendar to keep it in step with the true solar year, or they were not. Roger Beckwith[16] believes they were not, so the Qumran calendar became more and more out of step with the true solar year, falling back through the seasons as time went on. Let us think about the implications of this for the Qumran Passover. According to the book of Exodus, Passover was held in the first month of the year, originally called Abib and later called Nisan (Exodus 12:2 and 23:15). As the calendrical expert E. J. Bickerman states: 'Abib is the time of ripening barley',[17] corresponding to March/April. When the Qumran community started their solar calendar, the first month would therefore have been in the spring (March/April), at the time of ripening barley.

The earliest date for the Qumran community to have settled in Qumran was in about 100 BC.[18] They would have started their calendar so that the first month fell in the spring (as instructed in the books of Exodus, 1 Enoch and Jubilees, see later in this chapter). If Beckwith is correct, and the Qumran community did not intercalate their calendar (add leap days), then the 364-day year of their calendar would have become out of step with the true solar year of 365¼ days, falling behind it by 1¼ days each year. There were about 130 years between the crucifixion in AD 33 and the earliest possible start date of the Qumran calendar in about 100 BC. Hence by the time of the crucifixion, the first month of the Qumran calendar would have been about (130 × 1¼ = 160) days adrift from spring (March/April). Since 160 days is about five solar months, the first month of the Qumran calendar in the year of the crucifixion would have been in October/November if the Qumran calendar started in the spring in about 100 BC.

The latest date for the Qumran community to have started their calendar was when they reoccupied the Qumran site in about 4 BC. The time interval between 4 BC and the year of the crucifixion, AD 33, is about forty years. In that time period the Qumran calendar would have become (40 × 1¼ = 50) days out of step with the true solar year. Hence, if Beckwith is correct and the Qumran calendar ran on without intercalation, at the time of the crucifixion the first month of the Qumran calendar would have been in January/February if the Qumran calendar started in the spring in 4 BC. Since the Qumran community started their calendar on a date some time between about 100 BC and 4 BC, if leap days were not added to keep this calendar in step with the true solar year, then Passover in the Qumran calendar at the time of the crucifixion could not have been in the same week as Passover in the official Jewish calendar, which did keep in step with the true solar year. For Beckwith and Jaubert both to be right, the Qumran calendar would have had to start in about 260 BC, so that by the time of the crucifixion the calendar had temporarily come back into step with the solar year. Archaeology rules out the Qumran community occupying Qumran as early as this. Jesus could therefore not have used the Qumran calendar to celebrate his last supper as a Passover meal if intercalary days were not added to this calendar.

Time of Passover in the Qumran solar calendar with no intercalation	
Start date of Qumran calendar	Time of Qumran Passover in AD 33
Earliest date about 100 BC	October/November
Latest date about 4 BC	January/February

THE QUMRAN SOLAR CALENDAR WITH INTERCALATION

We will now consider the possibility that the Qumran community *did* intercalate their calendar (by adding additional days) so that the first month always fell in the spring. The problem is, as Talmon states: 'The intercalation system of the Qumran calendar with the true solar year still escapes our knowledge.' Even though we do not know *how* the Qumran community intercalated their calendar, I believe we can use information from the book of 1 Enoch to find out conclusively if Jesus *could* have used the Qumran calendar to celebrate his last Passover. The solution to this puzzle is fascinating; it involves understanding the 'gates of heaven', and I believe it has not been given before.

THE GATES OF HEAVEN

The section of 1 Enoch called 'The Book of Heavenly Luminaries (Lights)' is a wonderful description, based on keen observation, of the sun and the moon. For example, 1 Enoch correctly described that, viewed from the earth, the sun and the moon appear to have the same size ('In size the two are equal', 1 Enoch 72:37). 1 Enoch also observed that the moon obtained its light from the sun ('Light is beamed into the moon from the bright sun', 1 Enoch 78:4) and that the moon had a face ('it appears like a man', 1 Enoch 78:17): an early reference to what we call 'the man in the moon'.

Just as ancient peoples would have passed through gates to enter a city, so, they imagined, the sun and the moon must pass through gates in a celestial dome as they entered the observable sky.[19] The dome separated earth from heaven, and the gates through which the sun and the moon entered and left were called the gates of heaven. This imagery we still have today, when we talk about the pearly gates guarded by Saint Peter, as the gateway to heaven. The reference to pearls is inspired by the description of the New Jerusalem in Revelation: 'The twelve gates were twelve pearls, each gate made of a single pearl' (Revelation 21:21).

The image of gates through which the celestial bodies entered or exited the visible sky appears in texts from throughout the ancient Near East. For example, an ancient Egyptian Coffin Text states: 'I know that middle gate from which Re [the sun] issues in the east ... I know those two sycamores which are of turquoise between which Re goes forth, which go strewing shade at every eastern gate from which Re shines forth.'[20] The sun, of course, rises in the east on the horizon, and the above text states that from where the author was writing it appeared to rise between two sycamores (perhaps these were studded with turquoise because of their significance). As the year proceeds, the position on the eastern horizon at which the sun rises moves north and south, so the ancient world believed that the sun entered through different adjacent eastern gates in different months of the year, hence the words in the coffin text above: 'at every eastern gate from which Re shines forth'.

Let us now consider the book of 1 Enoch. Genesis 5:23 states: 'The days of Enoch were three hundred and sixty-five years.' It is unlikely to be a coincidence that the biblical age of Enoch is the number of days in a solar year. This association of Enoch in the book of Genesis with the sun is reflected in the later book of 1 Enoch, in which Enoch first learned the laws of the sun (1 Enoch 72).

The writer of 1 Enoch built on the gates of heaven imagery of the ancient Near East to develop his solar calendar. He observed that, at different times of the year, the sun rose in the east at different places on the horizon, and it set in the west also at different places on the horizon. Following Near Eastern tradition, he called the places where the sun rose and set 'the gates of heaven', and he matched the gates to months of the year. He defined six gates in the east through which the

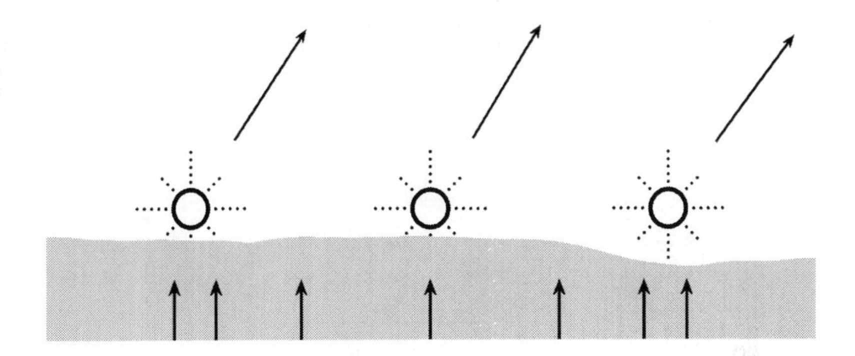

Fig. 7.2 The gates of heaven. The gates of heaven mark out the position of sunrise (and sunset) throughout the year. The sun rises for one month through each gate in turn. The boundaries between the gates are marked with vertical lines in the diagram. In practice these could have been standing stones. The sun's position is shown (from left to right) for the summer solstice, the two equinoxes and the winter solstice. In each case the direction of the rising of the sun is shown with an inclined arrow.

sun rose (entered), and six in the west through which it set (exited) (1 Enoch 72:5–37). He noted that on the longest day of the year, the sun rises and sets through the northernmost pair of gates, while on the shortest day it rises and sets through the southernmost pair (fig. 7.2). Incidentally, this information in the book of 1 Enoch is precisely that required to construct a 'henge' – an observatory like Stonehenge made from posts or standing stones, using which it is possible to intercalate (add) days to the calendar to ensure that the sun always rises through a certain gate (say the gap between two posts) in a given month.

1 Enoch clearly and carefully defined the first month of his calendar: 'It [the sun] rises in the first month in the large gate, namely it rises in the fourth of those six gates which are towards the east . . . and on those days the day grows daily longer and the night grows nightly shorter' (1 Enoch 72:6–9). What does this mean? Enoch is telling us that in the first month of the year, the sun rises through a given gate, the fourth gate, that is, it rises in that position on the horizon. He also tells us that throughout this month the days are lengthening and the nights

are getting shorter. This is a critical piece of information, because it means that the first month fell *after* the vernal (spring) equinox, when the lengths of the day and of the night are equal (equinox derives from the Latin words aequus (equal) and nox (night)).

We can confirm from the book of 1 Enoch that our interpretation above is correct because it states that in the last month of the year the sun 'rises in the third gate for thirty one mornings and sets in the west of heaven. And on that day the night becomes shorter, and amounts to nine parts, and the day amounts to nine parts, and the night becomes equal with the day' (1 Enoch, 72:31–33). In other words, it is in the *last* month of the year that the spring equinox occurs. Hence 1 Enoch is clear that the first day of the first month of his solar calendar, later used at Qumran, falls *after* the spring equinox. The Qumran community could only comply with this if they intercalated their calendar when required. The easiest way to have done this would have been to add an extra week to the year at the end of the last month, when required, to ensure that the first day of the first month always fell after the spring equinox (this is easily done because it is simple to detect the spring equinox, when the hours of the day and night are equal). This would have kept their 'leap year' divisible by seven so that a given date continued to fall on the same day each year. They would have needed to add an extra week in this way every five or six years. There are, of course, other ways in which they might have intercalated their calendar. However, irrespective of *how* the Qumran community may have added leap days, if they intercalated their calendar so that the first month of their year fell *after* the spring equinox, as instructed in the book of Enoch, we can determine the earliest possible date of Passover in their calendar as set out below.

At my request, the astrophysicist Graeme Waddington has calculated the date of the spring equinox in Jerusalem in AD 30 and 33, the only two possible years for the crucifixion. It was on March 22. Since the first day of the first month, Nisan, of the Qumran calendar had to fall *after* the spring equinox, March 22, and since the first day of the first month always fell on a *Wednesday*, the earliest possible date for Nisan 1 in AD 30 in the Qumran calendar was Wednesday, March 29. So the earliest possible date for Nisan 14 in AD 30 in the Qumran calendar was Tuesday April 11. But, as we have seen in Chapter 5, Nisan 14 in the official Jewish calendar in AD 30 was on Friday, April 7. Hence in AD 30, Passover in the Qumran calendar fell *after* Passover in the Jewish calendar.

In AD 33, using similar reasoning, the earliest possible date for Nisan 1 in the Qumran calendar was Wednesday, March 25. Hence Nisan 14 in AD 33 in this calendar fell on Tuesday, April 7. But in the Jewish calendar, Nisan 14 in AD 33 was on Friday, April 3. Therefore in AD 33, Passover was celebrated by the Qumran community *after* the official Passover.

Dates of Nisan 14 in the Jewish and Qumran calendars with intercalation

Year	Jewish lunar calendar	Qumran solar calendar
AD 30	Friday, April 7	Tuesday, April 11
AD 33	Friday, April 3	Tuesday, April 7

Hence, if the Qumran calendar was intercalated so that Nisan 1 fell after the spring equinox as described in 1 Enoch, then in the only two possible years for the crucifixion, AD 30 and 33, Passover in the Qumran calendar fell *after* Passover in the official Jewish calendar. Indeed, it was *generally* the case that Passover in the Qumran calendar fell *after* Passover in the Jewish calendar. This occurred because the two calendars were intercalated according to different rules. As we saw in Chapter 4, in the first century AD (and today) the Jewish calendar was intercalated so that *Passover* must fall after the spring equinox.[21] However, the Qumran community followed 1 Enoch, which stated that *Nisan 1* must fall after the spring equinox. Since Passover (in the middle of Nisan) necessarily falls after Nisan 1, it follows that Passover in the Qumran calendar, if it was intercalated, *always* fell after Passover in the Jewish calendar. If the Qumran calendar was not intercalated, as suggested by Beckwith, then, as I have shown, Passover in the Qumran calendar would not have fallen even in the same month as Passover in the official calendar. I believe it follows, beyond reasonable doubt, that Jesus could not have used the solar calendar of the Qumran community to celebrate his last supper as a Passover meal.

SUMMARY

The most strongly supported different calendar theory for the last supper is that proposed by Annie Jaubert, who argued that Jesus used the Qumran solar calendar to celebrate his last supper as a real Passover meal. In this calendar, Nisan 14 is always on a Tuesday. Jaubert proposed that Jesus held his last supper on Tuesday, Nisan 14 in the Qumran calendar, before being crucified on Friday, Nisan 14 in the official Jewish calendar. Jaubert suggested that the synoptics correctly described the last supper as a real Passover meal, using the Qumran calendar, whereas John correctly described the crucifixion as occurring before the Passover meal in the official Jewish calendar. Jaubert assumed, without question, that Nisan 14 in the Qumran calendar fell before, and in the same week as, Nisan 14 in the official calendar. Jaubert's theory has recently been given strong support by Pope Benedict XVI.

There are two possibilities for how the Qumran calendar operated, neither considered by Jaubert. The 364-day year in the Qumran calendar is 1¼ days shorter than the true solar year. One possibility is that this calendar was allowed to roll on from year to year without intercalation (without adding leap days), getting more and more out of step with the true solar year. Since the official Jewish calendar was kept in step with the solar year, I have shown that, at the time of the crucifixion, Passover in a Qumran calendar without intercalation would not have fallen even in the same month as Passover in the official calendar.

The other possibility is that the Qumran calendar *was* kept in step with the true solar year. According to the book of 1 Enoch, the first day of the year in the Qumran calendar must fall after the spring equinox and it must also be a Wednesday. Using these two pieces of information, we can show that in the only possible years for the crucifixion, AD 30 and 33, Passover in the Qumran calendar fell in the week *after* Passover in the official calendar.

We conclude that Jesus could not have used the Qumran calendar to celebrate his last supper as a Passover meal since, whether it was intercalated or not, Passover in the Qumran calendar did not fall in the same week as Passover in the official Jewish calendar. However, Pope Benedict XVI was almost right, as we will see in Chapter 10. In the next chapter I will follow up the claim in the Dead Sea Scrolls that the official Jewish calendar was not the calendar instituted by Moses. In particular, we will discover an ancient Jewish calendar which pre-dates the official Jewish calendar, and which the book of Exodus describes as going back to the time of Moses.

8 Does ancient Egypt hold a key to unlocking the problem of the last supper?

Now the length of time the Israelite people lived in Egypt was 430 years.

(Exodus 12:40)

As we have seen in the previous chapter, a different calendar theory is, in principle, an attractive way of explaining the apparent discrepancies between the synoptics and John concerning the date and nature of the last supper. However, the only 'different calendar' that has had any real support from scholars is the Qumran solar calendar and I have just shown conclusively that Jesus could not have used this calendar to celebrate his last supper as a Passover meal. So it seems we are no further forward in trying to understand the apparent disagreement between the synoptics and John on the last supper.

As I thought about this problem I tried to update it in my mind. Why do the Eastern Orthodox churches celebrate Easter on a different date from Catholics and Protestants? It is because Catholics and Protestants use the modern Gregorian calendar, but Eastern Orthodox Christians continue to calculate the date of Easter using the Julian calendar, which existed before the Gregorian calendar (see Chapter 2), because they have always celebrated Easter in the Julian calendar in their tradition. So in order to solve the date of the last supper problem in John and the synoptics, should we be looking for an ancient Jewish calendar that existed before the official Jewish calendar at the time of Christ, which a Jewish group (or groups) might have continued to use at the time of Christ to celebrate Passover, because they had always celebrated Passover in this calendar in their tradition?

Interestingly, a striking feature of *many* ancient Jewish writings is the claim that the official Jewish calendar had departed from the original calendar of Moses, and that the official Feasts, such as Passover, were therefore being held on the wrong days. As we saw in the previous chapter, the widely circulated books of Jubilees, 1 Enoch and the Damascus Document all make this claim. So when did the official Jewish calendar used at the time of Christ start, was there an earlier Jewish calendar and, if so, can we discover it? We will find the roots of this 'lost calendar' in this chapter. Fascinatingly, to solve this problem we must travel back in time to ancient Egypt.

THE ORIGIN OF THE OFFICIAL JEWISH CALENDAR AT THE TIME OF CHRIST

If we are to understand the origin of the Jewish calendar then we need to have a basic understanding of Jewish history. According to the Old Testament book of Joshua, when Joshua led the Israelites into Canaan he assigned portions of land to each of the twelve tribes (Joshua 13 and subsequent chapters). Canaan was divided into three main regions: Galilee, Samaria and Judah, see fig. 8.1. Although all the land of Canaan was allocated, it was not yet all conquered. For example, Jerusalem remained in the hands of people called the Jebusites for at least another two hundred years, until it was finally captured by the Israelite King David in about 1000 BC (2 Samuel 5:6–9). According to 2 Samuel, David established a unified Israelite monarchy ruling Judah, Galilee and Samaria from Jerusalem. After the death of David's son Solomon (about 930 BC) the tribes of Israel split into two kingdoms: the Northern Kingdom of Israel, comprising the ten tribes which lived in Galilee and Samaria, and the Southern Kingdom of Judah (the name 'Judea' used in the New Testament is a Greek and Roman adaptation of 'Judah' and it refers to the same region).

In 597/596 BC Babylon captured Jerusalem and deported many Jews to Babylon (2 Kings 24:10–17). In 586 BC the Babylonians returned, destroyed Jerusalem and its temple and deported more Judean Jews (2 Kings 25:1–21). This is known as the Babylonian exile of the Jews,

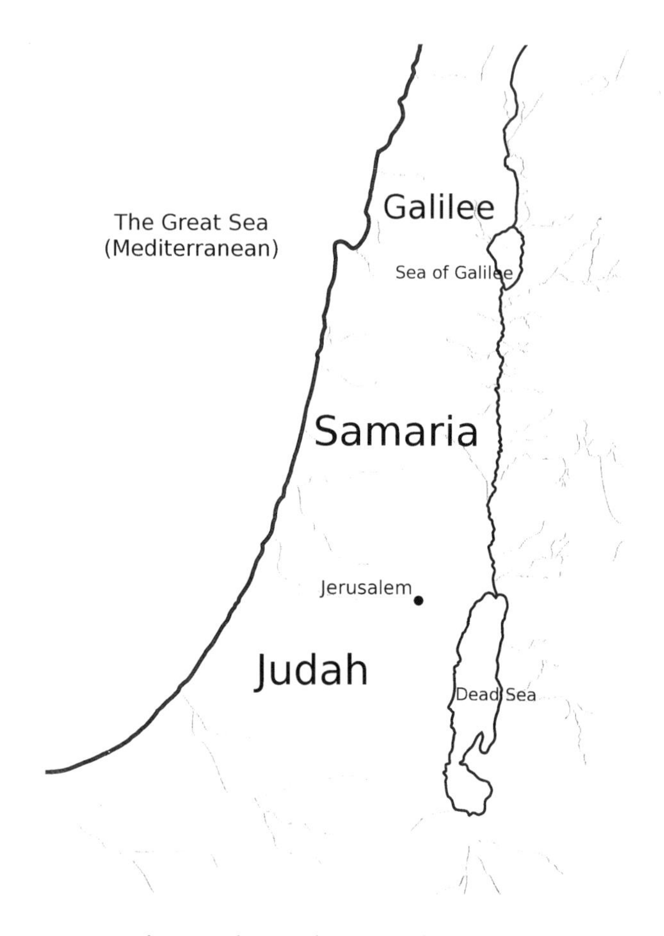

Fig. 8.1 Map of Canaan showing the regions of Galilee, Samaria and Judah.

often simply called 'the exile'. In about 537 BC Jews returned from Babylon to Jerusalem. When in exile in Babylon, the Judean Jews adopted the Babylonian calendar (they probably had no choice), and scholars agree (see below) that this was the origin of the official Jewish calendar at the time of Christ, which has continued until today (except that today the Jewish calendar is calculated and not based on observation). During the Babylonian exile the Jews in captivity adopted Babylonian names for their months: for example, the first month of the Jewish religious year, Nisan, was named after the Babylonian first month Nisannu;

the last (twelfth) month of the Jewish year, Adar, was named after the Babylonian last month Adaru. These Jewish month names are still in use today. As the calendrical expert Professor Bickerman states: 'In 586 [BC], after the annexation of Jerusalem by Nebuchadnezzar [the king of Babylon], the Jews began to reckon by the regnal years of the kings of Babylon and to use the imperial [Babylonian] calendar. As the ancient Rabbis already noted, the Jews had also adopted the Babylonian month names: Nisan is Nisannu, and so on.'[1]

The above Jewish calendar, which I have called the official Jewish calendar, is sometimes called the post-exilic Jewish calendar because it originated during the exile in Babylon. Like the Babylonian calendar, it was a lunar calendar. The first day of the month was determined by the first observation of the new lunar crescent and the day went from sunset to sunset. This was the calendar the Judean Jews took back with them after the exile and it was the official Jewish calendar at the time of Christ.

THE PRE-EXILIC JEWISH CALENDAR

What calendar did the Jews use before the exile? Here we have a problem because, as Bickerman states, 'The pre-Babylonian time reckoning of the Hebrews is virtually unknown.'[2] The Jewish scholar Sacha Stern writes: 'We return to the pre-exilic period ... calendar reckoning in the earlier biblical period remains completely obscure; we do not even know whether the calendar of the early Israelites was solar or lunar.'[3] To find this 'lost' pre-exilic calendar, an obvious starting point is to look for statements in the Old Testament about an ancient calendar which existed before the Babylonian exile, and the book of Exodus provides us with a key clue.

Exodus 12 introduces the story of the Passover Moses instituted in Egypt with a striking calendrical statement: 'The Lord said to Moses and Aaron in Egypt, "This month is to be for you the first month, the first month of your year"' (Exodus 12:1, 2).[4] God is here telling Moses and Aaron to change the first month of the calendar they were using to a new month, a month that will commemorate the time of the Exodus of the Hebrews from Egypt and their birth as a nation. As Houtman writes concerning these verses: 'YHWH's [God's] deliverance of Israel is such an impressive event, a turn around, that it is to be the start of a new time reckoning. The turn in Israel's fortune is given concrete shape in the change of the year.'[5] Just as, later, the coming of Christ marked the beginning of the Christian era, so the Exodus from Egypt marked the start of a new era for the ancient Hebrews.

Can we deduce what month is meant by 'this month' in Exodus 12:2? 'This month' was the month in which Moses held the Passover in Egypt, which followed the ten plagues, and those give a clue to the time of the year. Concerning the seventh plague, of hail, it says in Exodus: 'The flax and barley were destroyed since the barley was in the ear and the flax was in bloom. The wheat and spelt, however, were not destroyed, because they ripen later' (Exodus 9:31–32). We can deduce from these precise agricultural details and our knowledge of Egyptian crops that the plague of hail occurred in February–March.[6]

As argued in *The Miracles of Exodus*, the next (eighth) plague, of locusts, arrived just after the plague of hail, in February–March, the locusts being attracted by the wet soil.[7] The ninth plague was three days of darkness. The vivid description, 'darkness that can be felt' (Exodus 10:21), beautifully describes the darkness due to a khamsin dust-storm. The first of the khamsin storms each year in Egypt usually is the most severe, and it normally occurs in March (see Chapter 6), but sometimes in April. The tenth plague, the death of the firstborn, and the Passover Moses held in Egypt followed shortly after this ninth plague of darkness. We can therefore identify the time of the first Passover as March–April, and Exodus states that this was to be the first month of the calendar Moses established. This is consistent with the book of Exodus also calling the first month by the Canaanite name of Abib ('Today in the month of Abib you are leaving [Egypt]', Exodus 13:4), since the word Abib means the ripening ears of barley, which do indeed ripen in March–April (see Chapter 7). As we have seen, this month was later called Nisan. Thus, according to the book of Exodus, the first month of the Jewish religious year was established in the pre-exilic calendar as March–April by Moses in Egypt, and this first month propagated through to the post-exilic calendar.

WHAT CALENDAR(S) DID THE HEBREWS USE IN EGYPT?

The book of Exodus states that Moses was brought up in an Egyptian palace by Pharaoh's daughter (Exodus 2:10), and according to the New Testament he was 'educated in all the wisdom of the Egyptians' (Acts 7:22). Moses would therefore have had a detailed knowledge of Egyptian calendars because these were central to religious and civil life in ancient Egypt. In fact, at the time of Moses there were two main calendars in everyday use in ancient Egypt: one lunar and the other solar. The distinguished Egyptologist Professor Richard Parker has described these in detail,[8] and his findings have been revised and updated by Professor Marshall Clagett.[9] The original Egyptian calendar was lunar and it was in use from before 3000 BC until at least AD 180. Alongside this lunar calendar there was a solar calendar, introduced in about 2900 BC, which is known as the civil calendar because it was used for administrative, government and business purposes. From about 2900 BC the Egyptians used both of these calendars simultaneously, the lunar one for religious and the solar one for civil purposes. These would have been the Egyptian calendars in use at the time of Moses and they were still in use at the time of Jesus.

THE EGYPTIAN LUNAR CALENDAR

We know that the original Egyptian calendar was lunar because the Egyptian term for 'month' was written with a crescent moon surmounting a star, which was abbreviated in dates as just a crescent moon above the month number.[10] This lunar calendar then came to be used as the religious calendar of ancient Egypt, running alongside the civil solar calendar. The lunar calendar of ancient Egypt differed in several important ways from the official Jewish calendar at the time of Christ that I described in Chapter 4. In particular, instead of the first day of the month starting on the *evening* when the *new* lunar crescent was first seen, the first day of the Egyptian lunar month started in the *morning* on the first day of *invisibility* of the *old* lunar crescent. This day was the day of conjunction, when the earth, moon and sun are in line (see fig. 4.4a), and the ancient Egyptians regarded it as the day of the true new moon. In this lunar calendar, the day runs from sunrise to sunrise, not from sunset to sunset. The Egyptians were not alone in having a calendar based on the first *invisibility* of the *old* lunar crescent; the Maggi and Wadschaggas tribes of East Africa had a similar calendar.

The suggestion that the Egyptian lunar month began with the first invisibility of the waning lunar crescent was first proposed by Brugsch following his discovery in 1864 of an ancient Egyptian inscription, which can be translated as follows: 'He (Khons, the God of the Moon) is conceived on the Feast of *psdntyw*; he is born on the Feast of the Month; he comes to maturity on the Feast of the Half-Month.'[11] How should we interpret this curious statement? I asked John Ray, Professor of Egyptology at Cambridge, the meaning of the Egyptian word *psdntyw*. He said it means the 'day of the new moon'. Brugsch took this to be the first day of the Egyptian lunar month, being the day of conjunction, when the moon was conceived. He then took 'born on the Feast of the Month' to be the day when the crescent moon was first seen, when the moon was visibly born, the *second* day of the Egyptian lunar month. Finally he took the moon coming 'to maturity on the Feast of the Half-Month' to refer to the fifteenth day of the month, the day when the moon was full, that is fully grown.

The above interpretation was confirmed by Richard Parker, after analysing a host of Egyptian texts and performing detailed astronomical calculations. His studies showed that the Egyptians identified the *first* day of their lunar month as the day of *crescent invisibility*, which they took to be the day of conjunction, the true new moon. In 70 per cent of cases the new crescent moon was visible on the next day. In thc other 30 per cent of cases it was visible two days later. The Egyptians had a morning-to-morning day.[12]

Now for some important astronomy. As we have seen when we discussed the official Jewish calendar in Chapter 4, the thin, faintly glowing crescent of the new moon is first visible in the western sky shortly after sunset. The Jewish day therefore naturally begins in the evening. On the other hand, the thin, faintly glowing crescent of the *old* moon is *last* seen in the *eastern* sky shortly before *sunrise* (fig. 8.2). Hence the day in the Egyptian lunar calendar was a sunrise-to-sunrise

Fig. 8.2 Last and first visibility of the lunar crescent. The left-hand diagram shows the last visibility of the lunar crescent in the eastern morning sky (the day before the first day of the month in the Egyptian lunar calendar). The right-hand diagram shows the first visibility of the new lunar crescent in the western evening sky (the start of the month in the official Jewish calendar).

day. It may seem odd to us that a nation could choose to have the first day of its lunar month as the day of first *invisibility* of the lunar crescent. However, as the distinguished historical astronomer Otto Neugebauer pointed out, 'this is in all probability caused by the Egyptian reckoning of the day from sunrise, a procedure which in itself is most natural and does not require any astronomical motivation'.[13] In other words, because it is natural to start the day at sunrise, this led to the ancient Egyptians starting their lunar month on the first day of invisibility of the lunar crescent, because the lunar crescent is last seen in the morning sky just before sunrise.

Most scholars agree that the most probable date for Moses leading the Israelites out of Egypt in the Exodus was around 1270 BC, the Egyptian pharaoh at the time being Ramesses II, also called Ramesses the Great[14] (some scholars believe the Exodus was in about 1450 BC). Fascinatingly, we have really detailed documentary evidence from this time period of the Egyptian lunar calendar. The Temple of Amon-Re, built by the pharaoh Ramesses III (*c.*1194–1163 BC) at Medina Habu in Thebes, has on its southern wall a calendar consisting of lists of offerings to be prepared for feasts. The list is huge and contains a massive 1,470 lines of hieroglyphs. The chief source of this calendar was a similar calendar on the mortuary temple of Ramesses II (*c.*1290–1224 BC),[15] who, as we have seen, was probably the pharaoh at the time of the Exodus. So, we have considerable details of the lunar calendar and feast days of the Egyptians at the time of Moses (if the 1450 BC Exodus date were correct, this would not make any difference to my argument since the Egyptian lunar calendar was in use from before 3000 BC).

Clagett translates this lunar calendar of feasts at the Temple of Amon-Re and states that for the Feast of the First Day of the lunar month (*psdntyw*, the day of the new moon at conjunction) there is given 'an exceedingly long list of supplies, revealing the importance of this feast day'.[16] The next feast is called the Feast of the Month, being the second day of the lunar month. Parker calls this day 'new crescent day'. Clagett notes that this feast only has a short list of supplies.[17] Clagett also lists a feast on the third day of the lunar month, not mentioned on the calendar of feasts at the Temple of Amon-Re, but inscribed in temples and tombs elsewhere. This is called 'Feast of the First Mesper (or Arrival Day)'. Parker speculated that this feast was held because sometimes the new crescent moon appeared on the third day and not on the second day of the month.[18] These well-documented conclusions about the Egyptian lunar calendar are summarised in the table. We should remember that although I call this the Egyptian religious calendar, it was central to the life of ancient Egypt, possibly more so than the solar civil calendar, as attested by its numerous inscriptions on temples and tombs. Religion was at the heart of ancient Egypt.[19]

The Egyptian lunar calendar	
First day of the month, day of the new moon	Day of first invisibility of the moon, day of conjunction
Second day of the month	New lunar crescent usually appeared on this day
Third day of the month	New lunar crescent sometimes appeared on this day
Last day of the month	Day of last visibility of old lunar crescent
Start time of each day	Sunrise, since moon last seen in the morning sky shortly before sunrise

Many biblical scholars do not appreciate that in the Egyptian lunar calendar the day began at sunrise. For example, J. B. Segal makes the blanket statement, 'For calendric purposes the Israelite day – in the sense of the period of twenty-four hours – begins with sunset, *as in other countries where the moon provides the basis of time reckoning* [my italics].'[20] Statements like this, which totally ignore the lunar calendar of the great Egyptian civilisation, are frequently made and they are incorrect.

THE EGYPTIAN SOLAR CALENDAR

The Egyptian solar calendar, their civil calendar, was the calendar of business and government.[21] Like the Egyptian lunar calendar, each day in the solar calendar started at sunrise. Each month was thirty days long and there were twelve months in the year, totalling 360 days. The ancient Egyptians' knowledge of astronomy was so good that they knew a solar year was about 365 days long, so they inserted five extra days (called epagomenal days) before the New Year; hence the Egyptian solar year was 365 days long. However, the Egyptians' knowledge of astronomy was not quite good enough, because the true solar year is about 365¼ days long. The Egyptian solar calendar therefore slowly became out of step with the true solar year, by quarter of a day each year.

Many biblical experts, because they are not Egyptologists, seem to believe that the *only* ancient Egyptian calendar was the solar one and they are unaware of the Egyptian lunar calendar used for religious purposes, which lasted from before 3000 BC to at least AD 180. For example, the distinguished Old Testament scholar Professor Nahum Sarna, in his book *Exploring Exodus*, has a section headed 'The Calendar' in which he writes: 'Throughout most of Egyptian history the calendar was a solar one.'[22] As we have seen, throughout most of their history, the Egyptians had *two* calendars running side by side: a solar one used for government and business and a lunar one for religious feasts and festivals. Are either of these calendars relevant to the pre-exilic Jewish calendar? We will find out in the next chapter.

SUMMARY

Many ancient Jewish writings claim that the official Jewish calendar used at the time of Jesus had departed from the original calendar of Moses, and that the official feasts, such as Passover, were being held on the wrong days. The official Jewish calendar used in the first century AD has its origins in ancient Babylon. It was adopted by the Judean Jews when they were in exile in Babylon from 586 to 537 BC. In this chapter I have started to explore the calendar the Jews may have used before the exile in Babylon. I call this earlier calendar the pre-exilic calendar. Since, according to the Bible, the ancient Israelites spent hundreds of years in Egypt, I examine the ancient Egyptian calendars they might have used during this captivity. There were two such Egyptian calendars: one solar, for government and business, the other lunar, for religious festivals and feasts.

In the Egyptian lunar calendar, the first day of the month started in the morning, on the first day of invisibility of the old lunar crescent. This was the day of conjunction, when earth, moon and sun are in line. For the Egyptians it was the day of the true new moon. In this lunar calendar the day runs from sunrise to sunrise. This calendar lasted from before 3000 BC to at least AD 180. In the next chapter we will explore if the pre-exilic Jewish calendar might have been based on this ancient Egyptian calendar.

9 Discovering the lost calendar of ancient Israel

> The Lord said to Moses and Aaron in Egypt, 'This month is to be for you the first month, the first month of your year.'
>
> (Exodus 12:1–2)

As we saw in the previous chapter, the calendar expert Professor Bickerman stated, 'The pre-Babylonian time reckoning of the ancient Hebrews is virtually unknown',[1] and the Jewish scholar Sacha Stern wrote, 'We return to the pre-exilic period ... calendar reckoning in the early biblical period remains completely obscure.'[2] In this chapter we will find this 'lost calendar' of early Israel.

According to the book of Exodus, God instructed Moses and Aaron to change the first month of the calendar they were using so that the Exodus from Egypt marked the start of their new year. This was the *only* change in the calendar they were asked to make. Interestingly, Exodus pointedly states, 'The Lord said to Moses and Aaron *in Egypt*, "This month is to be for you the first month"' (Exodus 12:1–2). The readers of Exodus would have been well aware that Moses and Aaron were in Egypt; Moses and Aaron had been there throughout the ten plagues of the previous seven chapters of Exodus, so why specifically mention that they were in Egypt here, immediately before making a calendrical statement? I suggest the reason is explicitly to draw readers' attention to the fact that Moses and Aaron were in Egypt and therefore using an *Egyptian* calendar, the first month of which Moses was now to change.

Which Egyptian calendar would Moses have used to celebrate the religious Feast of Passover: the lunar one used for religious festivals or the solar one used for government and business? Moses had been brought up to know that the calendar used for the dates of religious festivals and feasts was the lunar calendar. To celebrate the Passover, Moses therefore would have used the existing religious lunar calendar of the Egyptians and modified this so that the first month was in the spring.

What was the first month in the Egyptian lunar year? Parker argued that the first month began with the first day of invisibility of the moon after the rising of Sirius, also known as Sothis, the brightest star in the sky. Calculations made for me by Graeme Waddington show that in 1200 BC Sirius rose around July 13 as seen from Luxor and around July 17 from Memphis. This roughly coincided with the start of the annual flooding of the River Nile, which was so important to the ancient Egyptians. An additional lunar month (an intercalary or leap month) was added when required (about one year in three) to keep the calendar in step with the 'Sirius year'. Incidentally, since the length of time between the annual risings of Sirius is only twelve minutes shorter than the true solar year, this would have kept the lunar calendar in close step with the true solar year.

Clagett believes that Parker may have been correct in his opinion that the lunar calendar was kept in step with the solar year, but that his statement that this was tied to the rising of Sirius is unproved.[3] I will not discuss this debate further because it is not relevant to the calendar Exodus states Moses used, except to say that the first month of the Egyptian lunar calendar was probably not in the spring. My interpretation of Exodus 12:1 is that Moses took the Egyptian religious lunar calendar and modified it so that the first month was in the spring, in the month the ears of barley ripened (Abib). Choosing the first month to be tied to agriculture in this way implies that this calendar was kept in step with the true solar year, and hence that Moses must have added an extra lunar month when required (about one year in three), probably at the end of the year. I am calling this calendar, that the book of Exodus states Moses instituted in Egypt, the pre-exilic calendar. On the basis that the only change recorded in Exodus 12 to the existing calendar in Egypt was the alteration of the timing of the first month, we can infer that the pre-exilic calendar had the characteristics given in the table.

The pre-exilic calendar	
Start of the day	Sunrise
First day of the month	First day of invisibility of the lunar crescent, conjunction, the true new moon
First month of the year	Abib, the month of ripening ears of barley, March/April in our calendar

Biblical scholars are of course well aware that, according to the book of Exodus, Moses inaugurated a new calendar in which the first month of the year was in the spring. However, because many biblical scholars are not aware of the Egyptian lunar calendar, in which the first day of the lunar month is based on the first *invisibility* of the *old* crescent moon, they assume that the calendar Moses instituted was a lunar calendar based on the first *visibility* of the *new* crescent moon. For example, Sarna writes: 'The new calendar of Israel is to be completely different . . . The month begins with the *new moon* [my italics], but the first month of the year is to fall in the spring.'[4] It is clear that by 'new moon' Sarna means 'new crescent moon', and not the true new moon at conjunction, because he is unaware of the Egyptian lunar calendar. Biblical scholars such as Sarna, Houtman and Segal all fail to consider that the calendar the book of Exodus uses to describe the Passover and the Feast of Unleavened Bread may have been a calendar in which the first day of the month was based on the first *invisibility* of the *old* lunar crescent.

THE HEBREW WORDS FOR MONTH AND MOON

The Bible usually uses the word *hodesh* for *month*. On a number of occasions *hodesh* is used interchangeably with the word commonly used for moon (*yerah*). For example 'in the month (yerah) of Ziv, which is the second month (hodesh)' (1 Kings 6:1). In addition, *hodesh* comes from the root *hadesh*, meaning 'new'. Many scholars believe that the primary meaning of *hodesh* (month) is 'new moon' and that it is only by extension that it came to mean 'month', the period between one new moon and the next. Similarly, as we have seen, the ancient Egyptian symbol for month was a moon.

The 'new moon' for the ancient Egyptians was the day of conjunction, taken to be the first day of invisibility of the lunar crescent, the day the moon was *conceived*, the *true* new moon. On the other hand, the 'new moon' for the priests of the temple at the time of Jesus was the first visible lunar crescent, denoting the *visible birth* of the new moon. I suggest that to Moses, 'educated in all the wisdom of the Egyptians' (Acts 7:22), 'new moon' meant the day of conjunction, the day of first invisibility of the lunar crescent (called the 'day of the new moon' by the ancient Egyptians). *Hodesh* in the Bible can therefore mean either the day of conjunction (if it refers to the pre-exilic calendar) or the day of the new crescent moon (if it refers to the later official Jewish calendar, the post-exilic calendar): both refer to the new moon, at conception and at birth, respectively.

THE CHANGE IN JEWISH CALENDARS

In the pre-exilic calendar described above, the day started at sunrise. However, in the time of Christ, in the official Jewish calendar the day started at sunset. This change almost certainly occurred when the Judean Jews were in exile in Babylon (596–538 BC), when they adopted the Babylonian calendar. Since the start of the month in the Babylonian calendar was based on the first visibility of the new lunar crescent in the evening sky, the Babylonian day started at sunset. Hence when the Judean Jews adopted the Babylonian calendar they would have changed the start time of their day from sunrise to sunset.

OLD TESTAMENT EVIDENCE FOR THE PRE-EXILIC DAY STARTING AT SUNRISE

If the pre-exilic Jewish calendar I have deduced is correct then we would expect to find evidence for a Jewish sunrise-to-sunrise day in the earlier events recorded in the Old Testament. Many biblical scholars agree that before the exile the Jewish day started at sunrise. For example, Finegan writes: 'In the Old Testament the earlier practice seems to have been to consider that the day began in the morning. In Gen 19:34, for example, the "next day" clearly begins with the morning after the preceding night.'[5] And Wagenaar states: 'An original custom to calculate the day from sunrise to sunrise eventually gave way to the custom to calculate the day from sunset to sunset.'[6] A detailed analysis of the account in 1 Samuel 30:17 of David fighting the Amalekites in about 1000 BC concludes that the text 'makes perfect sense as it stands, if it is assumed that the calendar day of the Amalekites began at sunset, whereas that of David resembled that of the Egyptian by starting at dawn'.[7] Roland de Vaux states: 'In Israel, the day was for a long time reckoned from morning to morning' and from an extensive analysis of biblical texts he concludes that the change to an evening to evening day probably began at 'the beginning of the Exile'.[8]

We will now see if the Passover instructions recorded in Exodus 12 are consistent with the day starting in the morning or in the evening. The relevant parts of Exodus 12 are as follows: 'The Lord said to Moses and Aaron in Egypt, "This month is to be for you the first month, the first month of your year. Tell the whole community of Israel that on the tenth day of this month each man is to take a lamb for his family . . . Take care of them until the fourteenth day of the month, when all the people of the community of Israel must slaughter them at twilight . . . That same night they are to eat the meat roasted over the fire, along with bitter herbs and bread made without yeast . . . Do not leave any of it till morning . . . it is the Lord's Passover"' (Exodus 12:1–11). The Hebrew words translated 'twilight' in the New International Version (NIV) Bible quoted above literally mean 'between the two evenings'. It is not certain what this expression means. It probably means the time interval between sunset and the first stars appearing but it may possibly mean late afternoon, between the decline of the sun and sunset.[9]

The Passover instructions in Exodus state that the Israelites should slaughter the lamb at twilight on the fourteenth day of the month (Exodus 12:6) and '*That same night* [my italics] they are to eat the meat roasted over the fire' (Exodus 12:8). Notice that the fifteenth day of the month is not mentioned at all in Exodus 12, only the fourteenth day. As Wagenaar states: 'In the Priestly festival calendar [in Exodus 12] Passover is firmly fixed to the fourteenth day of the first month.'[10] The natural reading of this account in Exodus 12 is that the slaughtering of the lambs and the eating of the Passover meal 'that same night' *both* occurred on the fourteenth day of the first month. This is consistent with a morning-to-morning day being used but inconsistent with an evening-to-evening day. The final instruction in Exodus concerning the Passover meal is: 'Do not leave any of it [the Passover lamb] till morning' (Exodus 12:10). In other words, do not leave any of it until the next day, the fifteenth day of the first month, using our pre-exilic calendar with its morning-to-morning day.

Exodus 12:14–16 instructs how the 'generations to come' should celebrate the Exodus from Egypt. 'For seven days you are to eat bread made without yeast. On the first day remove the yeast from your houses ... On the first day hold a sacred assembly and another one on the seventh day. Do no work at all on these days, except to prepare food for everyone to eat – that is all you may do.' Are these instructions consistent with a sunrise-to-sunrise day or a sunset-to-sunset day? The Israelites were instructed to remove the yeast from houses on the first day of the seven days of eating unleavened bread. Clearly this removal of yeast was in the daytime on day 14 of the first month, irrespective of whether the day started at sunrise or at sunset. However, apart from the preparing of food, this 'first day' was to be a day of rest, a day which later became called the Sabbath of the Passover, as we saw in Chapter 5. Clearly this special holy day of rest was the day on which the Passover meal was eaten, the first meal in the seven-day Feast of Unleavened Bread, which was eaten *after* sunset. This was the day on which families assembled for a sacred meal. Since Exodus 12:15–16 calls the first day of these seven days *both* the day on which leaven must be removed from houses *and* a sacred day of rest on which the Passover meal was eaten, a calendar with a sunrise-to-sunrise day must be being used in which both events occurred on Nisan 14.

TRANSFERRING THE PASSOVER MEAL BETWEEN CALENDARS

We have just shown that, according to Exodus 12, the Passover lambs were both killed and eaten on the fourteenth day of the first month. However, at the time of Christ, the Passover lambs were killed on Nisan 14 and then eaten on the night of Nisan 15, and it was Nisan 15 which was the day of rest called the Sabbath of the Passover. Why is there this apparent discrepancy?

I have already suggested the solution. The pre-exilic calendar had a morning-to-morning day. When the calendar changed to an evening-to-evening day it became necessary to transfer the feasts from the old to the new calendar. In the pre-exilic calendar used in Exodus 12, with its morning-to-morning day, the Passover lambs were slain 'between the two evenings' on day 14 and the roasting of the lambs and the eating of the Passover meal followed later that night, which was still part of day 14. But when the same events were transferred to the post-exilic Jewish calendar, with its evening-to-evening day, the Passover meal which was eaten in the evening/night was necessarily held on Nisan 15, because Nisan 15 commenced at sunset. By the time of Jesus, the killing of the lambs had been advanced to 3 p.m., because of the large number to be slain. Thus in the official Jewish calendar at the time of Christ the slaughter was on Nisan 14, and the Passover meal was on Nisan 15, which was also now the first day of the Feast of Unleavened Bread. It is therefore clear how the date of the Passover meal transferred from one calendar to the other and we have a consistent explanation that fits the different dates of the Passover meal, and the first day of the Feast of Unleavened Bread, in the pre-exilic Jewish calendar and in the official Jewish calendar in the first century AD. The table summarises the situation.

Transferring Passover from the pre-exilic calendar to the official Jewish calendar

Event	Date in pre-exilic calendar (morning-to-morning day)	Date in official Jewish calendar (evening-to-evening day)
Passover lamb sacrificed	Nisan 14	Nisan 14
Passover Feast and first day of the Feast of Unleavened Bread	Nisan 14	Nisan 15

Interestingly, Parker demonstrates that there was a similar transfer of feasts in Egypt from the lunar to the solar calendar. Parker writes: 'It is not to be supposed that there was a complete and wholesale transfer of feasts from the lunar to the civil calendar at one given time. No doubt it was a gradual process over the early years of the dual calendar ... The **fact** of such a transfer is beyond question.' In addition, after this transfer, Parker then shows that 'double dates' were given in Egyptian texts for each feast, one in the lunar and the other in the solar calendar, so that: 'From then on one might have two dates for each festival, one fixed to the civil year, the other determined by the lunar year.'[11] This provides an important precedent for what I am suggesting happened in ancient Israel.

THE TRANSITION FROM THE PRE-EXILIC TO THE POST-EXILIC JEWISH CALENDAR

As we saw in Chapter 2, the transition from the Julian calendar to the Gregorian calendar we use today was a gradual process. Pope Gregory XIII introduced the Gregorian calendar in AD 1582, but many people in England and the USA did not adopt this until AD 1752 and the Scottish island of Foula still has not adopted it. Although countries such as Greece and Russia use the Gregorian calendar for their everyday life (it is their civil calendar), Greek and Russian Orthodox churches still celebrate their religious festivals using the Julian calendar (still their religious calendar). Similarly, Parker states that the transfer of feasts from one calendar to another in ancient Egypt would have been a gradual process.

We can therefore expect that the transfer of feasts in ancient Israel from the pre-exilic to the post-exilic calendar (the official calendar used at the time of Christ) may have been a gradual process. In addition, only the Judean Jews were in exile in Babylon, so we cannot assume that Galilean Jews and Samaritans adopted the post-exilic calendar. Further, some Judean Jews may have objected to using the post-exilic calendar for religious feasts and festivals and preferred to keep to their traditional pre-exilic calendar. Do we have any biblical evidence for a gradual transfer of feast dates?

Some parts of this book are more tentative than others, so let me say here that what I am about to write is tentative, because we do not have enough evidence to be more certain. However I believe the little evidence we have is consistent with a gradual transfer of feast dates from the pre-exilic to the post-exilic calendar, with objections to this transfer from at least one eminent Judean Jew.

Analysing the transfer of feast dates is complicated by two factors. First, scholars are uncertain about when the first five books in the Old Testament were written. Second, these original texts were copied and recopied by scribes. Although experienced scribes were able to copy texts very accurately, they routinely 'modernised' the texts they were copying. For example, if a place name had changed or a feast date had changed, the scribe if called upon would update the text to use the new place name, or the new feast date, and they would also modernise outdated spellings and grammar. This was standard practice in the ancient world in Egyptian, Hebrew, Mesopotamian and other texts.[12] Somewhat similarly, most of the Bibles used today are in modern versions of the language being used. Hence many Old Testament books may have been updated to their 'final form' long after the original texts were written.

At first sight the Old Testament seems curiously confused about the dates of the Passover Feast and the related seven-day Feast of

Unleavened Bread (the Passover Feast being the first meal in the seven-day Feast of Unleavened Bread). According to the book of Exodus, the Feast of Unleavened Bread started on the *fourteenth* day of the first month (Exodus 12:17–19). However Leviticus and Numbers have the Feast starting on the *fifteenth* day of the first month (Leviticus 23:6 and Numbers 28:17), whereas in Ezekiel it is back on the *fourteenth* day (Ezekiel 45:21).

Interestingly, this double dating of the first day of the Feast of Unleavened Bread (the Feast of Passover) in the Old Testament is mirrored in New Testament times, where in the official Jewish calendar the first day of the Feast of Unleavened Bread (the Passover Feast) was on Nisan 15, but in the Qumran solar calendar it was on Nisan 14, as we saw in the previous chapter. In addition, this apparent discrepancy in the Old Testament is reflected in the apparent confusion in the New Testament over whether the last supper was on the fourteenth (John) or the fifteenth (synoptics) day of the first month. This raises a key question: could the solution to the synoptics/John last supper problem lie in the double dating for the Passover meal given in Exodus and Ezekiel (fourteenth day) and Leviticus and Numbers (fifteenth day)?

THE DIFFERENT DATES FOR THE PASSOVER MEAL AND THE FIRST DAY OF THE FEAST OF UNLEAVENED BREAD IN THE OLD TESTAMENT

The different dates in the Old Testament for Passover are well known to biblical scholars. For example, Bo Reicke writes: 'In the Mosaic laws, the evening of Passover (on which a meal lasting from about 7.00 pm until midnight inaugurated the festal week) is first dated Nisan 14 (Exodus 12:6, 8, 18); later passages, however, give the date as Nisan 15 (Leviticus 23:5f; Numbers 28:16f), and the latter date became general throughout Judaism.'[13]

Biblical scholars recognise that the Passover calendar in Ezekiel agrees with that in Exodus.[14] Scholars also acknowledge that Ezekiel's instructions 'are at variance with those recorded in Numbers and elsewhere',[15] and remain puzzled by the date of Passover given by Ezekiel.[16] How curious! Ezekiel was a priest (Ezekiel 1:3) and hence he would have been particularly familiar with the Passover calendar. Ezekiel 1:1 tells us that Ezekiel was among the Jews exiled to Babylon, by King Nebuchadnezzar in 596 BC, and Ezekiel wrote the book that bears his name while in exile, that is in the sixth century BC.

A key question is why the date of the Passover meal and the first day of the Feast of Unleavened Bread changes on going from Exodus to Leviticus and Numbers. This would not have been a minor matter for the Israelites because the book of Exodus instructs that the first day of the Feast of Unleavened Bread, when the Passover meal was eaten, should be celebrated on a *particular* day, because it commemorated 'the very day that I brought your divisions out of Egypt' (Exodus 12:17) and yet the date was apparently changed by one day after this clear instruction was given.

The date of the Passover Feast and the first day of the Feast of Unleavened Bread	
Exodus	Nisan 14
Leviticus	Nisan 15
Numbers	Nisan 15
Ezekiel	Nisan 14
Official calendar at the time of Jesus	Nisan 15
Qumran solar calendar	Nisan 14

This change of the date of the Passover meal and of the first day of the Feast of Unleavened Bread, from the fourteenth to the fifteenth day of the first month, is really quite extraordinary. Imagine being born on the fourteenth day of a certain month and then, after a period of years, changing your birthday celebration to the fifteenth day. You would not do this without an extremely good reason. The Passover meal is of much greater historical significance than any individual's birthday. It commemorated a new era for the Israelites, which started on a particular day in history. There must have been a compelling reason for the Israelites to change the date of this annual celebratory feast by one day.

THE REASON FOR THE DIFFERENT PASSOVER CALENDARS OF EXODUS, LEVITICUS, NUMBERS AND EZEKIEL

I suggest there is no discrepancy between the books of Exodus, Leviticus, Numbers and Ezekiel over the date of the Passover meal, eaten on the first day of the Feast of Unleavened Bread. There was simply a change of calendars. Exodus and Ezekiel use the pre-exilic calendar, with its morning-to-morning day. Leviticus and Numbers use the later post-exilic calendar, based on the Babylonian calendar, with its evening-to-evening day.

Let me very tentatively suggest *how* the above may have come about. Exodus 12 describes in considerable detail the Passover meal and it never mentions the fifteenth day of the first month, only the fourteenth day. Let us assume this was written before the exile and hence before the Jewish calendar change. Scribes copying this chapter during and after the exile could not easily have updated the text, and changed 'fourteenth' to 'fifteenth', because this would have required a major rewriting of the whole chapter, which was beyond the modernising of archaic usage routinely performed by scribes. Hence I suggest the Passover date in Exodus 12 faithfully preserves the original date in the pre-exilic calendar. On the other hand, I suggest that the passages from Leviticus and Numbers which refer to the Passover and the Feast of Unleavened Bread (e.g. Leviticus 23:6 and Numbers 28:17) come either from a post-exilic source or from a post-exilic editor/scribe who updated the pre-exilic source to give the dates of the Feast of Unleavened Bread in the official Jewish calendar of the time. Such updating would have been easy in Leviticus and Numbers because they do not give nearly such a detailed account of the Passover as Exodus 12.

The book of Ezekiel is of particular interest because it states it was written *during* his exile in Babylon. A key message of Ezekiel is that the Jews were in captivity because they had 'conformed to the standards of the nations around you' (Ezekiel 11:12). Chapters 40–48 describe Ezekiel's vision of a new temple that he had in the twenty-fifth year of his exile (Ezekiel 40:1). After this considerable length of time in exile let us assume that most of the Jewish priests had adopted the Babylonian-style calendar. Then the whole point of Ezekiel stating 'In the first month on the *fourteenth* day you are to observe the Passover' (Ezekiel 45:21) was to call his fellow Jews back to celebrating Passover according to the original pre-exilic calendar, and not to conform 'to the standards of the nations around you' (Ezekiel 11:12).

It appears from the above that in the sixth century BC one group of Judean Jews believed that the Passover meal and the first day of the Feast of Unleavened Bread should be celebrated on the fifteenth day of the first month, and a second group, including or led by Ezekiel, advocated celebrating the Passover meal on the fourteenth day of the month, as in the original pre-exilic calendar. In addition, those in Samaria and Galilee, who had not been taken into captivity in Babylon, would still have been celebrating the Passover Feast on the fourteenth day of the first month.

According to Ezekiel, one of the actions expected of the Messiah was to purify the temple's worship.[17] Would Jesus therefore choose, after his cleansing of the temple, to celebrate his last supper Passover meal on Nisan 14, according to the pre-exilic timetable advocated by Ezekiel, or on Nisan 15, as used by the priests of the temple in the first century AD? I will look at this question in Chapter 9.

SUMMARY

Exodus and Ezekiel appear to disagree with Leviticus and Numbers over the date of the Feast of Passover. In Exodus and Ezekiel this was on day 14 of the first month, and in Leviticus and Numbers it was on day 15. I have argued that before the exile of Judean Jews into Babylon in 586 BC, the original Jewish calendar was based upon the Egyptian lunar calendar. In this calendar, the first day of the month was the first day of *invisibility* of the *old* lunar crescent. This was the day of conjunction, the true new moon, and the day ran from sunrise to sunrise. In Exodus 12, the only change Moses was instructed to make to this Egyptian lunar calendar was to start the year in the spring, to commemorate the Exodus from Egypt at this time. I call this modified Egyptian calendar the pre-exilic Jewish calendar. The Judean Jews changed this pre-exilic calendar during their exile in Babylon to a Babylonian-style calendar, based on the first *visibility* of the *new* lunar crescent. This later calendar had a sunset-to-sunset day.

This change of calendar necessitated a transfer in the dates of feasts. In the pre-exilic calendar, with its sunrise-to-sunrise day, the Passover lamb was slain on the same day, day 14, as the Passover meal was eaten. In the later official Jewish calendar, with its sunset-to-sunset day, the Passover lambs were slain on Nisan 14 and the Passover meal was eaten on Nisan 15. This calendrical change explains the apparent discrepancy in the dates of the Passover meal in Exodus relative to Leviticus and Numbers. The ancient Egyptians had a similar transfer of the dates of their feasts from one calendar to another, leading to a similar double dating of feasts. In more recent times, the change from the Julian to the Gregorian calendar also resulted in a double dating of the Christian festivals of Christmas and Easter, with Catholics and Protestants celebrating these festivals according to the Gregorian calendar, and Orthodox churches keeping to the Julian calendar.

Ezekiel, in exile in Babylon in the sixth century BC, exhorted his fellow Jews to return to the pre-exilic Passover Feast date of Nisan 14. It therefore seems that following the transfer of feast dates outlined above, in the sixth century BC most Judean Jews believed the Passover meal should be eaten on Nisan 15, using a calendar with a sunset-to-sunset day, whereas some Judean Jews plus those not taken into captivity in Babylon, particularly Galilean Jews and Samaritans, would have still celebrated this Feast on Nisan 14, using a calendar with a sunrise-to-sunrise day. However, what was the situation in the first century AD? I will explain this in the next chapter.

10 Was the lost ancient Jewish calendar used in Israel at the time of Jesus?

> He [Jesus] came to a town in Samaria called Sychar, near the plot of ground Jacob had given to his son Joseph . . . Many of the Samaritans from that town believed in him . . . they urged him to stay with them, and he stayed two more days. And because of his words many more became believers. They said . . . 'We know that this man really is the Saviour of the World.'
>
> (John 4:5, 39–42)

Today we use the Gregorian calendar. However, the earlier Julian calendar has persisted down to today and is still used by various groups (Greek Orthodox, Russian Orthodox, etc.) to calculate the date of Easter. In the previous chapter we discovered the lost pre-exilic Jewish calendar. Did Jesus choose to use this calendar to celebrate his last supper as a Passover meal, held at least one day before the date in the official Jewish calendar? Clearly he could only have done so if he knew about this calendar. Hence in this chapter I am going to ask the key question whether the pre-exilic calendar persisted down to the first century AD and whether it was used by one or more groups in Israel at the time of Jesus. We will start by considering the Samaritans.

THE SAMARITANS

The Samaritans are frequently mentioned in the gospels. For example, according to John 4, quoted above, Jesus had a group of followers in Samaria who declared him to be 'the Saviour of the World'. Jesus was not a Samaritan; his conversation with a Samaritan woman makes this clear (see John 4:27). However, the gospels record Jesus speaking favourably about the Samaritans. For example, in the parable Jesus told about being a good neighbour (Luke 10:30–36), the person who helped the man who was beaten and robbed was not a Jewish priest nor a Levite, but a Samaritan. Of the ten lepers whom Jesus healed, the only one who thanked him was a Samaritan (Luke 17:11–19). So who were the Samaritans?

There are three main schools of thought about the origins of the Samaritans.[1] The Samaritans themselves claim to be the direct descendants of the northern Israelite tribes and to be the true Israelites who are the keepers of the laws of Moses.[2] Another tradition claims that the Samaritans were pagans, displaying a veneer of Israelite religion, who were brought into Samaria by the Assyrians to repopulate the land.[3] The Bible records that the king of Assyria captured Samaria and deported the Israelites to Assyria (2 Kings 17:6). This was in about 722 BC. Shortly afterwards the king of Assyria repopulated Samaria by bringing in people from various lands the Assyrians had conquered (2 Kings 17:24).

A third interpretation of Samaritan origins combines the above two theories: although the Assyrians deported some Israelites, significant numbers of the early Israelite population survived in Samaria and the Assyrians also brought in other people to join them. These two groups then intermingled to form the Samaritans of New Testament times.[4] Many scholars accept this third view. Because it takes into account all, rather than only part, of the available evidence this is the understanding of Samaritan origins that I will follow.

As we saw in Chapter 8, according to the Bible, Joshua led the Israelites into Canaan, which was divided into three main regions: Samaria, Galilee and Judah. Do we have any archaeological evidence that the Israelites were in Canaan at the time of Joshua? In 1896, the Egyptologist Flinders Petrie discovered a black granite slab known as the Merneptah Stele at the temple of the Pharaoh Merneptah at Thebes in Egypt. The slab has on it hieroglyphs commemorating Merneptah's campaign in Canaan in about 1210 BC. The stele states: 'Canaan is plundered with every evil; Ashkelon is conquered; Gezer is seized; Yanoam is made non-existent.' And then comes the line: 'Israel is laid waste, his seed is no more' (fig. 10.1). This document recognises that in about 1210 BC, not only were the Israelites in Canaan, they were there in sufficient numbers to be worth mentioning as a group of

Fig. 10.1 The Merneptah Stele. The photograph shows the part of the inscription where it says: 'Israel is laid waste.'

people the Egyptians claimed to have destroyed. (It may be interesting to note a revised translation, 'Israel is laid waste, her grain is no more.'[5]) The Merneptah Stele is the earliest reference outside the Bible to Israel as an entity.

The Bible records that Joshua assembled all the tribes of Israel at Shechem in Samaria (Joshua 24:1) and said to them: 'You crossed the Jordan and came to Jericho. The citizens of Jericho fought against you, as did also the Amorites ... but I gave them into your hands. I sent the hornet ahead of you, which drove them out before you. You did not do it with your own sword and bow.' What did Joshua mean by: 'I sent the hornet ahead of you'? Northern Egypt used the hornet as its national symbol, so Joshua is referring to Egypt's military campaign in Canaan. Joshua is saying that the Egyptian army (the hornet) conquered much of Canaan, as recorded on the Merneptah Stele, and that the Israelites then took over the conquered land as the Egyptian army withdrew.

Joshua established the Ark of the Covenant at Shiloh, near Shechem in Samaria (Joshua 19:51). From various Old Testament books it is clear that Shiloh was the major centre for Israelite worship in this period from about 1200 to 1000 BC. For example, Judges 18:31 calls Shiloh the 'house of God' and 1 Samuel 1:1–4 describes how people travelled to Shiloh to make sacrifices. If the pre-exilic calendar of ancient Israel was the calendar I deduced in the previous chapter, then this would have been the calendar Joshua and the Israelites used in Canaan. It would have been regulated from either Shechem or Shiloh in Samaria. (By 'regulated' I mean the Jewish priests would have proclaimed the first day of the lunar month, based on observing the first day of invisibility of the old lunar crescent, and would have added an extra month when required, so that the first month of the year remained in the spring.)

As we will see below, Samaritans claim that the modern Samaritan calendar, which is different from the modern Jewish calendar, has been handed down to them from the original calendar of Moses. We will therefore now examine the modern Samaritan calendar and see if it bears any resemblance to the pre-exilic calendar that I deduced in the previous chapter.

THE SAMARITAN CALENDAR

The most comprehensive account of the Samaritan calendar is given by Sylvia Powels.[6] As she points out: 'Few scholars have dealt with the Samaritan calendar. The reason for neglecting this subject is primarily that the Samaritans have made a secret of the rules of calculation of their calendar until recent times.'[7] The Samaritan calendar is therefore not well known by most biblical scholars.

The Samaritans claim that the official Jewish calendar is in error. In AD 1355, a Samaritan document written in Hebrew called *Taulida* (which means genealogy) claimed that God revealed the true calendar to Adam, who passed it on to his descendants, and finally to Moses, who changed the first month to be in the spring. Moses then taught the calendar, called by the Samaritans 'the True Reckoning', to Pinhas, Aaron's grandson. The *Taulida* claims that Pinhas established this calendar of Moses at Mount Gerizim, near Shechem in Samaria, when the Israelites entered the Promised Land.[8]

Interestingly, the Bible records that *Phinehas* was the grandson of Aaron (Exodus 6:25, Numbers 25:7). The ancient Hebrew alphabet used in the Old Testament consisted only of consonants. Hence we can identify Pinhas, the grandson of Aaron according to the Samaritan *Taulida*, with Phinehas, the grandson of Aaron according to the Old Testament. The Old Testament represents Phinehas as a leader of ancient Israel. Not only was he a priest (Numbers 25:7), but God conferred on Phinehas and his descendants the 'covenant of priesthood forever' (Numbers 25:13, 1 Maccabees 2:54). Phinehas was the chief priest in his time, because it was Phinehas who 'stood before the Ark of the Covenant in those days' (Judges 20:28). The Samaritan claim that Pinhas (Phinehas) was responsible for establishing the calendar of Moses in the Promised Land is clearly consistent with the biblical description of Phinehas as the chief priest.

Today's Samaritan calendar and Jewish calendar have much in common. Both are based on calculation, rather than on observations of the moon. Both are lunar calendars with the lunar year being composed of twelve lunar months of twenty-nine or thirty days each.[9] The lunar calendar year has 354 days, and in order to keep their lunar year in step with the solar year of about 365¼ days, both the Samaritan and the Jewish calendars add an additional lunar month when required.

The modern Samaritan calendar has one key difference from the modern Jewish calendar. The first day of the month in the Jewish calendar is the calculated appearance of the *new crescent moon* but the first day of the month in the Samaritan calendar is the calculated *conjunction* of the moon with the sun (at conjunction, the moon, earth and sun are in line and the moon is invisible).[10] The Samaritan month always starts before the Jewish month, because conjunction always occurs before the lunar crescent is first visible.[11]

THE SAMARITAN CALENDAR AND THE LUNAR CALENDAR OF ANCIENT EGYPT

It is clear from the above that the modern Samaritan calendar is closely linked to the lunar calendar of ancient Egypt and the pre-exilic calendar of ancient Israel. No scholar appears to have made this key connection before. Let me explain.

As we have seen in Chapters 4 and 8, on average, the moon is invisible for sixty hours in a lunar month. That is, there are sixty hours, on average, between the last visibility of the old lunar crescent and the first visibility of the new lunar crescent. Conjunction, when the sun, moon and earth are in line, occurs at the middle of this invisibility period. Hence there are thirty hours, on average, between the last visibility of the old lunar crescent and conjunction, followed by another thirty hours, on average, between conjunction and the first visibility of the new lunar crescent. Since there are twenty-four hours in a day, on average conjunction will be one day after the last visibility of the old lunar crescent and one day before the first visibility of the new lunar crescent. The first day in the month of the Samaritan calendar is the day of conjunction, so the Samaritan month starts, on average, one day before that of the official Jewish calendar.

As I stated in Chapter 8, the ancient Egyptians used the first day of invisibility of the old lunar crescent as the start of the month in their religious calendar. Thus the Egyptians, like the later Samaritans, started their month with conjunction. For both the Samaritans and the ancient Egyptians, conjunction was the day of the *true* new moon, the day when the moon was conceived. It is interesting to note that, as mentioned in Chapter 8, it was not until 1864 that Brugsch discovered the ancient Egyptian lunar calendar in which the first day of the month was the day of conjunction.[12] However, much earlier than Brugsch, in the twelfth century AD, the Samaritan scholar Abu'l-Hasan as-Suri explained that conjunction signified the true new moon, which was the first day of the month in the Samaritan calendar. Clearly as-Suri had not learned about a lunar calendar, in which the first day of the month was conjunction, from Egyptologists such as Brugsch, who lived much later. We have no evidence that the Samaritans were expert astronomers. They must therefore have derived their calendar from another culture, where such astronomers existed. A possible candidate from the period before Christ is ancient Egypt, which would fit with their traditions that their calendar dates back to Moses in Egypt, and that Pinhas brought this calendar into Canaan. I will investigate this further below.

THE SAMARITAN CALENDAR AND THE PRE-EXILIC JEWISH CALENDAR

Since about the fourth century AD, the official Jewish calendar has been a *calculated* calendar, as described above. Earlier than this, and in particular at the time of Christ, the start of the month in the official Jewish calendar was determined by *observing* the first visibility of the lunar crescent (see Chapter 4).

The Samaritan calendar has been a calculated calendar from at least the ninth century AD, when it is believed that the Samaritans calculated the time of conjunction from the tables of Arabian astronomers.[13] However, as Sylvia Powels says: 'It is assumed that before the adoption of the Arab astronomical tables they [the Samaritans] practiced observation.'[14] This clearly must have been the case in the first century AD. At that time not only the Jewish calendar but also the Samaritan calendar would have been based on observation, because they did not yet know how to calculate the calendar. However, for the Samaritans, the start of their month in their tradition was determined by the conjunction of the sun and moon. The problem is that the conjunction is not observable, so how did the Samaritans identify the start of their month? The obvious solution is that the Samaritans determined conjunction in the same way as the ancient Egyptians did, by looking for the *last* visibility of the *old* lunar crescent. The next day, the first day of invisibility of the lunar crescent, would then have been taken to be the day of conjunction, the first day of the month for the Samaritans, just as it was for the ancient Egyptians. The old lunar crescent is last seen in the morning sky just before sunrise so such an observational calendar naturally has a morning-to-morning day. Hence I suggest the Samaritan calendar in the first century AD had a sunrise-to-sunrise day, just as the ancient Egyptian lunar calendar had a sunrise-to-sunrise day.

If that is correct, then the only difference between the ancient observational Samaritan calendar and the ancient Egyptian lunar calendar was that the Samaritans started their year in the spring in the month of Abib. In other words, the Samaritan calendar was identical with the pre-exilic Jewish calendar. This pre-exilic calendar was used by Joshua and the Israelites in Canaan, and it was regulated from either Shechem or Shiloh in Samaria, as described earlier. As I explained in Chapter 8, it was the Judean Jews who deviated from this calendar during their exile in Babylon, when they adopted the Babylonian-style calendar. However, I suggest that the Samaritans, who were not captured by the Babylonians, have faithfully kept and transmitted the original pre-exilic Jewish calendar down to the present day, except that it is now a calculated calendar.

Similarities between the pre-exilic Jewish calendar and the modern Samaritan calendar	
Lunar or solar?	Lunar
First day of the month	Day of conjunction of the moon
First month of the year	Passover time in the spring. Intercalary 'leap months' added to keep calendar in step with solar year

I have written above that there is a period of thirty hours, on average, between conjunction and the first visibility of the new lunar crescent, and that, since there are twenty-four hours in a day, the Samaritan month starts, *on average*, one day before that in the official Jewish calendar. However, there will be occasions on which the Samaritan month starts two, or even more, days before the Jewish month, because the thirty-hour period mentioned above is only an average value.[15] We cannot therefore assume that the Samaritan (or pre-exilic calendar) month always starts one day before the start of the month in the official Jewish calendar. I will return to this in the next chapter, when we determine the date of the last supper.

As we have seen in Chapter 4, the Jews used to light beacons to indicate the first day of the month to Jewish groups throughout Palestine and beyond (e.g. in Syria and Babylon). Similarly, it seems that the Samaritans used to light beacons to let Samaritans outside Samaria know the first day of the month in the Samaritan calendar. Since the Samaritan month started before the Jewish month, the potential for confusion is clear. The Jewish Talmudic text Rosh Hashanah (i.3; ii.2), written not later than the beginning of the third century AD, states that the Jews had to abandon the lighting of beacons and instead had to send out messengers to announce the start of the month because of 'malpractices' by the Samaritans, presumably meaning the lighting of beacons on what the Jews regarded as the wrong day.

The sending out of messengers was introduced before the destruction of the Jerusalem temple in AD 70.[16]

THE SAMARITAN PASSOVER

The Jewish historian Josephus (*Antiquities* 11.325) writes that the Samaritan Sanballat built a temple on Mount Gerizim in about 388 BC.[17] Sanballat appointed Manasses as the first high priest of the Samaritan temple and many Jewish Judean priests left Jerusalem and joined Manasses in Samaria (Josephus, *Antiquities* 11.306–12). However, there was continuing hostility between Jews and Samaritans. The Jewish Judean high priest, John Hyrcanus, destroyed the Samaritan temple in 128 BC and the Samaritan city of Shechem in 107 BC.[18]

The Samaritan Passover has been continuously observed since antiquity.[19] It is the most important feast for the Samaritans, and it was (and still is today) celebrated on Mount Gerizim, irrespective of whether the Samaritan temple existed or not. It consists of the slaughter, roasting and subsequent eating of lambs as prescribed in Exodus 12.[20] However, there were times in the past, because of the political situation, when it was impossible for the Samaritans to celebrate Passover on Mount Gerizim. What did the Samaritans do then? As John Wilson explained in 1847: 'This ceremony [Passover] should be performed on Mount Gerizim, but on account of opposition and exactions of the Turks and Arabs, it is now gone through at their own houses ... The paschal lamb they eat with unleavened bread and bitter herbs, according to the law.'[21] Hence, when unable to sacrifice on Mount Gerizim, the Samaritans sacrificed Passover lambs in their own houses, just as in the account of the original Passover in the book of Exodus.

The following account from *Israel Travel* of the Samaritan Passover in 2007 shows the striking similarity between the modern Samaritan Passover and the original Passover instructions in the book of Exodus: 'A day before the Jewish Seder is held on the eve of the Passover holiday [note the Samaritan Passover being held on the day before the Jewish Passover in 2007], the Samaritan community gathers on the holy Mount Gerizim in the West Bank to hold their most important religious ceremony: the Passover sacrifice, during which every family must sacrifice and eat a lamb ... At precisely 7:10 pm [note this is during twilight: after sunset, but before the first stars appear] the great priest gives the signal to begin the sacrifice of dozens of sheep ... Once the sheep are killed they are placed in ovens for about three hours ... Close to midnight each family takes its lamb home where it will be quickly eaten together with matzas and bitter herbs.'[22] The similarity of this modern Samaritan timing with that described in the book of Exodus (the lambs being slain during twilight, etc.) rather than the revised practice of the priests of the Jerusalem temple in the first century AD (lambs slain before sunset) is consistent with the Samaritans' claim to be using the pre-exilic calendar. Having shown that the Samaritans used the pre-exilic Jewish calendar, I will now explore whether other groups did so as well.

THE LUNAR CALENDAR OF THE QUMRAN COMMUNITY

As we saw in Chapter 7, the main calendar of the Qumran community was a solar one. Yet, there are at least four different Dead Sea Scroll texts from the Qumran caves that refer in detail to a *lunar* calendar.[23] From the texts it is clear that this lunar calendar had a year of 354 days divided into twelve lunar months of length twenty-nine and thirty days. Every three years an additional thirty-day month was added (intercalated), so as to keep in step with the solar year. In these respects the calendar is similar to both the official Jewish calendar and the pre-exilic calendar.

A key question is when the month started in the Qumran lunar calendar. As Sacha Stern says, this 'has been subject to intense controversy'. However, from a detailed analysis of the texts, Talmon and Knohl concluded that the first day of the month in the Qumran lunar calendar corresponded to the *day of conjunction*.[24] This is consistent with the statement in one of the texts that the month begins and ends when the moon is *dark*. It is also consistent with an interesting comment made to me by Graeme Waddington, who notes that it is impossible to observe the new crescent moon from Qumran because there is a high mountain range immediately to the west of Qumran (see fig. 7.1). Since the new crescent moon is first visible in the western sky, just above the horizon, shortly after sunset, *the new crescent moon cannot be seen from Qumran*: the mountains block it out. On the other hand, the last visibility of the old lunar crescent, which occurs in the eastern sky, shortly before sunrise, *is* visible from Qumran. The conclusion reached by Talmon and Knohl therefore appears to be secure for geographical reasons as well as astronomical ones.

Thus the lunar calendar of Qumran appears to have been the same as the pre-exilic Jewish calendar. We do not know for certain if the Qumran lunar calendar was a 'theoretical' calendar or if it was actually used, but since at least four different Dead Sea Scrolls refer to it, and since these contain detailed observations of the moon, it would seem reasonable to infer that it was used. This would then mean that there was a group of Essenes who used the Qumran lunar calendar, which was probably identical to the pre-exilic Jewish calendar.

Why do the Dead Sea Scrolls describe this lunar calendar as well as the solar calendar? One possibility is that the Qumran community started to use their solar calendar, but they did not intercalate (add leap days, see Chapter 7), either because they did not know how to or because they believed their calendar was perfect as it was. So their calendar became more and more out of step with the true solar year. It must have been a shock to the Essenes to realise that their solar calendar did not keep in step with the sun. They would then have seen that this calendar could not be the true calendar of Moses, in which the first month must fall in the spring. I suggest that at least some Essenes then switched to the lunar calendar described in the four Dead Sea Scrolls. This calendar was already in use by the Samaritans, so they would have been aware of it, and they would have known that in this calendar the year did start in the spring. Incidentally, modern Samaritans believe that Passover should not fall on a Sabbath, so when it would do in their calendar they simply bring it forward. The Essenes could have done the same to keep to their rule that Passover should not fall on a Sabbath.

There is therefore evidence that two major groups, the Samaritans and at least some Essenes, used the pre-exilic Jewish lunar calendar in the first century AD. In this calendar both the Passover sacrifice and the Passover meal were on Nisan 14.

THE CALENDAR OF THE ZEALOTS

The Zealots were Jewish revolutionaries who engaged in resistance and war against the Romans. Historians disagree on when the Zealot movement started. Josephus depicts Judas the Galilean as leading a resistance movement against the Romans in AD 6, and founding a fourth sect, the others being the Pharisees, Sadducees and Essenes (*War* 18.23; *Antiquities* 14.4–10). Some scholars argue that this fourth sect was the start of the Zealot movement. Others argue that the Zealots did not emerge until after AD 44 or AD 66.[25]

One of the twelve inner disciples of Jesus was 'Simon the Zealot' (Luke 6:15; Acts 1:13). If the Zealots as a sect did not exist at this time, then the word 'Zealot' here simply means 'zealous'. However, various scholars suggest that Luke did mean that Simon was a Zealot.[26] If so, Jesus had a Zealot in his inner circle. We can deduce from Josephus that the Zealots celebrated the first day of the Feast of Unleavened Bread on Nisan 14 and not Nisan 15.[27] This is consistent with them using the pre-exilic calendar and not the official Jewish calendar. Hence not only the Samaritans and at least some Essenes used the pre-exilic calendar in the first century AD, it appears that the Zealots did so as well.

WHAT CALENDAR DID GALILEAN JEWS USE TO CELEBRATE PASSOVER?

The first mention of Galilee in the Bible is in Joshua 20:7. As we saw in Chapter 8, according to the book of Joshua, when Joshua led the Israelites into Canaan, Canaan was divided into three main regions: Galilee, Samaria and Judah. The Israelites in Canaan would have used the pre-exilic lunar calendar with its sunrise-to-sunrise day.

In 596 and 586 BC, as we have seen, Jerusalem was conquered by Babylon, and the Judean Jews were taken into exile. As I argued earlier, it was almost certainly during their exile in Babylon that the Judean Jews changed their calendar from the pre-exilic calendar to a Babylonian-style calendar. However, there was no reason for the inhabitants of Galilee and Samaria to make this change, since they were not taken into captivity in Babylon. We know from earlier in this chapter that the Samaritans did not make this change. Hence it is possible that at least some Galileans kept the pre-exilic calendar for their feasts and festivals, even if they went over to using the official Jewish calendar, with its sunset-to-sunset day, for their everyday life.

THE GALILEAN PASSOVER AT THE TIME OF CHRIST

Unfortunately we have almost no information about how Galilean Jews celebrated Passover at the time of Jesus.[28] I have found only one piece of information. This is from the Mishnah, which states: 'And sages say, "In Judah they did work on the eve of Passover up to noon, but in Galilee they did not do so at all".'[29] The New Testament scholars Bock and Herrick write concerning this Mishnah statement: 'There seem to have been different [Passover] customs in different parts of Israel.'[30] In particular, the Mishnah states that it was the Galilean custom to do no work on the entire day of the eve of Passover, which the New Testament scholar Harold Hoehner believed is consistent with the Galileans having a day that started at sunrise. Hoehner stated: 'It was the custom of the Galileans to do no work on the day of the Passover while the Judeans worked until midday. Since the Galileans' day began at sunrise they would do no work on the entire day of the Passover. On the other hand the Judeans' day began at sunset and they would work in the morning but not the afternoon.'[31]

If it is correct that some Galileans used a Passover calendar with a sunrise-to-sunrise day, which calendar did they use? Hoehner assumes that they simply shifted the start of their day from the Judean one by twelve hours, bringing it forward from sunset to sunrise, but the calendar which would then result is not a plausible option. One cannot simply move the start of the first day of the Judean lunar month to twelve hours earlier, as Hoehner suggests, because the moon is in its period of invisibility then, so the start of the month cannot be detected.[32] As is evident from our previous discussions of calendars, there are only two realistic options for a calendar with a sunrise-to-sunrise day: the solar calendar of the Essenes or the pre-exilic lunar calendar. It seems clear that the Mishnah here is discussing a Galilean Passover practice and not an Essene practice. Hence if the Galileans used a Passover calendar with a sunrise-to-sunrise day, this calendar must have been the pre-exilic calendar.

How confident can we be that some Galileans used the pre-exilic calendar at the time of Christ? For the historical reasons I have given above, I think this is likely. However, the passage from the Mishnah I have quoted, which Hoehner uses, is not really strong evidence. This passage states that in Judah they worked on the eve of Passover up to noon, but this does not mean the Judean Jews had a day which started at noon! Similarly, just because the passage states the Galileans did no work on the eve of Passover, we cannot deduce that they necessarily had a sunrise start to their day. The reality is that we do not have enough evidence to know with any certainty the Passover calendar the Galileans used. I therefore conclude that although it is probable, for historical reasons, that some Galileans used the pre-exilic calendar at the time of Jesus, we cannot be certain of this. I therefore omit them from the table.

Groups that used the pre-exilic calendar for Passover in the first century AD
The Samaritans
The Zealots
Some Essenes

SUMMARY

We have shown that the pre-exilic Jewish calendar persisted down to the first century AD and was used by the Samaritans. A number of other groups also used the pre-exilic calendar for their religious feasts (such as Passover) including some Essenes, the Zealots and possibly some Galileans. Some of these groups may have used the official Jewish calendar for their everyday life, just as Orthodox Christians today use the Gregorian calendar for their everyday life and the Julian calendar for their religious festivals such as Easter.

The Samaritans claim that their calendar has been handed down to them from Moses. The first day of each lunar month in the calendar is the day of conjunction of the moon with the sun (when the moon, sun and earth are in line and the moon is invisible). This differs from the Jewish calendar, in which the first day of the month is the first appearance of the new crescent moon. The Samaritan month always starts one, two, or even more, days before the Jewish month because conjunction always occurs before the lunar crescent appears. The Samaritans, like the ancient Egyptians, start their lunar month with conjunction, because they regard this as the day of the true new moon, the day on which the moon is 'conceived', whereas the first lunar crescent marks the day on which the moon is visibly 'born'.

In the first century AD, in the official Jewish calendar, the first day of the month was determined by observing the first visibility of the new lunar crescent. Since conjunction of the moon is not observable, the Samaritans almost certainly would have determined conjunction in the same way as the ancient Egyptians did, and as I suggest the pre-exilic Israelites did, by looking for the last visibility of the old crescent moon, and taking the next day, the day of conjunction, as the first day of the month.

When the Judean Jews changed their calendar from the pre-exilic calendar to a Babylonian-style calendar during their exile in Babylon, the Samaritans, who were not in exile in Babylon, did not do this and kept the original pre-exilic calendar. The Samaritan Passover has been continuously observed since antiquity. It is normally celebrated on Mount Gerizim in Samaria, but when this proves impossible it is held in their own houses, complete with a Passover lamb sacrificed outside the house, like the biblical description of the original Passover.

Four Dead Sea Scrolls describe a lunar calendar as well as the solar calendar of the Qumran community. It is clear from these texts that the first day of the month in this lunar calendar is the day of conjunction, therefore it is the same as the pre-exilic calendar. Hence at least some Essenes used the pre-exilic calendar. We can deduce from the writings of Josephus that a Jewish sect called the Zealots used the pre-exilic calendar, at least for celebrating Passover. In addition, it is possible that some Galilean Jews celebrated Passover using the pre-exilic calendar.

Hence the use of the pre-exilic calendar for celebrating Passover was not uncommon in the first century AD. Those groups using this calendar (including the Samaritans, some Essenes, the Zealots and possibly some Galilean Jews) would have held their Passover meal on Nisan 14, using a sunrise-to-sunrise day, and not on Nisan 15, as in the official Jewish calendar, with its sunset-to-sunset day.

In the next chapter we will explore whether the gospels describe Jesus as using the pre-exilic calendar to celebrate his last supper as a Passover meal and we will determine the date of the last supper.

11 The date of the last supper: the hidden clues in the gospels

On the first day of the Feast of Unleavened Bread, when it was customary to sacrifice the Passover lamb, Jesus' disciples asked him, 'Where do you want us to go and make preparations for you to eat the Passover?'

(Mark 14:12)

As you enter the city [Jerusalem], a man carrying a jar of water will meet you. Follow him to the house that he enters, and say to the owner of the house, 'The Teacher asks: Where is the guest room, where I may eat the Passover with my disciples?' He will show you a large upper room, all furnished. Make preparations there.

(Luke 22:10–12)

When it was almost time for the Jewish Passover, many went up from the country to Jerusalem.

(John 11:55)

In March 2010 I was invited to be an observer at a murder trial at the Old Bailey, the Central Criminal Court in London. The murder had occurred eight months previously and the witnesses disagreed on the details of what had happened. The prosecution and defence lawyers skilfully commenced their questioning of the witnesses by first trying to establish the background circumstances. Where had the murder occurred? At about what time? Who was present? Only then did the lawyers home in on the details. Who had thrown the first punch? Was the murder victim kicked when he was lying on the ground or up against a wall?

In this book we have carefully established some background circumstances to the gospels which many scholars have ignored. For example, what Jewish calendars were in use in the first century AD? We are now in a position to use this knowledge and to home in on the details of the apparent disagreements in the gospels about the date of the last supper. As we will see, a fascinating story unfolds.

THE DATE OF THE LAST SUPPER IN THE SYNOPTIC GOSPELS

If the synoptic gospel writers used a different calendar from the official one to describe the last supper as a Passover meal, we might expect them to have at least hinted at this. I believe that they did. Indeed, I believe that they gave a clear clue that their original audience would have had no difficulty in understanding. However, I suggest that modern scholars have not understood the clue the synoptics provided: this is why I call it a 'hidden clue' in the title of this chapter. Let me explain.

Mark introduces his account of the last supper with the words quoted at the start of this chapter. Matthew (26:17) and Luke (22:7–8) introduce their accounts with similar words. The purpose of the synoptic writers seems simple and straightforward: to tell their audience the day on which the disciples of Jesus prepared the Passover. However, immediately we have a problem. Biblical scholars have said for a long time that these verses apparently do not make sense. Mark tells us that Jesus' disciples made preparations for him to eat the Passover 'on the first day of the Feast of Unleavened Bread' (Mark 14:12) which, as we have seen in earlier chapters, was on Nisan 15 in the official Jewish calendar used at the time of Christ. However, in the very same sentence, Mark also tells us that the disciples made these preparations 'when it was customary to sacrifice the Passover lamb', which in the official calendar was on Nisan 14, *not* Nisan 15. So Mark appears to contradict himself. A modern-day equivalent would be for me to write: 'On Boxing Day [December 26], when it was customary to prepare the dinner for Christmas Day [December 25].'

How do biblical experts react to this apparent contradiction? There are three main schools of thought. The first is that Matthew, Mark and Luke are simply wrong. For example, Rudolf Bultmann, one of the most influential theologians and biblical scholars of the twentieth century, writes that Mark 14:12 is 'completely impossible'.[1] And so it is, according to the official Jewish calendar. However, is it really likely that three gospel writers would each make statements about the timing of events as well known as Passover and the Feast of Unleavened Bread that were 'completely impossible'? It would be like my writing that Boxing Day comes before Christmas Day, and then two other writers making the same mistake again, either independently or through carelessly copying my mistake.

Another school of thought argues that there has been a translation error. For example, the distinguished New Testament scholar Joachim Jeremias says that the contradiction in Mark 14:12 is 'most probably due to a translation error' (in going from Aramaic to Greek) and that the words 'on the first day of the Feast of Unleavened Bread' should be translated as 'on the day before the Feast of Unleavened Bread'.[2] However, Jeremias' suggestion of a translation error has not found wide support.

A third interpretation of Mark 14:12 (and the similar verses in Matthew and Luke) is to point out that, according to the Mishnah, in preparation for the Passover Feast, which was the first meal in the seven-day Feast of Unleavened Bread, held on Nisan 15, all leaven (yeast) was removed from Jewish houses on the preceding day, Nisan 14.[3] Many scholars argue that when Mark refers to 'the first day of the Feast of Unleavened Bread', he is writing loosely and means to refer to Nisan 14, when all leaven was removed from houses. For example, R. T. France writes: 'Properly speaking the feast of Unleavened Bread ran from Nisan 15 to 21, but Passover day itself, Nisan 14, was loosely included in that period, and so it is referred to as the first day of Unleavened Bread.'[4] France, and other scholars, also cite Josephus (*War* 5.99) as stating that Nisan 14 was the first day of unleavened bread. However, as we have seen in the previous chapter, Josephus here appears to be referring to a group of Jews called the Zealots who used a different calendar, probably the pre-exilic calendar, in which Nisan 14 *was* the first day of unleavened bread. Elsewhere, Josephus is clear that Nisan 15 was the first day of unleavened bread in the official calendar (see, for example, *Antiquities* 3.249).

Although it is indeed correct that the Mishnah states that all leaven was removed from Jewish houses on Nisan 14, this third interpretation is not the natural interpretation of Mark 14:12. If we had asked any Judean rabbi in the first century AD which day in the official calendar was 'the first day of the Feast of Unleavened Bread', all the evidence suggests he would have replied, without hesitation, 'Nisan 15'. Similarly, if we had asked him on which day the Passover lambs were sacrificed, he would again have replied, without hesitation, 'Nisan 14'. This is why Bultmann described Mark 14:12 as 'completely impossible'. Mark 14:12, and the similar statements in Matthew and Luke, simply do not make sense if the official Jewish calendar was being used.

The three main interpretations of Mark 14:12 if the official Jewish calendar was used

Interpretation	Source
Completely impossible	Bultmann (for example)
Translation error	Jeremias
Loose writing	France (for example)

THE NATURAL INTERPRETATION OF MARK 14:12

My suggestion is that we should take Mark 14:12 at face value. Mark is telling us that the day for sacrificing the lamb was the same day as the first day of the Feast of Unleavened Bread. This makes perfectly good sense if Mark is thinking of a calendar with a sunrise-to-sunrise day. In the official calendar, in which the day starts at sunset, the lambs are sacrificed in the afternoon of Nisan 14 and the meal is eaten after sunset, the date now being Nisan 15. But if a sunrise-to-sunrise calendar is used, the lamb is sacrificed and the meal is eaten both on the same calendar date.

Dates of Passover events

Event	Official calendar (sunset-to-sunset day)	Calendar with a sunrise-to-sunrise day
Passover lambs sacrificed	Nisan 14	Nisan 14
First day of the Feast of Unleavened Bread	Nisan 15	Nisan 14

If Jesus and his disciples sacrificed a Passover lamb on Nisan 14, and if this was also the first day of the Feast of Unleavened Bread, then they must have been using a calendar with a sunrise-to-sunrise day. Hence when Mark introduced his account of the last supper with the words I quoted at the start of this chapter, he was deliberately and pointedly telling his audience that in his description of the last supper as a Passover meal he was using a calendar with a sunrise-to-sunrise day. I suggest this would have been obvious to his original audience, who were familiar with the different calendars of their time. In particular, they would have known about the widely used pre-exilic calendar. However, over the centuries a knowledge of the different Jewish calendars in use at the time of Jesus has been forgotten. In particular the pre-exilic calendar is largely unknown today, and so scholars have assumed that Jesus used the official Jewish calendar for his last Passover. They have then had difficulty in interpreting Mark 14:12 and the similar verses in Matthew and Luke.

If Jesus held his last supper as a Passover meal using a calendar with a sunrise-to-sunrise day, which calendar did he use? The number of different calendars that were actually used in the ancient world is limited and those having a sunrise-to-sunrise day are given below. I include for completeness a calendar (number 3 below) which was never used in the ancient world, but which nevertheless some scholars have suggested that Jesus used.

1 The solar calendar of Qumran

As shown in Chapter 7, Passover in the Qumran solar calendar occurred *after* Passover in the official calendar and we can therefore rule out this theory.

2 The solar calendar of ancient Egypt

There is no evidence that Passover was a feast in this calendar, and even if it was it is highly unlikely that it would have fallen in the same week as Passover in the official Jewish calendar, because no leap days or months were added to the Egyptian solar calendar and so it became out-of-step with the true solar year (see Chapter 8). We can therefore rule out Jesus using this calendar to celebrate his last Passover.

3 A new-crescent-moon lunar calendar with a sunrise-to-sunrise day

Various scholars suggest that Jesus used a calendar with a sunrise-to-sunrise day, the first day of the month being determined by observing the first visibility of the new crescent moon.[5] However, since the new crescent moon is only visible in the evening sky, for a short period of time after sunset, *all* known calendars in the ancient world that were based on observing the new crescent moon had an evening-to-evening day (see Chapter 4). We can therefore rule out Jesus using a new-crescent-moon lunar calendar with a sunrise-to-sunrise day.

4 The pre-exilic calendar of ancient Israel

There is only one remaining possibility for a calendar with a sunrise-to-sunrise day: the pre-exilic calendar described in Chapter 9. In the pre-exilic calendar, with its sunrise-to-sunrise day, the Passover lambs were slain on the same day as the Passover meal was eaten, this being the first day of the Feast of Unleavened Bread, Nisan 14.

Let me summarise my argument. The natural interpretation of the synoptic gospels is that, for his last supper Passover meal, Jesus chose to use a calendar in which it was customary to sacrifice the Passover lamb on the first day of the Feast of Unleavened Bread. If this interpretation is correct, Jesus used a calendar with a sunrise-to-sunrise day, in which the Passover meal was prepared on Nisan 14 and the meal was eaten that same night, still Nisan 14. I have considered four possible calendars with a sunrise-to-sunrise day that Jesus might have used and ruled out three of them, leaving the pre-exilic calendar as the only possible solution. Hence Jesus must have used the pre-exilic calendar to celebrate his last supper as a Passover meal. As we saw in the previous chapter, the pre-exilic calendar was widely used to celebrate Passover in the first century AD. It was used by the Samaritans, the Zealots and at least some Essenes. That it was used by the Essenes fits in with our next clue.

THE CLUE OF THE MAN CARRYING A JAR OF WATER

Some scholars believe the arrangements Jesus made for his last supper, quoted from Luke at the start of this chapter, suggest a pre-arranged sign. For example, Howard Marshall states: 'As the disciples enter the city, they will be met by a man carrying a jar of water. This would be an unusual sight, since men normally carried leather bottles and women carried jars or pitchers [containing smaller quantities]. The instruction sounds like a reference to a pre-arranged sign.'[6] A modern-day equivalent might be to say that a man wearing a skirt will meet you.

Why would a man be apparently acting like a woman and carrying a water jar in Jerusalem? Let us update the situation. Why would a man today be wearing a skirt? A good reason would be if he was Scottish. Men from Scotland sometimes wear a kind of skirt called a kilt because this is their traditional clothing. So was there a group of Jewish men who traditionally *did* carry water jars? The answer is 'yes'. The Essenes were largely celibate, hence their men necessarily carried both water jars and leather bottles. Thus, as Bargil Pixner points out, the man carrying a jar of water must have been an Essene.[7] The Essenes did not only have a community in Qumran. Josephus tells us that the Essenes 'occupy no one city, but settle in large numbers in every town' (*War* 2.124). Evidence that the Essenes had a community in Jerusalem comes from several sources, including the Dead Sea Scrolls themselves. For example, the War Scroll refers to the forces of light returning 'from battle against the enemy when they journey to their community in Jerusalem' (1QM 3.10–11; 1QM is the technical name of the 9½ feet long section of the War Scroll found in Cave 1 at Qumran). Josephus mentions an Essene teacher living in Jerusalem (*Antiquities* 13.311).

It may seem strange that the Pharisees and Sadducees would have allowed the Essenes, with their different solar and lunar calendars, to have a community in the holy city of Jerusalem, but they probably had no choice. Josephus tells us that the Essenes were favoured by Herod the Great since an Essene prophet called Menachem predicted that Herod would rule over the Jews, and 'from that time he

[Herod] continued to hold all Essenes in honour' (*Antiquities* 15.373). Hence if the Essenes wished to have a community in Jerusalem we can expect royal privilege to have made this happen. One of the gates into the walled city of Jerusalem was called 'the Gate of the Essenes' (Josephus, *War* 5.145), presumably because it was through this gate that the Essenes entered their community in Jerusalem. From the information given by Josephus (*War* 5.145) we can deduce that this was in the south-west of Jerusalem, overlooking the Hinnom valley, although its precise location is still disputed (fig. 11.1). Interestingly, the traditional site of the last supper is located on Mount Zion, which is also in the south-west of Jerusalem. Although the present building dates from the twelfth century AD, it is possible that it stands over or near the original site.

If Jesus wished to hold his last supper in Jerusalem as a Passover meal using the pre-exilic calendar, then his options were limited. He could hardly have asked to use the upper room of an orthodox Jew living in Jerusalem, because celebrating Passover on a day other than the official one would have been a heresy. Hence I suggest he made arrangements with an Essene to use his upper room, celebrating Passover using the pre-exilic lunar calendar that we know from the Dead Sea Scrolls some Essenes also used. So a consistent story emerges. When Jesus asked his disciples to enter Jerusalem and meet a man carrying a jar of water, they knew he meant they were to meet an Essene and hence they would have entered Jerusalem through the Essene Gate. Pixner argues that the disciples, being non-Essenes, could not enter the Essene compound without an invitation, which Jesus had pre-arranged, and that the Essenes, who were known for their hospitality (Josephus, *War* 2.124), could be expected to have a guest room. Since an Essene man carrying a water jar would not have been an unusual sight in and around the Essene compound in Jerusalem, I do not think we can deduce from the account in Luke whether the meeting was pre-planned or not. Jesus was not an Essene, but we can expect he had Essene followers just as he had Samaritan, Galilean and Judean followers. Choosing an Essene upper room, together with the pre-exilic calendar used by at least some Essenes, enabled Jesus to celebrate his last supper as a Passover meal.

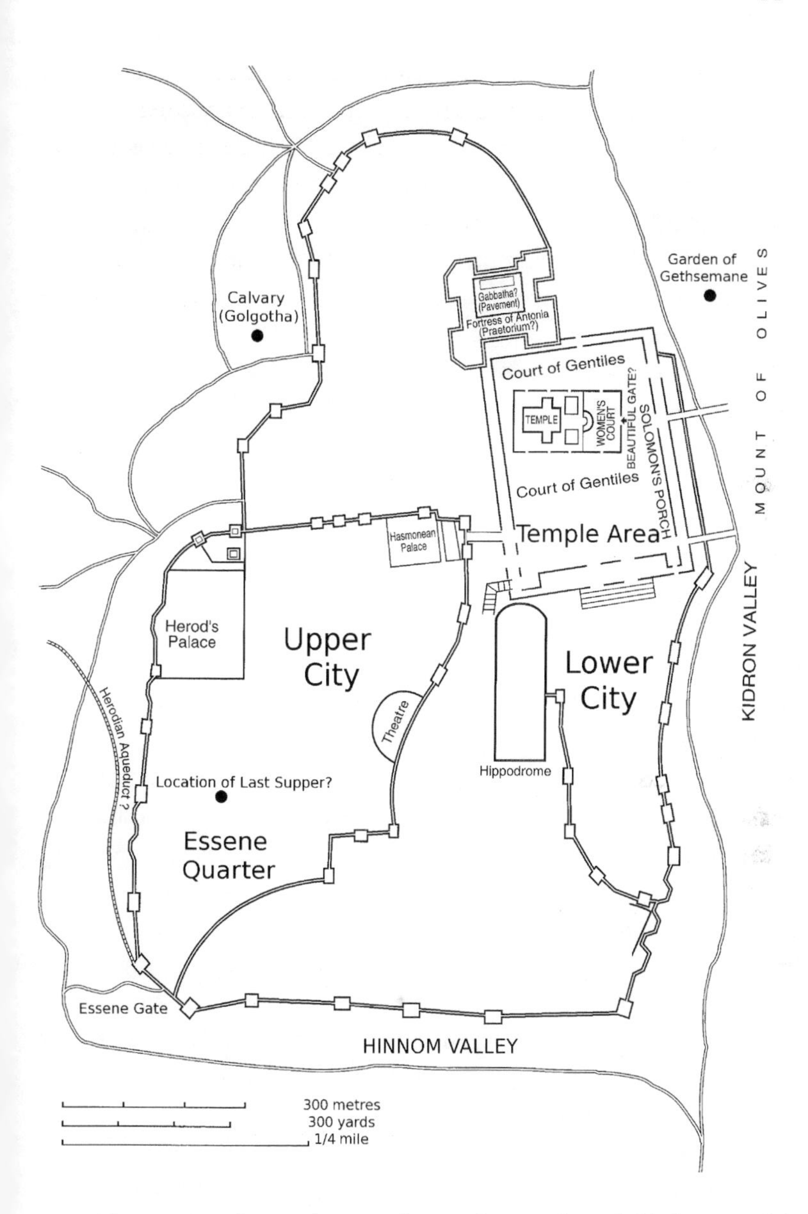

Fig. 11.1 Jerusalem at the time of Jesus, showing the probable location of the Essene Gate, the Essene quarter, the last supper and the Garden of Gethsemane.

If Jesus held his last supper in an Essene house then this throws light on his act of washing the disciples' feet at the last supper, particularly his puzzling statement: 'A person who has had a bath needs only to wash his feet' (John 13:10). The Essenes interpreted the Old Testament rules of bathing and ritual purity very strictly. Jesus' disciples would almost certainly have taken a bath before eating a Passover meal, but in walking to the Essene house their feet would have become dirty. The allusion to Essene practice would have been a natural one for Jesus to make at an Essene house, and out of respect for his Essene hosts Jesus made sure everyone was ritually clean by washing the feet of his disciples.

I have shown how Jesus chose to celebrate his last supper as a Passover meal by using the pre-exilic calendar and holding this meal at the house of an Essene in Jerusalem. However, was there another reason why Jesus chose to use the pre-exilic calendar? In particular, was it consistent or inconsistent with his ministry and message?

JESUS THE NEW MOSES

It is clear from the gospels that Jesus understood his role as that of a new Moses. For example, in the Sermon on the Mount Jesus went up on a mountain to teach the people about the law, just as the book of Exodus records that Moses had done on Mount Sinai. In this Sermon, Jesus said: 'Do not think that I have come to abolish the Law [given by Moses] or the prophets: I have not come to abolish them but to fulfil them' (Matthew 5:17). Jesus then gave a new interpretation of the law by saying, 'You have heard it said . . . but I say to you' regarding murder, adultery, etc. (Matthew 5:21–48).

Jesus compared himself directly with Moses, for example: 'Just as Moses lifted up the snake in the desert, so must the Son of Man be lifted up' (John 3:14). 'If you believed Moses, you would believe me, for he wrote about me' (John 5:46). John saw Jesus as the new Moses. He said: 'For the law was given through Moses; grace and truth came through Jesus Christ' (John 1:17). One of the first disciples of Jesus, Philip, said: 'We have found the one [Jesus] Moses wrote about in the law' (John 1:45). It is clear from his words and actions that Jesus saw himself as fulfilling the Old Testament promise of a new Moses: 'The Lord your God will raise up for you a prophet like me [Moses] from among you' (Deuteronomy 18:15).[8] By adopting the pre-exilic calendar for his last Passover Jesus was pointedly and deliberately identifying himself with a calendar which was believed to have been initiated by Moses.

References to Jesus as the new Moses permeate the New Testament, reflecting the way Jesus thought of himself. For example: 'He [Jesus] was faithful to the one who appointed him, just as Moses was faithful in all God's house. Jesus has been found worthy of greater honour than Moses, just as the builder of a house has greater honour than the house itself' (Hebrews 3:2–3).

The gospels link various events in the life of Jesus with Moses and the Exodus. For example, Luke records that at the Transfiguration, Moses and Elijah appeared and talked with Jesus. Luke says: 'They spoke about his departure [Greek *exodos*] which he was about to bring to fulfilment in Jerusalem' (Luke 9:31). Luke seems to use the Greek word *exodos* deliberately in his account of the conversation *Moses* had with Jesus to link in his readers' minds the first Exodus, in which Moses led the Israelites out of slavery in Egypt, with the new Exodus, in which Jesus leads God's people out of the slavery of sin and death.

Jesus chose to hold the last supper as a Passover meal, thus linking this supper directly with the first Passover of Moses. However, despite their similarities, this last Passover meal of Jesus was also fundamentally different from a normal Passover meal: Jesus, the new Moses, used it to mark the start of a new era, just as the first Passover of Moses marked the start of a new era. At the last supper Jesus said: 'This cup is the *new* covenant in my blood, which is poured out for you [my italics]' (Luke 22:20), echoing the words of Moses over one thousand years earlier: 'This is the blood of the covenant that the Lord has made with you' (Exodus 24:8). At his last Passover Jesus said: 'Do this in remembrance of me' (Luke 22:19); at the first Passover God said to Moses: 'This is a day you are to commemorate' (Exodus 12:14).

It seems that Jesus, even when he was radically departing from the words said at a traditional Passover, was deliberately choosing his words at the last supper to remind his disciples of the words recorded in the book of Exodus at the first Passover of Moses. How fitting then, for Jesus, the new Moses, to have chosen to celebrate his last meal with his disciples on the *exact* anniversary of the original Passover meal held by Moses and the Israelites in Egypt, by using the *same* lunar calendar that Moses used with its sunrise-to-sunrise day. Indeed, Jesus could *only* have held his last supper on the *exact* anniversary of the first Passover of Moses by using the pre-exilic calendar. As we saw in Chapter 9, Ezekiel 33–48 promise that God will revive his people through a new temple and a new king, taken to be the Messiah, teaching the people to follow his Laws. How appropriate for Jesus, a few days after cleansing the temple (Mark 11:15), to have celebrated the Passover Feast on the date specified by Ezekiel, Nisan 14 (Ezekiel 45:21) in the pre-exilic calendar, and not on Nisan 15 in the later official calendar, as used by the priests who had allowed the temple to become defiled (Mark 11:17). The words of Jesus at the last supper, including his choice to celebrate it as a Passover meal using the pre-exilic calendar, appear to have been a deliberate symbolic action by Jesus.

THE PASSOVER CALENDAR IN JOHN'S GOSPEL

As we have seen, the synoptic gospels indicate right at the start of their account of the last supper that they are using a calendar with a sunrise-to-sunrise day. Does John similarly indicate the calendar he is using? I suggest that he does. When John introduces his account of the last week of Jesus he states: 'When it was almost time for *the Jewish Passover*, many went up from the country to Jerusalem [my italics]' (John 11:55). I suggest that John deliberately and pointedly introduces his account of the last week of Jesus by referring not to 'the Passover' but to 'the Jewish Passover', since he wishes to specify that he is referring to *the official Jewish Passover* as distinct from the Essene Passover, the Samaritan Passover, etc. On the other hand, Matthew,

Mark and Luke *never* use the term 'the Jewish Passover', but simply 'the Passover'. Hence both the synoptics and John give clear clues that they are using different calendars, clues which would have been understood by many of their original audience.

THE DATE OF THE LAST SUPPER

Just as we can use astronomical calculations to reconstruct the official Jewish calendar, in which the first day of the month is based on the first visibility of the lunar crescent, so we can use similar calculations to reconstruct the pre-exilic calendar in the first century AD, based on the first invisibility of the old lunar crescent, corresponding to conjunction. At my request Graeme Waddington has performed these calculations for AD 33, which I have shown is the most probable year of the crucifixion, and, out of interest, for AD 30, the only other possible year. The results of his calculations for Nisan 14 in AD 30 and 33 are shown in the table.

Date of Nisan 14 in Jerusalem

Year	Official Jewish calendar	The pre-exilic calendar
AD 30	Sunset, Thursday, April 6 to sunset, Friday, April 7	Sunrise, Monday, April 3 to sunrise, Tuesday, April 4
AD 33	Sunset, Thursday, April 2 to sunset, Friday, April 3	Sunrise, Wednesday, April 1 to sunrise, Thursday, April 2

If the crucifixion was in AD 30, then the above calculations show that the last supper, according to the pre-exilic calendar, would have had to be on Monday evening, four days before the crucifixion the following Friday (this is one of only 1 per cent of cases where the time interval between the lunar invisibility and visibility calendars is as long as four days[9]). On the other hand, if the crucifixion was in AD 33, then the last supper, according to the pre-exilic calendar, was on the Wednesday evening before the Friday crucifixion. Can we rule out one of these possibilities?

John's gospel explicitly makes the following time statement: 'Six days before the Passover, Jesus arrived at Bethany, where Lazarus lived' (John 12:1). If John intended 'the Passover' to mean the Passover meal, then in the official Jewish calendar, used by John, this was held on Nisan 15, which in both AD 30 and 33 was from sunset Friday to sunset Saturday. Counting back six days leads to the Jewish day Nisan 9, which runs from sunset Saturday to sunset Sunday. 'The next day' (John 12:12) after Jesus arrived in Bethany was the 'Triumphal Entry' of Jesus into Jerusalem. This was therefore on Monday. On 'the next day' (Mark 11:12), Jesus cursed the fig-tree. This was then on Tuesday. Following this, 'In the morning' (Mark 11:20) the fig-tree was seen withered. This would have been on Wednesday. Hence the last supper, which occurred after the withering of the fig-tree, cannot have been on Monday evening if the gospel chronology of the last week of Jesus is even approximately consistent.[10] In addition, although I argued in the first chapter of this book that having the last supper on Thursday evening with the crucifixion on Friday morning did not give enough time for all the intervening events recorded in the gospels, having the last supper on Monday evening gives too *much* time (as we will see from the analysis in the next chapter). Hence we can rule out Monday as the day of the last supper. This also rules out once again AD 30 as the year of the crucifixion. We therefore have one, and only one, remaining possibility. The last supper was on Wednesday, April 1, AD 33, with the crucifixion on Friday, April 3, AD 33.

Many readers will understandably be sceptical that the last supper was on a Wednesday. It is a well-established Catholic and Protestant assumption that the last supper was on Thursday (although in his Easter Thursday Homily of 2007 Pope Benedict seemed to be moving away from this, see chapter 7). Every year at Easter time, millions of people throughout the world attend church services on the Thursday of Holy Week to commemorate the last supper Jesus held with his disciples. In the UK, at least, this day has been given a special name: Maundy Thursday. It seems almost inconceivable that the major Christian churches in the world, and the leading biblical scholars in the world, could be mistaken over the day of the last supper.

Yet the New Testament nowhere says that the last supper was on the day before the crucifixion (I will analyse what the New

Testament does say in the next chapter). Probably the earliest account of the last supper we have is given by the apostle Paul in his first letter to the Corinthians, in about AD 55. He starts his account by reminding his audience of the time when the last supper was held. Paul does *not* say it was on the night before the crucifixion, he says it was 'on the night he [Jesus] was betrayed' (1 Corinthians 11:23).

WAS THERE A PASSOVER LAMB AT THE LAST SUPPER?

Would it have been possible for someone following the pre-exilic calendar in AD 33 to sacrifice a lamb in Jerusalem on the Wednesday? Although no Passover lamb is mentioned in the gospel accounts of the last supper, the natural interpretation of 'so they [the disciples] prepared the Passover' (Mark 14:16) is that a Passover lamb was prepared. According to the book of Exodus, the original Passover of Moses was a household celebration: the Israelites in Egypt slaughtered their Passover lambs at home. I showed in Chapter 10 that the Samaritans sometimes sacrificed their Passover lambs at home. Professor Alan Millard tells me that Jews from Galilee and other regions, who were unable to travel to Jerusalem to celebrate Passover, would almost certainly have celebrated Passover where they lived, sacrificing a lamb outside their house. The disciples of Jesus might therefore have 'prepared the Passover', including killing and roasting the Passover lamb, at the house where they later held their Passover meal, probably in the Essene quarter of Jerusalem.

On the other hand, Deuteronomy instructs that the Passover lamb must be sacrificed 'In the place he [God] will choose as a dwelling for his Name' (Deuteronomy 16:6), which Judean Jews interpreted as the temple of Jerusalem. An important question is whether the priests of the Jerusalem temple would have allowed Passover lambs to be sacrificed in the temple on a day other than the official one. An analysis of Jewish rabbinical writings suggests this may have been the case; for example, there is evidence that the temple priests allowed Passover lambs to be sacrificed 'under another name' in the temple on Nisan 13.[11] I suggest that the most likely reason for this is a calendrical one.

If there was a Passover lamb at the last supper on Wednesday it would have been killed 'between the two evenings' according to the original instructions in Exodus 12. In the official Jewish calendar this was Nisan 13, which commenced at sunset on Wednesday, April 1, AD 33. So it seems that the disciples might have been able to sacrifice the lamb at the temple on this day. I therefore suggest that there was a Passover lamb at Jesus' last supper, sacrificed either at the Jerusalem temple or at the house with the upper room where Jesus held this supper.

In the next chapter we shall explore the timing of events between the last supper and the crucifixion, free of the constraint that scholars normally impose, either explicitly or implicitly, that the last supper was on a Thursday evening. A key question, of course, is whether the sequence of events between the last supper and the crucifixion recorded in the gospels better fits with the last supper being on a Wednesday or a Thursday evening. We will find that the analysis throws new light upon events such as the trials of Jesus. First we summarise our findings in this chapter.

SUMMARY

Matthew, Mark and Luke introduce their accounts of the last supper by stating that it was held on the first day of the Feast of Unleavened Bread, when the Passover lamb was sacrificed. This statement has puzzled biblical scholars for centuries because it makes no sense using the official Jewish calendar, with its sunset-to-sunset day, in which the Passover lamb is sacrificed on Nisan 14 and the first day of the Feast of Unleavened Bread is Nisan 15. However, the natural interpretation of the synoptic gospels here is that they are reporting Jesus celebrating Passover using a different calendar, one with a sunrise-to-sunrise day. In this calendar, the Passover lamb is sacrificed on Nisan 14 and the Passover meal, held on the first day of the Feast of Unleavened Bread, is eaten that same evening and night, still Nisan 14 in a calendar with a sunrise-to-sunrise day.

I therefore suggest that the words of Mark 14:12 (quoted at the start of this chapter), and the similar words in Matthew 26:17 and Luke

22:7–8, were intended to be calendrical statements, setting the scene and telling readers that out of the variety of calendars in use in Israel in the first century AD, Jesus chose one with a sunrise-to-sunrise day to hold his last supper as a Passover meal. An analysis of calendars having a sunrise-to-sunrise day shows that the pre-exilic calendar is the only one possible. I suggest that many of the original gospel audience would have understood this, since they would have been familiar with the official Jewish calendar and with the pre-exilic calendar, still widely used for celebrating Passover by the Samaritans, some Essenes, the Zealots, etc.

Did Jesus have any motivation to use the pre-exilic calendar for his last Passover? The answer is a clear yes. Jesus understood his role as the new Moses. By choosing to use the pre-exilic calendar for his last Passover, Jesus held this meal on the *exact* anniversary of the first Passover of Moses. Jesus thus deliberately and pointedly linked his last supper with this first Passover. The effect would not have been lost on his disciples, particularly when Jesus spoke of the new covenant he was establishing, superseding the original covenant established by Moses.

The synoptic gospels' account of the last supper as a Passover meal is consistent with a calendar having a sunrise-to-sunrise day being used, which is consistent with that calendar being the pre-exilic calendar. John's gospel, on the other hand, describes the Passover around the time of the crucifixion as being 'the Jewish Passover'. Hence the Jewish Passover referred to by John is the official Jewish Passover in the official Jewish calendar with its sunset-to-sunset day. Thus the synoptic gospels and John's gospel are using different calendars when they refer to Passover. The synoptics are using the pre-exilic calendar, with its sunrise-to-sunrise day, in which the last supper was a true Passover meal. On the other hand, John is using the official Jewish calendar, with its sunset-to-sunset day, in which the last supper, the trials of Jesus and the crucifixion were all before the official Passover meal. All four gospels are consistent in their treatment of the last supper when it is recognised that they are using different calendars.

We can use astronomy to reconstruct both the official and the pre-exilic Jewish calendars in the first century AD. We have done this for AD 30 and AD 33, the only plausible years for the crucifixion. Once again we find that we can rule out AD 30 for the year of the crucifixion since this results in the last supper being on a Monday evening, which is too early, for reasons given in this chapter and the next. This means we have a single solution to the date of the last supper. The last supper was on Wednesday, April 1, AD 33, with the crucifixion being on Friday, April 3, AD 33.

In the next chapter we will examine the events between the last supper and the crucifixion and see if the gospel accounts are consistent or inconsistent with the last supper being on a Wednesday. As we will see, placing the last supper on a Wednesday throws new light on our understanding of the gospel records of the last week of Jesus, and it enables us to solve several previously puzzling problems.

12 From the last supper to the crucifixion: a new analysis of the gospel accounts

They bound him [Jesus] and brought him first to Annas.

(John 18:12–13)

At daybreak the council of the elders of the people, both the chief priests and teachers of the law, met together, and Jesus was led before them.

(Luke 22:66)

Very early in the morning, the chief priest, with the elders, the teachers of the law and the whole Sanhedrin, reached a decision. They bound Jesus, led him away and turned him over to Pilate.

(Mark 15:1)

In this chapter we will consider the sequence of events recorded in the gospels, from the last supper to the crucifixion, paying particular attention to their timing.

THE CONDENSED NATURE OF THE GOSPELS

Let us start by reminding ourselves that all biographies are compressed versions of history. In a biography a person's rich and varied life is condensed into a few hundred pages, with only the highlights usually recorded. The gospels are of necessity similarly selective, and as John writes at the very end of his gospel: 'Jesus did many other things as well. If every one of them were written down, I suppose that even the whole world would not have room for the books that would be written' (John 21:25).

Our study of the gospels in this book has shown that they each compress events differently: they are four separate narratives telling the story of the same person. For example, it is clear from John that the ministry of Jesus lasted for longer than one year since John mentions three Passovers in his ministry (including the one at the crucifixion). If we did not have John's gospel we could well conclude from Matthew, Mark and Luke that the ministry of Jesus lasted for only one year. Nearly all scholars accept that the longer ministry described by John is correct. The synoptic gospels are not incorrect: they simply give us fewer time markers. When we study the events the gospels record between the last supper and the crucifixion, we should therefore not be surprised to find that each gospel condenses the events in different ways.

A problem all the gospel writers must have had when writing about the events between the last supper and the crucifixion was the lack of witnesses they could consult. The gospels record that at the arrest of Jesus after the last supper all the disciples fled. Only Peter, and possibly another disciple, was present in the courtyard of the high priest when Jesus was interrogated inside by Annas (John 18:15–16). It seems likely that no disciples were present at the subsequent trials of Jesus before the Sanhedrin, before Pilate and before Herod. The gospel writers would have had to piece together what information they could from the most reliable sources, and leave out anything they were unsure about. For example, Luke may well have consulted Joseph of Arimathea about the trials: he was a member of the Sanhedrin who had not consented to their decision to put Jesus to death (Luke 23:50–52). I believe this largely explains why, for example, only John mentions the interrogation of Jesus before Annas and only Luke mentions his trial before Herod. We can therefore understand why different gospels record some events and not others, and hence why they compress events in different ways.

BACKGROUND TO THE TRIALS OF JESUS

It is helpful to understand the possible Jewish legal background to the trials of Jesus. The Jewish rules regarding trials for capital cases are stated in the Mishnah (a compendium containing regulations attributed to about 150 rabbis who lived from about 50 BC to about AD 200[1]): 'In capital cases they hold the trial during the daytime and the verdict must also be reached during the daytime ... In capital cases a verdict of acquittal may be reached on the same day, but a verdict of conviction not until the following day. Therefore the trials may not be held on the eve of a Sabbath or on the eve of a Feast day' (Mishnah *Sanhedrin* 4.1). Trials could also not be held on the Sabbath, nor on a Feast day itself, because work such as the writing of minutes was forbidden on these days.

If these legal rules, written down in about 200 AD but based on earlier practice, applied at the time of the trials of Jesus, then they present major problems to the conventional understanding of these trials. For example, consider the rule: 'Trials may not be held on the eve of a Sabbath or on the eve of a Feast day.' The Passover meal was eaten on the first day of the feast of Unleavened Bread, Nisan 15 in the official Jewish calendar. The eve of this Feast day was Nisan 14. The conventional belief is that the last supper was on a Thursday, with the trials early on Friday, before the crucifixion on Friday morning. As we saw in Chapter 3, about 50 per cent of scholars support the 'synoptic chronology' in which the last supper was a Passover meal in the official calendar, held at the start of Nisan 15. These scholars would therefore place the trials later that Jewish day, still Nisan 15, a feast day. The other 50 per cent of scholars support the 'Johannine chronology' in which the crucifixion was on Nisan 14, so that the trials were earlier that Jewish day, still Nisan 14, the eve of a feast day. Either way, this is clearly contrary to the Jewish law described in the Mishnah.

The Mishnah also states that in capital cases the Sanhedrin must meet on two successive days. The main trial is on the first day, and if the person is convicted the Sanhedrin must sleep on their decision and confirm it the next day. Clearly if the last supper was on Thursday night with the crucifixion the following morning then this rule could not have been followed.

Finally, the Mishnah states that the trials must be held in the daytime. However, many scholars believe that the main Sanhedrin trial was held at night, before sunrise on Friday morning, for two reasons. First, fitting in all the events the gospels record in the extremely limited time available virtually necessitates a night-time trial. Second, these scholars interpret the description of the main Sanhedrin trial in the gospels of Matthew and Mark as implying a night-time trial.

It is clear that having the last supper on a Thursday evening with the crucifixion the following morning blatantly flouts the Jewish legal proceedings documented in the Mishnah. Yet although the gospels claim that there were many false witnesses at the trials, not one of the gospels claims that the trials were illegal. They implicitly accept the legality of the trials. How do scholars respond? The almost universal response of Christian scholars is to say that these rules in the Mishnah were written down in about 200 AD and we cannot assume they applied at the time of Jesus. For example, John Robinson writes: 'Obviously the trial or interrogation of Jesus as described in the Gospels was not conducted according to the rabbinic rules ... however ... we are not certain about the extent to which 1st century Pharisees already practised 2nd century rabbinic rules in judicial proceedings.'[2]

Many Jewish scholars offer a different viewpoint. For example Geza Vermes writes: 'The oldest rabbinical traditional law code, the Mishnah, has a special tractate [treatise] called Sanhedrin ... it is clear that the tractate Sanhedrin preserves a number of legal traditions which are considerably older than AD 200 ... Some New Testament scholars are in principle unwilling to accept rabbinic literature as providing valid evidence for the age of Jesus. But if they object to the use of the Mishnah ... they are not at liberty to reject first century AD sources, such as Philo and the Dead Sea Scrolls ... which also testify to the illegality of court business on Sabbaths/feast days ... [In addition] it is hard to imagine in a Jewish setting of the first century AD that a capital case would be tried at night.'[3]

We cannot be certain whether all, some or none of the legal rules for capital cases recorded in the Mishnah applied at the time of the trials of Jesus. However, since they may have done, we should keep them in mind as we now read the gospel accounts of these trials, particularly in the light of the suggestion in the previous chapter that the last supper was on a Wednesday evening. If this new chronology is correct then this opens up the possibility that the main trial by the

Sanhedrin was not on a feast day nor on the eve of a feast day. There could also have been two Sanhedrin trials on successive days, and, in addition, these trials could both have been in the daytime. In other words, our new chronology could be fully consistent with the legal rules in the Mishnah.

THE LAST SUPPER PASSOVER MEAL

First, we will look at the start and finish times of the official Jewish Passover in the first century AD. Josephus tells us that the Passover lambs were sacrificed between the ninth and the eleventh hour, that is, approximately between 3 p.m. and 5 p.m., on Nisan 14 (*War* 6.423). The lambs were then roasted and the Passover meal was eaten after sunset that evening (at the start of Nisan 15 in the official calendar). The Passover meal ended at midnight (Mishnah *Pesahim* 10:9) and just after midnight the priests reopened the temple gates.[4]

Did the start and finish times of the last supper Passover differ from those of the official Passover? If Jesus used the pre-exilic calendar and followed the Passover timings in Exodus 12, then the Passover lambs would have been sacrificed at twilight 'between the two evenings' (Exodus 12:6) on Nisan 14 in the pre-exilic calendar. As I said in Chapter 8, 'between the two evenings' probably means between sunset and when the first stars appeared.[5] Sunset on April 1, AD 33 was at 6.14 p.m.,[6] so the lambs would have been sacrificed between 6.14 and about 7.45 p.m., either outside the house with the upper room in Jerusalem or in the Jerusalem temple. (As noted in Chapter 11, sunset on April 1, AD 33 marked the start of Nisan 13 in the official calendar, when it seems that lambs for Passover were allowed to be slain in the Jerusalem temple.) When were the Passover lambs eaten according to Exodus 12? Cornelis Houtman writes: 'In view of the time when the animal was to be slaughtered, the time needed to prepare it for roasting (an hour to an hour and a half) and the actual roasting, one may assume that it was *about midnight when the meal began* [my italics].'[7] In addition, as we saw in Chapter 10, the Samaritans, who use the pre-exilic calendar, *start* to eat their Passover meal close to midnight. Exodus 12:10 states: 'Do not leave any of it [the Passover lamb] until the morning.' As Houtman notes, this is 'an instruction about the time length of the meal',[8] which it appears could continue until the morning. Jubilees, written in about 200 BC, states: 'They shall eat it [the Passover lamb] at the time of the evening until the third part of the night' (Jubilees 49:12). Jubilees appears to be dividing the night into three parts, suggesting that the meal must be finished by 2 a.m. Since Jubilees was widely used by the Qumran community it appears that the Essenes believed the Passover meal should finish by 2 a.m.

What does the Bible say about the timing of the last supper? Joachim Jeremias points out that the last supper was a lengthy meal which lasted 'into the night'.[9] Paul writes: 'The Lord Jesus, on the *night* he was betrayed [my italics], took bread' (1 Corinthians 11:23). John says: 'As soon as Judas had taken the bread, he went out. And it was *night* [my italics]' (John 13:30). The gospels give no indication that the last supper was a rushed event; indeed the opposite is the case. First, Jesus washed his disciples' feet (John 13:2–17), then he took bread and wine with them (Luke 22:17–19), Judas left to betray Jesus (John 13:18–30) and Jesus predicted Peter would deny him (Luke 22:31–38). Interspersed with these actions John records that Jesus gave various long discourses (John 14:1–16:33). After these discourses Jesus prayed for himself (John 17:1–5), for his disciples (John 17:6–19) and for all believers (John 17:20–26). It was only after all these discourses and prayers that Jesus and his disciples left the upper room. The earliest time the last supper ended would have been at midnight, if Jesus had been following the official Passover calendar. However, if Jesus was following the pre-exilic calendar, and if he was celebrating his last supper as a Passover meal in an upper room in the Essene section of Jerusalem (see Chapter 11), then the last supper could have lasted until 2 a.m., for the reasons given above. Incidentally, I have always been puzzled as to why, when Judas betrayed Jesus, he did not bring the arresting party back to the upper room to arrest Jesus there. This would have been the obvious thing to do. However, if the upper room was in the Essene quarter of Jerusalem, the temple guards would not have dared to enter for fear of antagonising the Essenes.

FROM THE LAST SUPPER TO GETHSEMANE

The last supper took place in an upper room, probably in the Essene quarter in the south-west corner of Jerusalem. If so, Jesus and his disciples would have left Jerusalem by the Essene Gate, and walked along the Hinnom valley to the south of Jerusalem and then up the Kidron valley to an olive grove (John 18:1) called Gethsemane (Matthew 26:36) on the slopes of the Mount of Olives (Luke 22:39) which is to the east of Jerusalem (see fig. 11.1). *Kidron* is derived from a Hebrew word meaning 'dark' and the bottom of the Kidron valley is over 200 feet below the platform of the outer court of the temple.[10] We do not know the detailed route Jesus and his disciples took, but it was along this deep and dark valley that they walked, crossing the dried-up river bed at the bottom, and then climbing up the slope of the Mount of Olives on the other side. They may well have used the ancient paths drawn on fig. 11.1. They would have walked by the light of the full moon (in the middle of the lunar month).

How long did their journey take? The distance between the traditional site of the upper room and the traditional Gethsemane via the Essene Gate is at least 1.5 km (and about 3 km using the ancient paths shown on fig. 11.1). Given the time of night and the difficult terrain I suggest the journey took at least 15–30 minutes.

PRAYERS IN GETHSEMANE

In the garden of Gethsemane the gospels record that Jesus asked Peter, James and John to keep watch while he prayed, but they fell asleep. Jesus prayed again but the disciples fell asleep again. Jesus prayed a third time, and the disciples fell asleep yet again (Mark 14:32–41). After the first time the disciples fell asleep, Jesus said: 'Could you not keep watch for one hour? Watch and pray.' The gospels give no indication that Jesus was rushing his prayers: again the reverse is the case. When Jesus said, 'Could you not keep watch for one hour?', he may not have been exaggerating the time. Can we estimate the time these prayers took, with the disciples falling asleep three times, despite trying to stay awake? It is unlikely to have been less than one hour and may well have been longer.

THE ARREST OF JESUS

All four gospels describe the arrest of Jesus in Gethsemane. It is worth noting that Gethsemane overlooked Jerusalem. Jesus would have seen the arrest party coming. He could have fled into the desert and hidden undetected, but he chose to stay. The arrest is full of drama. Judas arrived with the arresting party, he identified Jesus with a kiss and Jesus was seized. Peter cut off the ear of the servant of the high priest with his sword; Jesus told Peter to put his sword away and healed the wounded man. Jesus asked why the arresting party had come at night armed with swords and clubs when he was teaching daily in the temple courts. The disciples of Jesus deserted him and fled, one of them running away naked when his garment was seized. Jesus was then bound and taken back to Jerusalem. The arrest of Jesus and the surrounding events must have taken 15–30 minutes, and the journey back to Jerusalem, presumably back across the Kidron valley, another 15–30 minutes.

We are now in a position to estimate the time Jesus arrived back in Jerusalem. If the last supper ended between midnight and 2 a.m., the journey to Gethsemane took 15–30 minutes, the prayers at Gethsemane lasted about one hour, the arrest took 15–30 minutes, and the journey back to Jerusalem about 15–30 minutes, then it was between 1.45 a.m. and 4.30 a.m. when Jesus arrived back in Jerusalem. Taking an average of these figures, we can say that Jesus probably arrived back in Jerusalem at about 3 a.m., with an uncertainty of about 1 hour and 30 minutes.

INTERROGATION BY ANNAS

Only John records that after his arrest Jesus was first taken to Annas for a preliminary and informal interrogation (John 18:13–24). This is a clear example of the compression of events in the gospels, in this case in the synoptic gospels. Who was Annas? John tells us he was 'the father-in-law of Caiaphas, the high priest that year' (John 18:13). Annas had himself been high priest from AD 6 to 15 and Caiaphas had been appointed as high priest in AD 18 (being removed from office in AD 36).[11] Many scholars believe that Annas was the 'power behind the throne' who still enjoyed the courtesy title of 'high priest'.[12] I am reminded of visiting Singapore in 1992, two years after the President, the powerful Lee Kuan Yew, had stepped down from office, but he remained in the cabinet as senior minister. I asked how the President was performing and was asked 'Do you mean Lee Kuan Yew?' because he was still effectively the President.

It is clear from both the Bible and Josephus that the Jews regarded Annas as the 'honorary' high priest even after (and perhaps because of) his being deposed by the Roman procurator in AD 15. Thus Luke 3:12 states: 'In the fifteenth year of the reign of Tiberius Caesar ... during the high priesthood of Annas and Caiaphas.' We know that Caiaphas was the official high priest at that time, but Luke is correctly pointing out that Annas was the effective high priest, so not only does he list both Annas and Caiaphas, but he also places Annas first, in recognition of his seniority. Similarly Acts 4:6 states: 'Annas the high priest was there, and so were Caiaphas, John ... '. Again at that time Caiaphas was the official high priest but the powerful Annas was in charge in reality.

Given that at the time of the trials of Jesus both Annas and Caiaphas were called the high priest, there is clearly cause for confusion if the high priest is not named. We find this potential for confusion in John's account of the interrogation of Jesus by Annas. John says that Jesus was brought first to Annas (John 18:13), then 'the high priest [Annas or Caiaphas?] questioned Jesus' (John 18:19), then an official asked Jesus: 'Is this the way you answer the high priest [Annas or Caiaphas?]?' (John 18:22). John ends his account of the interrogation with: 'Then Annas sent him [Jesus] bound to Caiaphas the high priest' (John 18:24). This last sentence is, of course, the key to understanding what John meant in earlier sentences. John is saying that Caiaphas was not present at the interrogation by Annas, since

Annas, when he was finished with Jesus, sent him [Jesus] bound to Caiaphas. As Raymond Brown states, these words have 'the clear implication that Caiaphas was (and had been) elsewhere'.[13]

John gives no indication of how long the questioning by Annas lasted. In order to estimate this, we consider the time clues given in the gospel accounts of the denials of Jesus by Peter.

THE THREE DENIALS BY PETER AND THE TWO COCK CROWS

At the last supper, according to Mark, Jesus predicted that Peter would deny him: 'Today – yes, tonight – before the cock crows twice you will deny me three times' (Mark 14:30). The other gospels have Jesus predicting only one cock crow (Matthew 26:34; Luke 22:34; John 13:38). Some manuscripts of Mark omit the word 'twice', but early reputable manuscripts of Mark do contain the word 'twice' and many scholars believe that the reference to two cock crows is preserving the story in its original form.[14] I will take the two cock crows to be factual. Note that Jesus predicted that the denials and cock crows would take place that night and not in the daytime.

After Jesus was arrested, John states he was taken to Annas, interrogated and then sent to Caiaphas. Mark describes how Peter had followed Jesus, and as he was standing in the courtyard of the house of the high priest,[15] warming himself by a fire, a servant girl accused him of being with Jesus. Peter denied this and the cock crowed (Mark 14:68). The servant girl accused him once more, and Peter denied a second time. Those standing near Peter accused him yet again, Peter denied a third time, and 'immediately the cock crowed a second time' (Mark 14:72).

I would like to concentrate initially on the first denial of Peter. John pointedly separates the first denial of Peter from the second and third, as if they were separated significantly in time. According to John, Jesus was brought bound to Annas (John 18:12–14) and in the very next verses Peter's first denial is reported (John 18:15–18). John therefore places the first denial of Peter shortly after Jesus arrived to be interrogated by Annas. I have estimated above that Jesus was probably taken to Annas at about 3 a.m., with an uncertainty of about 1 hour and 30 minutes. The first denial of Peter was therefore probably in this time period.

What do we know about cock crowing in Jerusalem? It is expressly stated in rabbinic literature that the breeding of cocks was forbidden in Jerusalem.[16] On the other hand, the Mishnah in three places refers to cocks crowing in Jerusalem.[17] So it would seem that there was a difference between what rabbis wanted to happen and what actually happened, and that some cocks, although probably not many, were in Jerusalem at the time of Christ.

Josephus (*War* 5.244) says there was a cohort of Roman soldiers permanently based in the Antonia fortress in Jerusalem. The Romans divided the night into four watches of three hours each, roughly 6 p.m. to 9 p.m., 9 p.m. to midnight, midnight to 3 a.m., and 3 a.m. to 6 a.m. The Romans signalled the end of the third watch, at 3 a.m., with a trumpet call known as the cock crow (gallicinium in Latin). Jesus refers to this in Mark 13:35, where he asks his followers to exhibit the same watchfulness as the four watches of Roman soldiers: 'Therefore keep watch because you do not know when the owner of the house will come back – whether in the evening, or at midnight, or when the cock crows, or at dawn.' Note that when Jesus refers to the cock crow here he evidently means the 3 a.m. Roman trumpet call known as the gallicinium.

Although there have been a variety of claims that cocks crow at 12.30 a.m., 1.30 a.m., 2.30 a.m., etc.,[18] the reality is that cocks, like many other birds, mainly crow as dawn is approaching (and then continue to crow throughout the day). The 'dawn chorus', including cock crow, normally starts with a few calls about one hour before sunrise and then builds up to a crescendo at sunrise. Graeme Waddington has calculated for me that sunrise in Jerusalem on April 2, AD 33 was at 5.46 a.m. For a cock to crow at about 3 a.m., my estimated time of Peter's first denial, would therefore be unusual (but not impossible if it was disturbed). However, we have another candidate for this first cock crow: the Roman trumpet call at 3 a.m. called the gallicinium (cock crow). Although various commentators are not keen on the idea that the cock crow at Peter's denial was the gallicinium,[19] I find it highly plausible. The Antonia fortress, which was the barracks of the Roman garrison in Jerusalem, was adjacent to, and overlooked, the temple. The house of the high priest would have been close to the temple (indeed, the two main traditional sites are close to the temple[20]). Peter was outside, in the courtyard of the high priest. I believe there can therefore be little doubt that he would have heard the 3 a.m. gallicinium trumpet call loud and clear.

It seems to me to be too much of a coincidence that the first denial of Peter was probably at approximately 3 a.m. and the Roman trumpet call known as cock crow was also at 3 a.m. In addition, as we have seen, Mark reports Jesus specifically calling the 3 a.m. Roman trumpet call the cock crow (Mark 13:35), and *in the next chapter* (Mark 14:68) he refers to the cock crow at the time of Peter's first denial. We should also remember that Jesus enjoyed plays on words,[21] and for him to have had the first cock crow as the gallicinium and the second from a live bird would, I suggest, have been consistent with the element of surprise to Peter, hinted at in the gospels, when he heard these two *different* cock crows. If my argument is accepted then we can pinpoint the time of the first denial of Peter, and the time of the start of the interrogation by Annas, as 3 a.m. I suggest that Matthew and Luke did not refer to this gallicinium cock crow because they compressed the account in Mark, as they did when reporting many other events.[22]

Luke gives us the most detailed information about the second and third denials of Peter. He states that the second denial was 'a little later' than the first (Luke 22:58) and that the third denial was 'about an hour later' (Luke 22:59) than the second. If the first denial was at 3 a.m. this places the third denial at about 4.30 a.m., which fits well with sunrise at 5.46 a.m. and the first dawn chorus cock crowing approximately one hour earlier. So we have a consistent story, and a consistent set of times, for the denials of Peter and the two cock crows. Luke records that, immediately following the final cock crow, Jesus turned and looked straight at Peter (Luke 22:61). This would have been as Jesus was being led from Annas across the courtyard to Caiaphas.

MAIN TRIAL BY THE SANHEDRIN

The synoptic gospels make it clear that this was a lengthy trial. Matthew writes: 'The chief priests and the whole Sanhedrin were looking for false evidence against Jesus so that they could put him to death. But they did not find any, though *many false witnesses* [my italics] came forward' (Matthew 26:59–60; Mark 14:55–56 is similar). After hearing from these many false witnesses, Matthew continues: '*Finally* [my italics] two came forward and declared, "This fellow said, 'I am able to destroy the temple of God and rebuild it in three days'"' (Matthew 26:61; also Mark 14:58). The terminology used, 'Many false witnesses ... finally', suggests an unhurried trial in which witness after witness gave evidence, but they all disagreed with each other (Mark 14:56).

The high priest then changed tactics and all three synoptic gospels record him asking Jesus: 'Are you the Christ?' (Matthew 26:63; Mark 14:61; Luke 22:67). Jesus replied that he was the Son of God, and that they would see him seated at the right hand of God (Matthew 26:64; Mark 14:62; Luke 22:68–70). The Sanhedrin then pronounced that he had blasphemed and was worthy of death (Matthew 26:65–66; Mark 14:63–64; Luke 22:71). The close agreement in wording of Matthew, Mark and Luke concerning the latter part of this trial (Luke does not mention the false witnesses at the start) makes it clear that all three gospels are describing the same event: the main trial of Jesus by the Sanhedrin.

We have shown that according to John, and using timings for the denials provided by Luke, Jesus was first interrogated by Annas, and this questioning ended at about 4.30 a.m. Jesus was then taken bound to Caiaphas, which would have taken 15 minutes, say, and sunrise was at 5.46 a.m. There was therefore no time for a protracted *night-time* trial by Caiaphas and the Sanhedrin. If my interpretation is correct, after his arrest Jesus spent most of the rest of that night being interrogated by Annas, and he was then taken to Caiaphas at dawn. Hence all or most of the trial by Caiaphas and the Sanhedrin must have been in the daytime.[23]

WAS THE SANHEDRIN TRIAL BY NIGHT?

Only Luke records when the main trial by the Sanhedrin started. He states: '*At daybreak* [my italics] the council of the elders of the people, both the chief priests and teachers of the law, met together, and Jesus was led before them' (Luke 22:66). Luke's statement is consistent with the timetable in John, which we have deduced above, that Annas sent Jesus bound to Caiaphas (John 18:24) about one hour before sunrise. I therefore conclude that this was a daytime trial, starting at daybreak and probably a lengthy trial because of the many witnesses that were called.

If Luke and John agree that this was a daytime trial, why do most scholars believe it occurred at night? There are two main reasons: first, if the last supper was on Thursday evening with the crucifixion at about 9 a.m. on Friday, the time pressure this produces on the many events recorded between the last supper and the crucifixion virtually forces this main Sanhedrin trial to have been before sunrise on Friday. Second, many scholars believe that Matthew and Mark imply that this was a night-time trial, for the reasons given below.

Whereas John interweaves his account of the denials by Peter with the night-time interrogation of Jesus by Annas, Matthew and Mark interweave their accounts of the denials by Peter with the trial of Jesus by the Sanhedrin. Since the denials by Peter occurred at night, many scholars think that Matthew and Mark imply that the trial by the Sanhedrin must also have been at night. This raises the following key issue of biblical interpretation.

The gospel writers were not modern professional historians and they did not therefore necessarily write down events in strict chronological order (and even professional historians do not always do this today). Sometimes the order of events mattered to them, and sometimes it did not, because it was not important to the story. An example is the temptations of Jesus in the wilderness. According to Matthew, the first temptation was to tell stones to become bread, the second was for Jesus to throw himself off the top of the temple and survive, and the third was to worship the devil in exchange for ruling the world

(Matthew 4:1–11). Luke describes the temptations, but in a different order (first, stones becoming bread; second, worshipping the devil; and third, Jesus throwing himself off the top of the temple, Luke 4:1–13). So Matthew and Luke do not state these events in the same order, but the order is unimportant and of no concern to them. A modern example may be helpful. At the weekend I pulled some weeds out of my garden and then mowed the lawn, in that order. However, when my wife phoned her mother later that day she said: 'Colin mowed the grass and did some weeding.' It would be ludicrous to accuse my wife of being inaccurate: the order of these events was of no importance, either to her or to her audience (her mother). Similarly, the order of events at the temptations of Jesus was of no importance to the gospel writers, nor to their audience. However, when the gospel writers explicitly give time markers, we should then take seriously the order of events they give. Hence, when Luke explicitly states that the trial of Jesus by the Sanhedrin started at daybreak, this specific time marker we should take seriously.

Both Matthew and Mark describe the denials by Peter (Matthew 26:69–75; Mark 14:66–72) *after* they describe the trial by the Sanhedrin (Matthew 26:57–68; Mark 14:53–65). On the other hand Luke places the denials by Peter (Luke 22:54–62) *before* the trial by the Sanhedrin (Luke 22:66–71). To my mind, the situation is similar to the different order of events between Matthew and Luke regarding the temptations of Jesus. We therefore need to ask which of these writers cared more about having the denials of Peter and the Sanhedrin trial in the correct order. I think the answer is obvious: it was Luke. He alone tells us that the Sanhedrin trial started at daybreak. He then consistently places the night-time denials by Peter before this daytime Sanhedrin trial. This totally agrees with John, who has the denials by Peter running in parallel with the interrogation by Annas. We can tentatively speculate on why Luke and John were concerned about the order of these events and Matthew and Mark were not. Most scholars believe that the gospels of Mark and Matthew were written before those of Luke and John. In addition, most scholars believe that Mark formed the basis for Matthew, so their common order is not surprising. When Mark and Matthew wrote their gospels perhaps neither they nor their audience were concerned about whether the denials by Peter were before or after the trial by the Sanhedrin. However perhaps questions were then asked about the order of these events, and also people wanted to know if the Sanhedrin trial was at night or in the daytime, particularly if a trial at night would have been illegal. So both Luke and John decided to clarify the situation. It is also worth noting that it was recognised as early as the second century AD that the gospel of Mark was not in strict chronological order.[24]

Concerning a night-time trial, Geza Vermes writes: 'Although the arrest of Jesus was sudden and unprepared, the evangelists declare that the whole august body of the Sanhedrin – consisting of seventy-one members according to the Mishnah – was already assembled in the high-priest's palace at night, and on Passover night of all nights. Not only were the councillors present, but there was also a whole bunch of witnesses ready to testify against Jesus. Was all this carefully organised when it was still uncertain whether Jesus would actually be found let alone detained?'[25] Even if it was not Passover night in the Judean calendar, the argument of Vermes still has some force. Does it not make more sense that it was during the night-time interrogation by Annas that the Sanhedrin and the witnesses were located and brought to the palace of Caiaphas, ready for the trial in the morning?

Mark ends his account of the first Sanhedrin trial with the words: 'They all condemned him as worthy of death' (Mark 14:64). Immediately following these words, Mark writes: 'Then some began to spit at him; they blindfolded him, struck him with their fists, and said, "Prophesy!" And the guards took him and beat him' (Mark 14:65). The message of these verses is that the main Sanhedrin trial had ended with Jesus being condemned to death. Jesus was then spat at, blindfolded, hit and handed over by the Sanhedrin to the guards, who took him and beat him. The procedure of Jesus being handed over by the Sanhedrin to the guards is similar to that recorded in Matthew 5:25: 'The judge may hand you over to the officer, and you may be thrown into prison.' Rawlinson writes that the last words of Mark 14:65 should perhaps be translated as: 'And the attendants took Him into custody with blows.'[26]

Taking the evidence from all four gospels into account, the conclusion to me is clear. The main trial by the Sanhedrin started at daybreak and probably lasted a number of hours. It followed the night-time denials by Peter and the night-time interrogation by Annas. At the end of the trial Jesus was handed over to the guards.

THE SECOND SANHEDRIN TRIAL

We turn now to the second short confirmatory Sanhedrin trial. Matthew and Mark introduce their account of this trial with the following explicit time statement: 'Very early in the morning, the chief priests, with the elders, the teachers of the law and the whole Sanhedrin, reached a decision. They bound Jesus, led him away and turned him over to Pilate' (Mark 15:1). Matthew similarly states: 'Early in the morning, all the chief priests … came to the decision to put Jesus to death. They … handed him over to Pilate' (Matthew 27:1–2). R. T. France writes that the phrase translated 'very early in the morning' in Mark 15:1 means 'at or even before daybreak'.[27]

The above words of Matthew and Mark are hugely significant. If the trial by Annas was at night, before sunrise, and Jesus was then transferred to Caiaphas (John 18:12–24), and if *the first trial* by Caiaphas and the Sanhedrin was a lengthy trial *starting at daybreak* (Luke 23:66), and if the *second short trial* by Caiaphas and the Sanhedrin *also started at daybreak* (Matthew 27:1–2 and Mark 15:1), following which Jesus was led from Caiaphas to Pilate, it still being early morning (John 18:28), then *the two trials by the Sanhedrin must have been on successive days.* This, I suggest, is the natural reading of all four gospels.[28] Interestingly, this interpretation fully accords with the statement in the Mishnah that the Sanhedrin can only meet by day, and that in capital trials the Sanhedrin must meet on successive days, the second short meeting being to confirm their decision to impose a capital sentence. In addition, the Mishnah states that trials may not be held on the eve of a Sabbath nor on the eve of a feast day (Mishnah Sanhedrin 4.1). If the chronology suggested in the previous chapter is correct, then the last supper was held on Wednesday evening, the main trial by the Sanhedrin was on Thursday morning, Nisan 13 in the official Jewish calendar, with Nisan 15 being the first day of the Feast of Unleavened Bread. So on this new chronology, the trial was not held on Nisan 14, the eve of a feast day, but on the previous day, again in accordance with the Mishnah. Incidentally, our new chronology, which brings the arrest and trials forward in time, is also consistent with the religious authorities looking 'to arrest Jesus and kill him. "But not during the Feast," they said, "or the people may riot"' (Mark 14:1–2).

I suggest that the natural interpretation of the gospels gives the following sequence of events: last supper on Wednesday evening, probably ending between midnight and 2 a.m. Arrest in the early hours of Thursday followed by interrogation by Annas lasting until dawn (John). Denials by Peter at the same time as the questioning by Annas (John). Trial by Caiaphas and the Sanhedrin, starting at daybreak on Thursday (Luke). Jesus sentenced to death and handed over to guards (Matthew, Mark). Thursday night spent in prison. Short session of Sanhedrin confirming the death sentence at daybreak on Friday (Matthew, Mark). Jesus taken to Pilate.

From the last supper to the trial by Pilate

Event	Day and time
The last supper	Wednesday evening and night
Arrest of Jesus	Thursday – early hours
Interrogation by Annas and denials by Peter	Thursday about 3 a.m. until dawn
Trial by Caiaphas and the Sanhedrin	Thursday – starting at daybreak
Jesus sentenced to death and handed over to the guards	Thursday
Jesus spends night in prison	Thursday night
Sanhedrin meets to confirm the death sentence	Friday – daybreak
Trial by Pilate	Friday – early morning

TRIAL BEFORE PILATE

John tells us that the Jews took Jesus to Pilate because, although the Sanhedrin had condemned Jesus to death, they did not have the authority to carry out the death sentence (John 18:31). This agrees with a statement in the Jerusalem Talmud that 'forty years before the destruction of the temple the right to inflict the death penalty was taken away from the Jews'.[29] The temple was destroyed in AD 70, so presumably this rule would have been in place in AD 33, the year of the crucifixion.

John states that Jesus was brought into the praetorium of Pilate in the early morning (John 18:28). We know that Roman officials liked to begin their work at dawn.[30] If the second short confirmatory trial by the Sanhedrin started at sunrise on Friday, April 3, AD 33, which was at 5.46 a.m., Jesus was probably with Pilate shortly after 6.00 a.m. After questioning, Pilate found out that Jesus was from Galilee, so he sent him to Herod Antipas, because he was the official in charge of Galilee, and, after further questioning, Herod Antipas sent him back to Pilate (Luke 23:6–12).

THE CURIOUS DREAM OF THE WIFE OF PILATE

While Pilate was judging Jesus, Matthew records that his wife sent him the following message: 'Don't have anything to do with that innocent man, for I have suffered a great deal today in a dream because of him' (Matthew 27:19). This is curious if the conventional chronology is correct, because if Jesus was arrested in the early hours of Friday, how did Pilate's wife know about this before she went to sleep on Thursday evening and had her dream? However, in our new chronology, if Jesus was arrested in the early hours of *Thursday* morning, tried by the Sanhedrin that day and sentenced to death, then Caiaphas would have given Pilate advance notice on Thursday afternoon that Jesus had been condemned to death, that the Sanhedrin would be meeting again early the next day to confirm their decision, and that they would then bring Jesus to him so that he could authorise the death penalty. Pilate's wife could then have known about this on Thursday and had her dream on Thursday night, relaying her message to Pilate on Friday morning. The ancient historian Bruce Winter informs me that the Jews would not have been able simply to 'drop in' on Pilate on Friday morning. They would have had to present a written petition to him in advance for him to try Jesus.[31] An appropriate time would have been on Thursday, after the main Sanhedrin trial. This is when Pilate's wife would have learnt that Jesus would be tried by Pilate. This is another small, but important, example of how having the last supper on Wednesday fits the gospel accounts much better than having it on Thursday.

THE CRUCIFIXION

The gospels record how Pilate offered to release Jesus or Barabbas, the crowd chose Barabbas, Jesus was then flogged, the soldiers mocked him, Simon carried his cross and Jesus was crucified. As is well known, the gospels apparently give different times for the crucifixion. Mark writes: 'It was the third hour when they crucified him' (Mark 15:25); John says that when Pilate handed over Jesus to be crucified it was 'about the sixth hour' (John 19:14). As we have seen, the usual Jewish method of counting the hours of daylight was from sunrise. However, Roman officials such as Pilate used the Julian calendar introduced by Julius Caesar, and counted the hours of their day from midnight (as we do today).[32] It is possible that the source of information for John about the time when Pilate handed over Jesus to be crucified was from a Roman official, who told him that it was about the sixth hour (Roman time), that is about 6 a.m. This is consistent with Mark saying that Jesus was crucified at the third hour (Jewish time), about 9 a.m. Jesus died at the ninth hour (Mark 15:34), that is at about 3 p.m., at the same time as the first Passover lambs were being slain (Josephus, *War* 6.423), on Friday Nisan 14 in the official Jewish calendar. The timetable of events between the last supper and the crucifixion is given in the table.

From the last supper to the crucifixion

Event	Gospels	Time
Last supper	All	Wednesday evening and night ending between midnight and 2 a.m. Thursday
Walk to Gethsemane	All	Early Thursday morning
Prayers in Gethsemane	Synoptics	Early Thursday morning
Jesus arrested	All	Early Thursday morning
Interrogation by Annas	John	About 3.00–4.30 a.m., Thursday
First denial by Peter and cock crow	All	About 3.00 a.m., Thursday
Third denial by Peter and cock crow	All	About 4.30 a.m., Thursday
Jesus taken to Caiaphas	All	About 5.00 a.m., Thursday
Main trial by Sanhedrin	Synoptics	Thursday after sunrise (at 5.46 a.m.), probably lasting for some hours
Sanhedrin hand over Jesus to the guards	Mark	Thursday at end of Sanhedrin trial
Second short Sanhedrin confirmatory trial	Matthew, Mark	Friday after sunrise (5.46 a.m.)
Trial before Pilate	All	Friday morning
Trial before Herod	Luke	Friday morning

Trial before Pilate	All	Friday morning
Pilate's wife reports dream	Matthew	Friday morning
Release of Barabbas	All	Friday morning
Jesus flogged	Matthew, Mark, John	Friday morning
Soldiers mock Jesus	Matthew, Mark, John	Friday morning
Simon carries cross	Synoptics	Friday morning
Crucifixion	All	Friday about 9.00 a.m.
Jesus dies	All	Friday about 3.00 p.m.

SUMMARY

The table above summarises the order and timing of events between the last supper and the crucifixion deduced from the four gospels. A detailed analysis of the gospels shows that the last supper was on Wednesday evening/night, the main Sanhedrin trial of Jesus was in the daytime on Thursday, followed by a short Sanhedrin trial at daybreak on Friday confirming the death sentence. This new chronology is consistent with the legal rules in the Mishnah concerning capital trials by the Sanhedrin. It is also consistent with Jesus using the pre-exilic calendar to celebrate his last supper as a Passover meal. In the year of the crucifixion we can calculate that the Passover meal in the pre-exilic calendar was on a Wednesday. A Wednesday last supper and a Friday crucifixion allow just the right amount of time to fit in all the events the gospels record as happening between the last supper and the crucifixion.

13 A new reconstruction of the final days of Jesus

> Therefore, since I myself have carefully investigated everything from the beginning, it seemed good also to me to write an orderly account for you, most excellent Theophilus, so that you may know the certainty of the things you have been taught.
>
> (Luke 1:3–4)

> Scholars who have looked at what we can know about the historical Jesus from the Gospels have generally decided that the answer is 'not much'.
>
> (Judith Redman[1])

The quotations above strikingly illustrate the difference between the claims of a gospel, in this case that of Luke, to have carefully investigated everything about the life of Jesus and the claims of many modern scholars, that we cannot reliably understand much about the historical Jesus from the gospels. Geza Vermes represents what is often thought to be the view of the majority of scholars about the gospels when he writes: 'They are filled with discrepancies.'[2]

In this book I have carefully investigated the last days of Jesus afresh. I have forensically examined the gospels, comparing them with each other and with historical sources. I have found that the major apparent discrepancies in the gospel descriptions of the final days of Jesus, including the last supper, do not exist. They arise because we have wrongly interpreted the gospel texts. When correctly understood, all four gospels agree with each other to a remarkable extent. They also agree with the relevant passages in the Dead Sea Scrolls and with Jewish and Roman historians.

This is not a devotional book, but at times as I was writing it I felt caught up in a most wonderful story. When we understand these final days of Jesus better, we see an even bigger picture than before.

Anyone who reads detective stories, or anyone who is a scientist, knows that the solution of a complex problem often turns out to be simple, once the problem has been understood. So it is with the problems surrounding the gospel descriptions of the last supper and the final days of Jesus, outlined in Chapter 1. The solution given in this book is as follows.

1. John places the last supper, the trials and the crucifixion of Jesus all before the official Jewish Passover meal. In John's account, Jesus died at the time the first Passover lambs were slain, at about 3 p.m. on the fourteenth day of the Jewish month Nisan.
2. In Matthew, Mark and Luke (the synoptic gospels), the last supper is a Passover meal. Jesus was therefore crucified *after* this Passover meal, on Nisan 15. Hence John and the synoptic gospels apparently disagree not only on whether the last supper was a Passover meal or not, but also on the date of the crucifixion.
3. The solution to the above problems given in this book is that, in their description of the last supper as a Passover meal, Matthew, Mark and Luke were using *a different calendar* to John. This book also identifies the different calendars used.
4. John was using the official Jewish calendar, the one used by the priests of the temple in Jerusalem in the first century AD. This calendar was a lunar calendar with a sunset-to-sunset day. In this calendar the Passover lamb was slain on Nisan 14, in the afternoon, and the Passover meal was eaten after sunset, the day then being Nisan 15.
5. In their description of the last supper, Matthew, Mark and Luke were using a different lunar calendar, one having a *sunrise-to-sunrise day*. In this calendar, both the sacrifice of the Passover lamb and the eating of the Passover meal were on Nisan 14. Nisan 14 in this calendar was *before* Nisan 14 in the official Jewish calendar.
6. The situation is similar to that today, where Greek and Russian Orthodox churches normally celebrate Easter before Catholics and Protestants, because the Orthodox churches

still use the earlier Julian calendar to determine the date of Easter whereas Catholics and Protestants use the modern Gregorian calendar.

7 Using a different calendar theory, all four gospels agree on the date and nature of the last supper. The last supper was a real Passover meal according to the calendar used by the synoptic gospels. However, the Passover meal in this calendar was eaten *before* that in the official calendar, hence John was correct in saying that the last supper was before the official Passover meal. All four gospels also now agree on the date of the crucifixion. It was on Nisan 14 in the official Jewish calendar, Jesus dying at 3 p.m. when the first Passover lambs were slain (John and also Paul).

8 All the evidence from the Bible and other early documents is consistent with the crucifixion being on Nisan 14 in the official calendar.

9 What was the different calendar that Jesus chose to celebrate his last supper as a Passover meal, as described by the synoptics? The only plausible calendar previously proposed by others is the solar calendar used by the Qumran community, probably members of a Jewish group called the Essenes, and described in the Dead Sea Scrolls. I have shown that this theory cannot be true, since Passover in this calendar fell *after* Passover in the official calendar.

10 The 'different calendar' I have identified that Jesus used to celebrate his last supper as a Passover meal was *the pre-exilic calendar of ancient Israel*. When the Judean Jews were in exile in Babylon in the sixth century BC they adopted the Babylonian calendar, including using Babylonian-style month names. This calendar was a lunar calendar, with a sunset-to-sunset day, and was the official Jewish calendar in the first century AD. Before this Babylonian-style calendar the Jews used an earlier, pre-exilic calendar.

11 I have identified this ancient pre-exilic Jewish calendar as being based on the lunar calendar of ancient Egypt, but with the first month changed to the spring (called the month of Abib, meaning

ripening ears of barley). The name of this first month was later changed to Nisan when the Judean Jews were in exile in Babylon (Nisan being the Hebrew equivalent of the name of the Babylonian first month, Nisannu).

12 This pre-exilic calendar was a lunar calendar with a *sunrise-to-sunrise day*, just as the ancient Egyptian lunar calendar had a sunrise-to-sunrise day. It persisted through to the first century AD and I have shown that it was used to calculate Passover by various groups, including the Samaritans, the Zealots and at least some Essenes. There would therefore have been nothing particularly unusual about Jesus choosing to use this calendar to celebrate his last supper as a Passover meal. It would be somewhat like a Christian today choosing to celebrate Easter according to the Julian calendar (as indeed I did when on holiday in Greece) rather than the Gregorian calendar (which I use when in England). We know from the Jewish historian Josephus that Samaritans, Essenes and Zealots all lived in Jerusalem in the first century AD.

13 With the aid of an astrophysicist I have reconstructed both the official Jewish calendar and the pre-exilic Jewish calendar for the first century AD. Passover in the pre-exilic Jewish calendar was always a few days before Passover in the official calendar.

14 From these calendar reconstructions we can identify the date of the crucifixion as Friday, April 3, AD 33, and the date of the last supper as Wednesday, April 1, AD 33.

15 It is clear from his words and actions that Jesus saw himself as the new Moses. By choosing to hold his last supper as a Passover meal using the pre-exilic calendar, Jesus was holding his last Passover meal on the *exact* anniversary of the first Passover meal described in the book of Exodus. Jesus was therefore symbolically identifying himself as the new Moses, which is consistent with his words at the last supper.

16 A Wednesday last supper goes against the widespread assumption that this was on a Thursday. However, Thursday is nowhere said to be the day of the last supper in the Bible. A detailed

analysis of the gospels shows that they do indeed place the last supper on a Wednesday.

17 A Wednesday last supper solves the problems outlined in Chapter 1 of this book. It explains what happened on 'lost Wednesday'. It solves the apparent discrepancy of John and the synoptics on the date and nature of the last supper. It allows sufficient time for all the events the gospels record between the last supper and the crucifixion. Finally, it means that the Jewish trials of Jesus were legal. Following the last supper on Wednesday evening/night, Jesus was arrested in the early hours of Thursday morning. The main trial by the Jewish Sanhedrin court was in the daytime on Thursday. They then met again early Friday morning to confirm the death penalty. This agrees with the Mishnah, which states that the Sanhedrin must only meet in the daytime and in capital cases it must meet again the next day to confirm its decision.

In closing, let me return to the statement by Richard Dawkins I quoted in Chapter 1: 'The only difference between *The Da Vinci Code* and the gospels is that the gospels are ancient fiction while *The Da Vinci Code* is modern fiction.' I have taken what the biblical scholar F. F. Bruce called 'the thorniest problem in the New Testament', the problem of the date and nature of the last supper. I have shown that even with this complex problem the gospels are in substantial agreement, when understood in the light of evidence from the Dead Sea Scrolls, ancient Egypt, and elsewhere. The extensive analysis in this book shows that the gospels give a coherent and detailed factual account of the last days of Jesus, days that changed the world. On the other hand, *The Da Vinci Code* is indeed a work of fiction.

Finally, let me emphasise the striking symbolism our new dating of the last days of Jesus has revealed. By using the pre-exilic calendar, Jesus held his last supper as a real Passover meal on the exact anniversary of the first Passover, described in the book of Exodus, thus identifying himself as the new Moses, instituting a new covenant and leading God's people out of captivity. Jesus died at about 3 p.m., on Nisan 14 in the official Jewish calendar, at the time the Passover lambs were slain, thus becoming identified with the Passover sacrifice. These powerful symbolisms are based on objective historical events. The details of the last days of Jesus I have reconstructed in this book are deep in meaning and significance and, I suggest, throw new light on God working to a climax within history.

Notes

1 FOUR MYSTERIES OF THE LAST WEEK OF JESUS

1. Richard Dawkins, *The God Delusion* (London: Transworld Publishers, 2006), pp. 122, 123, 319.
2. *The NIV Study Bible*, 'Chart of Passion Week' (London: Hodder and Stoughton, 1987), pp. 1492–3.
3. John P. Meier, *A Marginal Jew: Rethinking the Historical Jesus*, vol. I: *The Roots of the Problem and the Person* (New York: Doubleday, 1991), p. 395.
4. There are a large number of theories about the interdependence of the Passion narratives of Matthew, Mark and Luke. See, for example, Raymond E. Brown, *The Death of the Messiah*, 2 vols. (New York: Doubleday, 1994), vol. I, pp. 40–6.
5. The Sanhedrin was the highest court of the Jews and it was presided over by the high priest, who was Caiaphas at the time of the crucifixion.
6. Geza Vermes, *The Passion* (London: Penguin, 2005), p. 111.

2 DATING THE CRUCIFIXION – THE FIRST CLUES

1. Chart: 'The Life of Christ', in *The NIV Study Bible* (London: Hodder and Stoughton, 1998), p. 1452.
2. Josef Blinzler, *Der Prozess Jesu*, fourth edition (Regensburg: Pustet, 1969), pp. 101–26. See E. P. Sanders, *The Historical Figure of Jesus* (London: Penguin, 1993), pp. 282–90, for a discussion of the range of dates for the crucifixion.
3. It took the independently minded English, and their American colonies, until 1752 to fall into line and adopt the Gregorian calendar.
4. Jack Finegan, *Handbook of Biblical Chronology*, revised edition (Peabody, MA: Hendrickson, 1998), pp. 329–44.
5. A. Burnett, M. Amandry and P. P. Ripollès, *Roman Provincial Coinage*, vol. I: *From the Death of Caesar to the Death of Vitellius (44 BC–AD 69)*

(London: British Museum Press, 1992), pp. 608–26, at p. 621 states: 'The coinage of Tiberius can be dated very closely. The first issue is dated by year 1 of Tiberius and year 45 of Actium (August–November AD 14).' Fig. 2.1 is a photograph of this double-dated coin from which we know that Tiberius started to reign in AD 14.

6. John P. Meier, *A Marginal Jew: Rethinking the Historical Jesus*, vol. I: *The Roots of the Problem and the Person* (New York: Doubleday, 1991), p. 384.
7. *The Anchor Bible Dictionary* says around AD 18 to around AD 36. Finegan, *Handbook of Biblical Chronology*, p. 352, gives AD 18–36.
8. Finegan, *Handbook of Biblical Chronology*, p. 362, and Harold W. Hoehner, *Chronological Aspects of the Life of Christ* (Grand Rapids: Zondervan, 1977), p. 30. Rainer Riesner, *Paul's Early Period: Chronology, Mission Strategy, Theology* (Grand Rapids: Eerdmans, 1998), pp. 36–8, keeps AD 26 for Pilate's appointment and places his departure from Palestine after Passover in AD 36 but before Passover in AD 37.
9. For example, the book of Esther records that Queen Esther, the Jewish wife of the famous King Xerxes of Persia, said to her adopted father, Mordecai: 'Do not eat or drink for three days, night or day. I and my maids will fast as you do. When this is done, I will go to the king' (Esther 4:16). After fasting, Esther went to King Xerxes 'on the third day' (Esther 5:1). It therefore seems that fasting for part of the third day counted as fasting for the whole of it. King Xerxes ruled from about 486 to 465 BC, almost 500 years before Jesus.
10. Jerusalem Talmud, Shabbath ix, 3.
11. For example, the nineteenth-century Anglican bishop Brooke Foss Westcott, who, with Fenton Hort, produced a new Greek text of the New Testament, believed that the crucifixion was on a Thursday. This implies that he put the last supper on Wednesday, so perhaps he anticipated my date of the last supper, see Chapter 11.

3 THE PROBLEM OF THE LAST SUPPER

1. Leviticus states that the Passover meal is eaten on Nisan 15, and Josephus confirms that this was the case in the first century AD.
2. See, for example, F.F. Bruce, *The Gospel of John* (Grand Rapids: Eerdmans, 1983), p. 374.
3. For a good survey of views see I. Howard Marshall, *Last Supper and Lord's Supper* (Exeter: Paternoster Press, 1980), pp. 57–75.
4. Joachim Jeremias, *The Eucharistic Words of Jesus* (London: SCM Press, 1966).

5. C.K. Barrett, *The Gospel According to John: An Introduction with Commentary and Notes on the Greek Text*, second edition (Philadelphia: Westminster, 1978), p. 141.
6. D.A. Carson, *The Gospel According to John* (Leicester: Inter-Varsity Press; Grand Rapids: Eerdmans, 1991), p. 460.
7. Carson, *The Gospel According to John*, p. 589.
8. Craig L. Blomberg, *The Historical Reliability of John's Gospel* (Leicester: Inter-Varsity Press, 2001), p. 254. See also Carson, *The Gospel According to John*, p. 622.
9. John P. Meier, *A Marginal Jew: Rethinking the Historical Jesus*, vol. I: *The Roots of the Problem and the Person* (New York: Doubleday, 1991), p. 399.
10. N.T. Wright, *Jesus and the Victory of God* (Minneapolis: Fortress, 1996), p. 438.
11. Josephus, *The Jewish War*, 6.423.
12. Annie Jaubert, *La date de la cène* (EBib; Paris: Gabalda, 1957), and its English translation by Isaac Rafferty, *The Date of the Last Supper* (Staten Island, NY: Alba House, 1965).
13. Marshall, *Last Supper*, pp. 57–75.
14. Harold W. Hoehner, *Chronological Aspects of the Life of Christ* (Grand Rapids: Zondervan, 1977), pp. 81–90.
15. Mark A. Matson, 'The Historical Plausibility of John's Passion Dating', in *John, Jesus and History*, vol. II: *Aspects of Historicity in the Fourth Gospel*, ed. Paul N. Anderson, Felix Just and Tom Thatcher (Atlanta: Society of Biblical Literature, 2009), p. 307.
16. Meier, *A Marginal Jew*, p. 427.
17. R.T. France, *The Gospel of Mark* (Grand Rapids: Eerdmans; Carlisle: Paternoster, 2002), p. 559.

4 CAN WE RECONSTRUCT THE JEWISH CALENDAR AT THE TIME OF CHRIST?

Key books on the Jewish calendar include the following:

Jack Finegan, *Handbook of Biblical Chronology*, revised edition (Peabody, MA: Hendrickson, 1998).

Emil Schürer, *A History of the Jewish People in the Age of Jesus Christ: 175 BC – AD 135*, revised edition, ed. G. Vermes, F. Millar and M. Black (Edinburgh: T&T Clark, 1973), vol. I, Appendix III, pp. 587–601.

Sacha Stern, *Calendar and Community: A History of the Jewish Calendar 2nd Century BCE – 10th Century CE* (Oxford: Oxford University Press, 2001).

1. Jonathan Sacks, *The Chief Rabbi's Haggadah: Hebrew and English Text with New Essays and Commentary* (London: HarperCollins, 2003), p. 67.
2. Chapter 5 of this book shows that in the first century AD the first-fruits festival of the sheaf of barley being waved in the temple occurred on Nisan 16.
3. A good introduction to astronomy is *Astronomy and the Imagination: A New Approach to Man's Experience of the Stars* by Norman Davidson (London and New York: Routledge and Kegan Paul, 1985).
4. Mark E. Cohen, *The Cultic Calendars of the Ancient Near East* (Bethesda, MD: CDL Press, 1993), p. 4.
5. Davidson, *Astronomy and the Imagination*, pp. 69–74.
6. Nikos Kokkinos, 'Crucifixion in AD 36', in *Chronos, Kairos, Christos: Nativity and Chronological Studies Presented to Jack Finegan*, ed. Jerry Vardaman and Edwin Yamauchi (Winona Lake: Eisenbrauns, 1989), pp. 133–63.
7. Conjunction is in ecliptic longitude only, not in ecliptic latitude, otherwise there would be an eclipse every conjunction.
8. J.K. Fotheringham, 'The Evidence of Astronomy and Technical Chronology for the Date of the Crucifixion', *Journal of Theological Studies* 34 (1934), 146–62.
9. Joachim Jeremias, *The Eucharistic Words of Jesus* (London: SCM Press, 1966), p. 40.
10. Colin J. Humphreys and W. G. Waddington, 'Dating the Crucifixion', *Nature* 306 (1983), 743–6. Also C. J. Humphreys and W. G. Waddington, 'Astronomy and the Date of the Crucifixion', in *Chronos, Kairos, Christos*, pp. 165–81.
11. John Meier, *A Marginal Jew: Rethinking the Historical Jesus*, vol. I: *The Roots of the Problem and the Person* (New York: Doubleday, 1991), p. 431.
12. Meier, *A Marginal Jew*, p. 401.
13. Meier, *A Marginal Jew*, pp. 401–2.
14. E. A. Pearce and C. G. Smith, *The Hutchison World Weather Guide* (Oxford: Helicon, 2000), give monthly rainfall figures for Jerusalem (and elsewhere). However, the book incorrectly lists Jerusalem as being at an altitude of 557 m/1,485 ft. Neither is correct and the internal conversion is also wrong. The co-ordinates given for the meteorological site refer to 2 km north-west of the Temple Mount,

with an altitude of about 2,485 ft (757 m). Presumably, 757 m became incorrectly copied as 557 m.

15. John Wilkinson, *Jerusalem as Jesus Knew It* (London: Thames and Hudson, 1978). The quotation in the text is from the caption to his fig. 18.
16. The Jewish calendar had close links with the similar Babylonian lunar calendar, in which the first day of the month was also determined by observing the first crescent of the new moon. Stern states: 'It is most probable that the lunar calendar was adopted by the Jews under direct influence of the Babylonian calendar' (Stern, *Calendar and Community*, p. 29).

    The ancient Babylonians were expert astronomers who had been performing detailed astronomical calculations from well before the time of Christ. Stern writes: 'Solstices and equinoxes were calculated at least from 322 BCE.' The relevance of these calculations to false reports of seeing the new moon, and by implication the problem of a cloudy sky, is spelled out by Stern for both the Babylonian and the Jewish calendars. He writes: 'The Babylonian calendar was based not only on sightings but also on detailed calculations, which presumably eliminated, to a large extent, the incidence of false sightings. The same would apply to the early rabbinic [Jewish] calendar, when detailed interrogation of the witnesses was carried out in order to detect false sightings' (Stern, *Calendar and Community*, p. 111). Ben Zion Wacholder and David B. Weisberg ('Visibility of the New Moon in Cuneiform and Rabbinic Sources', *Hebrew Union College Annual* 42 (1971), 227–42) also point out the similarity between Babylonian and rabbinic methods of predicting the visibility of new moons.

    Many ancient civilisations relied on the moon for their monthly timekeeping. Ancient peoples would have been able to look at the moon and tell the day of the month, to within a day, from the moon's shape. Amateur astronomers can do the same today. The easiest time to do this is at half-moon time, when the moon appears as a 'D' in the sky: the precise shape of the half-moon means that this can be used to pinpoint the exact day of the month with confidence. Concerning predicting the day of the next new moon, Waddington has told me that in the first century AD the Jews would have known that a lunar month had to be either twenty-nine or thirty days long. By observing the phases of the moon in the previous month they would have been able to predict accurately the first visibility of the next crescent moon. The Babylonians had been predicting the day of the new crescent moon for many centuries previously.
17. The fact that the month had to be either twenty-nine or thirty days long is also the reason why the table 'The effect of a cloudy sky …'

does not need to have footnotes in the same way as the previous table, 'The date of Nisan 14 . . .'.

18. Meier, *A Marginal Jew*, p. 402.

5 THE DATE OF THE CRUCIFIXION

1. J. K. Fotheringham, 'The Evidence of Astronomy and Technical Chronology for the Date of the Crucifixion', *Journal of Theological Studies* 34 (1934), 146–62.
2. Robin Lane Fox, *The Unauthorised Version: Truth and Fiction in the Bible* (London: Viking, 1991), p. 34. Nikos Kokkinos, 'Crucifixion in AD 36', in *Chronos, Kairos, Christos: Nativity and Chronological Studies Presented to Jack Finegan*, ed. Jerry Vardaman and Edwin Yamauchi (Winona Lake: Eisenbrauns, 1989), pp. 133–63.
3. I. Howard Marshall, *The Gospel of Luke: A Commentary on the Greek Text* (Exeter: Paternoster Press, 1978), p. 43.
4. John P. Meier, *A Marginal Jew: Rethinking the Historical Jesus*, vol. I: *The Roots of the Problem and the Person* (New York: Doubleday, 1991), p. 384.
5. Rainer Riesner, *Paul's Early Period: Chronology, Mission Strategy, Theology* (Grand Rapids: Eerdmans, 1998), p. 40.
6. Meier, *A Marginal Jew*, p. 384.
7. Jack Finegan, *Handbook of Biblical Chronology*, revised edition (Peabody, MA: Hendrickson, 1998), pp. 340–1.
8. See, for example, Robert Jewett, *Dating Paul's Life* (London: SCM Press, 1979), pp. 99–100, and Ormond Edwards, *The Time of Christ: A Chronology of the Incarnation* (Edinburgh: Floris Books, 1986), pp. 170–4.
9. See, for example, Riesner, *Paul's Early Period*, pp. 64–71.
10. Jewett, *Dating Paul's Life*, diagram after p. 160.
11. Riesner, *Paul's Early Period*, pp. 64–71.
12. See, for example, Riesner, *Paul's Early Period* and Jewett, *Dating Paul's Life*, pp. 29–30.
13. Subsequent parts of my argument in this and the next chapter finally rule out AD 34 because AD 33 fits every feature of the available evidence, whereas AD 34 would conflict with nearly all the evidence.
14. Joachim Jeremias, *The Eucharistic Words of Jesus* (London: SCM Press, 1966), p. 41.
15. For the counting of days in the Bible, particularly between the crucifixion and the resurrection, see Chapter 2.

16. J.B. Segal, *The Hebrew Passover: From the Earliest Times to AD 70* (London: Oxford University Press, 1963), pp. 248–51. Segal states that the Sadducees interpreted the Sabbath of Leviticus 23:11 as the normal Sabbath (Friday evening to Saturday evening) which fell in Passover week. Since the barley sheaf had to be waved on 'the day after the Sabbath', the Sadducees interpreted this as the Jewish day from Saturday evening to Sunday evening that fell in Passover week. The Pharisees, on the other hand, interpreted the Sabbath of Passover week to be Nisan 15, because Leviticus 23:6–7 states, 'On the fifteenth day of that month [Nisan] the Lord's Feast of Unleavened Bread begins ... On the first day hold a sacred assembly and do no regular work.' So, as we saw in Chapter 3, Nisan 15 became known as the Sabbath of the Passover, and the Pharisees said that it was on the day after this, on Nisan 16, that the barley sheaf should be waved.
17. Finegan, *Handbook of Biblical Chronology*, p. 368.
18. Harold W. Hoehner, *Chronological Aspects of the Life of Christ* (Grand Rapids: Zondervan, 1977), pp. 45–63.
19. What date do modern biblical scholars favour for the crucifixion? The survey of Blinzler, reported in Chapter 2, showed that about 50 per cent supported AD 30 and about 25 per cent chose AD 33. Why do the majority of biblical scholars favour AD 30 over AD 33? Some scholars, for example Riesner, argue that the fifteenth year of the reign of Tiberius should be reckoned from Tiberius' joint rule with Augustus in AD 12, which means that John the Baptist started his ministry in AD 26/27, which is then compatible with the crucifixion of Jesus being in AD 30 (Riesner, *Paul's Early Period*, p. 40). However, as I have shown, there is no evidence to support this way of counting, whereas there is clear evidence that the fifteenth year of the reign of Tiberius should be counted from his appointment as the new emperor on September 17, AD 14.

    Other scholars, for example Meier, accept that the fifteenth year of the reign of Tiberius should be counted from his appointment on September 17, AD 14, but then he writes, 'We see that the fifteenth year of Tiberius could have included at least parts of AD 27, 28 or 29' (Meier, *A Marginal Jew*, pp. 385–6). Meier then hypothesises that Jesus began his ministry very early in AD 28, with the first Passover of his ministry in the spring of AD 28 and the crucifixion in the spring of AD 30. The problem with this analysis is that if Tiberius was appointed on September 17, AD 14, then his fifteenth year could not have included 'part of AD 27' using any reasonable calendar, Roman, Jewish religious or Jewish civil (see the table on p. 65 on the fifteenth year of Tiberius). Hence the first Passover of

Jesus' ministry could not have been as early as the spring of AD 28. I therefore believe the arguments of those who support an AD 30 crucifixion should be rejected, leaving April 3, AD 33 as the only possible date for the crucifixion.

20. Hoehner, *Chronological Aspects of the Life of Christ*, p. 23.
21. Hoehner, *Chronological Aspects of the Life of Christ*, p. 25.
22. Paul L. Maier, 'The Date of the Nativity and the Chronology of Jesus' Life', in *Chronos, Kairos, Christos*, ed. Vardaman and Yamauchi, p. 122.
23. Colin J. Humphreys, 'The Star of Bethlehem – a Comet in 5 BC – and the Date of the Birth of Christ', *Quarterly Journal of the Royal Astronomical Society* 32 (1991), 389–407. See also Humphreys, 'The Star of Bethlehem, a Comet in 5 BC and the Date of Christ's Birth', *Tyndale Bulletin*, 43.1 (1992), 31–56.
24. Finegan, *Handbook of Biblical Chronology*, p. 347.
25. F. F. Bruce, *The Gospel of John* (Grand Rapids: Eerdmans, 1983), p. 76.
26. Finegan, *Handbook of Biblical Chronology*, p. 348.
27. Edwards, *The Time of Christ*, pp. 127–8.
28. R. T. France, *The Gospel of Mark* (Grand Rapids: Eerdmans, 2002), pp. 437–8.
29. France, *The Gospel of Mark*, p. 438.
30. There is a possible piece of evidence that I have not discussed so far in this chapter. A few scholars (for example, Kokkinos, 'Crucifixion in AD 36') presume that John the Baptist died in AD 35, and since the gospels report that he died before Jesus (for example, Mark 6:14–29) they place the crucifixion in AD 36. Both Mark 6:14–29 and Josephus (*Antiquities* 18.117) record that Herod Antipas killed John the Baptist. Some time later, Herod Antipas was defeated in battle by Aretus in AD 36, and Josephus states that some of the Jews attributed his defeat to revenge by God for the beheading of John the Baptist (*Antiquities* 18.116–19). Kokkinos and others argue that the revenge of God would have been swift, so that if Herod Antipas was defeated in AD 36 then he must have killed John the Baptist shortly before this, in AD 35. However, as Hoehner points out (*Chronological Aspects of the Life of Christ*, p. 101), Josephus does not imply such a short interval of time at all, and clearly indicates that it was a series of *other* incidents (Herod Antipas getting rid of his first wife – it should be noted she was Aretus' daughter – boundary disputes, etc.) which finally led to war. As Hoehner says: 'This theory [of John the Baptist being beheaded in AD 35] makes havoc of the Gospels' chronology, whereas if one follows the Gospels' chronological framework one can fit in the events in Josephus very easily.' In addition, our reconstructed Jewish calendar shows that neither AD 35 nor 36 could have been the year of the crucifixion.

6 THE MOON WILL BE TURNED TO BLOOD

1. C. K. Barrett, *The Acts of the Apostles: A Shorter Commentary* (London and New York: T&T Clark, 2002), pp. 24–5.
2. The interpretation that Peter saw recent events as a fulfilment of the whole of Joel's prophecy does not exclude the possibility that he may have regarded them also as a foretaste of a greater fulfilment in the future, when Christ returned.
3. F. F. Bruce, *The Book of the Acts*, revised edition (Grand Rapids: Eerdmans, 1988), p. 61. The phrase 'In the last days' is used in Hebrews: 'In the past God spoke to our forefathers through the prophets at many times and in various ways, but *in these last days* he has spoken to us by his Son' (Hebrews 1:1). In his speech on the day of Pentecost, Peter is similarly saying that 'the last days' started with the coming of Jesus.
4. Bruce, *The Book of the Acts*, pp. 61–2.
5. Leviticus 23:15 and 16 spell out how the day of Pentecost was calculated: 'From the day after the Sabbath [of the Passover, the Sabbath of the Passover being Nisan 15], the day you brought the sheaf [of barley] of the wave offering [Nisan 16], count off seven full weeks. Count off fifty days up to the day after the seventh Sabbath and then present an offering of new grain [wheat] to the Lord.'

   The day of Pentecost was a first-fruits festival of the wheat harvest on which two leavened loaves made from new wheat and yeast were waved in the temple by the priests. The produce of the wheat harvest could not be eaten until this happened. Just as the offering of a sheaf of barley on Nisan 16 marked the beginning of the barley harvest season, so the offering of loaves made from new wheat marked the beginning of the wheat harvest. The length of time involved – seven weeks of seven days – is a 'perfect' period of time, seven being regarded as a special perfect number. The Feast of Pentecost was also called the 'feast of weeks' (e.g. Exodus 34:22; Deuteronomy 16:10) because it was held exactly seven weeks after the waving of the sheaf of barley.

   It turns out that for the only two possible dates for the crucifixion, April 7, AD 30 and April 3, AD 33, Nisan 16 falls on a Sunday. Fifty days, counting inclusively, after Sunday, Nisan 16 leads to another Sunday. The tradition of the church of celebrating the giving of the Holy Spirit on a Sunday, called Whit Sunday, is therefore correct.
6. William Neil, *The Acts of the Apostles* (London: Oliphants, 1973), p. 75.
7. Bruce, *The Book of the Acts*, p. 62.
8. Colin Humphreys, *The Miracles of Exodus* (San Francisco: Harper San Francisco; London: Continuum, 2003), pp. 134–6.

9. J. H. Charlesworth, *The Old Testament Pseudepigrapha*, 2 vols. (London: Darton, Longman and Todd, 1983), vol. I, pp. 354–80. The original Sibylline Oracles were written by prophetic priestesses (the Sibyls) and date back to the sixth century BC. However, most or all of the original Oracles were destroyed by fire, and the Sibylline Oracles we now possess are probably a collection of oracles written by Jewish and Christian authors in imitation of the pagan Sibylline Oracles. Charlesworth dates the portion of the Oracles I have quoted to 163–145 BC. However, it is known that the Oracles contain later Christian additions. If the above quotation is pre-Christian then it indicates that dust-storms can blot out the sun. If it is a Christian addition then it may suggest an early tradition that the darkness at noon at the crucifixion was due to a dust-storm.
10. Robert Hanbury Brown, *The Land of Goshen and the Exodus* (London: E. Stanford, 1919), p. 60.
11. M. R. James, *The Apocryphal New Testament* (Oxford: Oxford University Press, 1924), p. 154.
12. Tertullian, *Apologeticum* 5 and 21.
13. P. E. Pusey, *Cyrilli Archiepiscopi Alexandrini In XII Prophetas*, vol. I (1868), pp. 341–2, cited by G. R. Driver, 'Two Problems in the New Testament', *Journal of Theological Studies* 16 (1965), 334–5.
14. An eclipse of the moon occurs at full moon time when the earth is between the moon and the sun. The moon is in the earth's shadow, and one therefore might expect the moon to look black, or to be invisible against the night sky. However, some sunlight does fall on the moon because the light rays from the sun are bent around the earth by the earth's atmosphere (fig. 6.1; this bending is termed 'refraction').

    When the light rays from the sun pass through the earth's atmosphere, they are scattered by the air molecules they encounter. This preferentially removes the shorter (blue) wavelengths of light, which is why the sky looks blue.

    At sunset, the sun is just above the horizon and the light reaching us from the sun has had to travel through a greater thickness of the earth's atmosphere than when the sun is overhead. Hence even more light is scattered, not just blue, but also green, yellow and orange, and only red light is left. This is why the setting (or rising) sun looks red. At a lunar eclipse, the light from the sun reaching the moon is red because the sunlight has passed through a particularly long length of the earth's atmosphere. The moon then reflects back to earth the red light that strikes it and we see the eclipsed moon as blood-red. The actual colour of the moon during a lunar eclipse varies according to the atmospheric conditions on earth. Sometimes the moon is almost black, but often it is deep red: the colour of blood.

15. Bruce, *The Book of the Acts*, p. 62.
16. Let me mention some of the problems involved in calculating ancient eclipses. We have to wind back in time the equations that describe the motion of the moon around the earth and the earth around the sun. However, we must also take into account the speed at which the earth spins around on its axis, because this determines the places on earth from where an eclipse will be seen. Scientists used to believe that the earth's rate of rotation on its axis was constant, but we now know this is not the case. One problem is due to tidal friction. As tidal water flows across the bottom of the ocean, and up and down the seashore, energy is lost due to friction, hence the earth's rotation is slowing and our days are lengthening. Indeed, one day, far in the future, our earth will totally stop rotating. So the sand on the seashore is controlling the sands of time. Scientists can calculate the change of rotation of the earth due to tidal friction, and take it into account when calculating eclipses.

    However, there is another effect that scientists cannot yet calculate. The melting of polar icecaps changes the rate of rotation of the earth. As we go back in time there have been a number of ice ages, and mini ice ages, but we do not know in detail how the polar icecaps have varied with time. However, in a number of cases the time, date and place of observation of the same ancient eclipse have been recorded in several different texts, for example from Babylon and China. If all the sources describing the same ancient eclipse are consistent, then we can have confidence in them. We can then use this eclipse as a 'marker eclipse'. By using a number of such marker eclipses we can find out from eclipse calculations how the earth's rate of rotation must have varied going back in time. Having established in this way how the speed of rotation of the earth has varied in the past, we can then use this knowledge to perform calculations for other eclipses. We can cover the period from 700 BC to the present using this technique (it is difficult to rely on the accuracy of eclipse records before about 700 BC).
17. F. Richard Stephenson and David H. Clark, *Applications of Early Astronomical Records* (London: Adam Hilger, 1978), pp. 36–59. F. Richard Stephenson, *Historical Eclipses and Earth's Rotation* (Cambridge: Cambridge University Press, 1997).
18. Colin J. Humphreys and W. G. Waddington, 'Dating the Crucifixion', *Nature* 306 (1983), 743–6.
19. Colin J. Humphreys and W. G. Waddington, 'Astronomy and the Date of the Crucifixion', in *Chronos, Kairos, Christos: Nativity and Chronological Studies Presented to Jack Finegan*, ed. J. Vardaman and E. M. Yamauchi (Winona Lake: Eisenbrauns, 1989), pp. 165–81.

7 DID JESUS USE THE SOLAR CALENDAR OF QUMRAN FOR HIS LAST SUPPER PASSOVER?

1. Pope Benedict XVI's Holy Thursday Homily entitled 'Jesus is the New and True Lamb' was delivered on Easter Thursday, April 6, 2007 for the Mass of the Lord's Supper, celebrated in the Basilica of St John Lateran. My quotations are from the Zenit News Agency website, zenit.org, based in Vatican City.
2. Nearly all scholars believe that the Qumran community were members of a Jewish group called the Essenes. See James C. VanderKam and Peter Flint, *The Meaning of the Dead Sea Scrolls: Their Significance for Understanding the Bible, Judaism, Jesus and Christianity* (London: T&T Clark International, 2002), pp. 239–54.
3. Shemaryahu Talmon, 'Calendar Controversy in Ancient Judaism: The Case of the Community of the Renewed Covenant,' in *The Provo International Conference on the Dead Sea Scrolls: Technological Innovations, New Texts, and Reformulated Issues*, ed. Donald W. Parry and Eugene Ulrich (Leiden: Brill, 1999), pp. 379–85, at pp. 380–1.
4. The Damascus Document proclaims that whoever desired to return to the law of Moses must observe the 'book of the division of time' (Damascus Document 16.1–5), almost certainly a reference to the book of Jubilees. The Damascus Document further states that the whole of Israel had become blind because it had departed from the original calendar of Moses (Damascus Document 3.13–15). Large fragments of the Damascus Document were originally found in Egypt, in the Cairo Geniza, a room adjoining a synagogue in Old Cairo in which ancient documents were stored. Later, fragments of the Damascus Document were found in several caves in Qumran. Scholars date the text from the first century BC to the first century AD.
5. Y. Yadin, *The Temple Scroll*, 4 vols. (Jerusalem: Israel Exploration Society, 1983), vol. I, pp. 116–19.
6. Emil Schürer, *The History of the Jewish People in the Age of Jesus Christ: 175 BC – AD 135*, revised edition, ed. G. Vermes and F. G. B. Millar, with M. Black (eds. vols. I–II) and M. Goodman (vol. III), (Edinburgh: T&T Clark, 1987), vol. III, pp. 256 and 308–18. Jubilees, written in Hebrew, claims that its contents were directly revealed to Moses by an angel. Jubilees was widely circulated and we have found manuscripts translated into Greek, Ethiopic, Latin and Syriac. A major theme of Jubilees is that the official Jewish calendar used by the priests of the temple was *not* the calendar instituted by Moses, and that the priests were therefore committing the grave error of commemorating festivals on the wrong days.

Jubilees condemns those who use the official Jewish lunar calendar, 'For there are those who shall base their observations on the moon – even though it disorders the seasons and arrives from year to year ten days too soon. They shall make of a detestable day a day of witness, of an impure day a day of festival ... They shall be in error regarding the new moons, the seasons, the Sabbaths and the festivals' (Jubilees 6:35–38). A number of other Jewish writings, including 1 Enoch and the Damascus Document, also reject the official Jewish calendar. Most scholars believe that the documents found in the caves of Qumran had been used by the Qumran Community between about 100 BC and AD 68.

7. VanderKam and Flint, *The Meaning of the Dead Sea Scrolls*, pp. 198–9. Jubilees used 1 Enoch as a source (see, for example, O. S. Wintermute, 'Jubilees: A New Translation and Introduction', in *The Old Testament Pseudepigrapha*, ed. James H. Charlesworth, 2 vols. (New York: Doubleday, 1985), vol. II, pp. 49–50).
8. VanderKam and Flint, *The Meaning of the Dead Sea Scrolls*, p. 199. 1 Enoch and Jubilees are not accepted as part of the Bible by either Roman Catholics or Protestants.
9. Wintermute, *Jubilees*, pp. 43–4.
10. M. Black, J. C. VanderKam and O. Neugebauer, *The Book of Enoch: A New English Edition* (Leiden: Brill, 1985). See particularly Appendix A by Neugebauer on *The Book of the Heavenly Lights*, pp. 386–419.
11. E. Isaac, *1 Enoch: A New Translation and Introduction*, in *The Old Testament Pseudepigrapha*, ed. Charlesworth, vol. I, p. 7.
12. Wayne Horowitz, 'The 360 and 364 Day Year in Ancient Mesopotamia', *Journal of the Ancient Near Eastern Society of Columbia University* 24 (1996), 34–42, at 41.
13. We do not know if the Qumran community, or the writers of Jubilees or 1 Enoch, read the early chapters of Genesis literally or not. Genesis 1 was read figuratively by some people long before the rise of modern science.
14. Annie Jaubert, *La date de la cène* (EBib; Paris: Gabalda, 1957). A number of scholars misinterpret the solar calendar of the Qumran community and say that the Passover meal was held on Wednesday. This is wrong. As Jaubert shows, it was held on Nisan 14, which was always a Tuesday, because Nisan 1 was always a Wednesday. See also Martin G. Abegg, 'Does Anyone Really Know What Time It Is: A Reexamination of 4Q503 in Light of 4Q317', in *The Provo International Conference on the Dead Sea Scrolls*, pp. 396–406, at p. 397.
15. Talmon, 'Calendar Controversy in Ancient Judaism', p. 387. See also the discussion on the problem of intercalation by VanderKam in the *Anchor Bible Dictionary*, vol. I, pp. 819–20.

16. Roger T. Beckwith, *Calendar and Chronology, Jewish and Christian: Biblical, Intertestamental, and Patristic Studies* (Leiden: Brill, 2001), pp. 93–140.
17. E.J. Bickerman, *Chronology of the Ancient World*, revised edition (London: Thames and Hudson, 1980), p. 24. Some commentators say that Abib means young ears of corn rather than barley, but since corn and barley ripen at similar times, both interpretations refer to the same time in the solar year.
18. Unfortunately we do not know when the Qumran community started to use their calendar, but we can make a rough estimate of the time the community was established. The first Dead Sea Scrolls were found in 1947 by a Bedouin shepherd, who threw a rock into a cave at Qumran, heard the crash of an earthenware jar shattering, went in to explore, and found the scrolls (John C. Trevor, *The Untold Story of Qumran* (Westwood, NJ: Revell, 1965), pp. 103–4). Excavations at Qumran started in 1949, led by Roland de Vaux (VanderKam and Flint, *The Meaning of the Dead Sea Scrolls*, pp. 34–41). More recently, Professor Jodi Magness has offered a revised chronology of the site that is now widely accepted. She argues that the Qumran community settled in Qumran some time in the first half of the first century BC. They did not leave following the earthquake in 31 BC, but stayed and repaired the damaged buildings. The community left in about 9/8 BC following a violent fire, and returned and repaired the site early in the reign of Herod Archelaus, which was from 4 BC to AD 6, leaving when the Romans destroyed the site in AD 68. (Jodi Magness, *The Archaeology of Qumran and the Dead Sea Scrolls* (Grand Rapids: Eerdmans, 2002). See also VanderKam and Flint, *The Meaning of the Dead Sea Scrolls*, pp. 50–1.)
19. J. Edward Wright, *The Early History of Heaven* (Oxford: Oxford University Press, 2000), p. 19.
20. Coffin Text §159. In R.O. Faulkner, *The Ancient Egyptian Coffin Texts*, 3 vols. (Oxford: Aris and Phillips, 1973), vol. I, pp. 137–8; also in J.B. Pritchard (ed.), *Ancient Near Eastern Texts Relating to the Old Testament*, third edition (Princeton: Princeton University Press, 1969), p. 33.
21. For example, Anatolius, Bishop of Laodicea in Syria, wrote in *Canons of the Passover* in about AD 270: 'this [the rule of the equinox that Passover must fall after the spring equinox] is not our own reckoning, but it was known to Jews long ago even before Christ and it was carefully observed by them, as witness Philo, Josephus and Musaeus … when these writers explain questions concerning the Exodus, they say that it is necessary that all alike sacrifice the Passover after the vernal equinox, in the middle of the first month'.

8 DOES ANCIENT EGYPT HOLD A KEY TO UNLOCKING THE PROBLEM OF THE LAST SUPPER?

1. E. J. Bickerman, *Chronology of the Ancient World,* revised edition (London: Thames and Hudson, 1980), p. 24.
2. Bickerman, *Chronology of the Ancient World,* p. 24.
3. Sacha Stern, *Calendar and Community: A History of the Jewish Calendar 2nd Century* BCE – *10th Century* CE (Oxford: Oxford University Press, 2001), p. 28.
4. Scholars hold a wide range of views on the account of Moses and the Exodus recorded in the Bible but a discussion of this is outside the scope of this book. However, of particular interest is the origin of the pre-exilic calendar recorded in the book of Exodus.
5. Cornelis Houtman, *Exodus,* 2 vols. (Kampan: Kok Publishing, 1996), vol. II, p. 167.
6. Colin J. Humphreys, *The Miracles of Exodus* (San Francisco: Harper San Francisco; London: Continuum, 2003), pp. 130–45.
7. Humphreys, *The Miracles of Exodus,* pp. 131–4.
8. Richard A. Parker, *The Calendars of Ancient Egypt* (Chicago: University of Chicago Press, 1950).
9. Marshall Clagett, *Ancient Egyptian Science,* 3 vols. (Philadelphia: American Philosophical Society, 1995), vol. II: *Calendars, Clocks and Astronomy.*
10. Clagett, *Ancient Egyptian Science,* vol. II, p. 7.
11. Clagett, *Ancient Egyptian Science,* vol. II, pp. 280–1 and 285–6.
12. Parker, *The Calendars of Ancient Egypt,* pp. 13–23.
13. Otto Neugebauer, *A History of Ancient Mathematical Astronomy,* 3 vols. (Berlin: Springer, 1975), vol. II, p. 563, n. 3. It may also be worth mentioning that the atmosphere is clearer just before dawn than just after sunset, so last crescent observations are 'easier' than first crescent ones.
14. See, for example, Humphreys, *The Miracles of Exodus,* pp. 28–38.
15. Clagett, *Ancient Egyptian Science,* vol. II, pp. 253–4.
16. Clagett, *Ancient Egyptian Science,* vol. II, p. 268.
17. Clagett, *Ancient Egyptian Science,* vol. II, p. 269.
18. Clagett, *Ancient Egyptian Science,* vol. II, pp. 285–7.
19. There is also some evidence for a different Egyptian lunar calendar from an astronomical Egyptian text known as Papyrus Carlsberg 9, which was written in or after AD 144 (Parker, *The Calendars of Ancient Egypt,* p. 13). It is possible to deduce from this papyrus that this later lunar calendar was probably introduced in the fourth century BC. Since

this calendar is unlikely to have been used in pre-exilic times I will not consider it further (Parker, *The Calendars of Ancient Egypt*, p. 29). See also Leo Depuydt, *Civil Calendar and Lunar Calendar in Ancient Egypt* (Leuven: Peeters, 1997).

20. J. B. Segal, *The Hebrew Passover: From the Earliest Times to* AD *70* (London: Oxford University Press, 1963), p. 131.
21. Bickerman, *Chronology of the Ancient World*, p. 40. Also Clagett, *Ancient Egyptian Science*, vol. II, pp. 4–7.
22. Nahum Sarna, *Exploring Exodus* (New York: Schocken, 1996), pp. 81–2.

9 DISCOVERING THE LOST CALENDAR OF ANCIENT ISRAEL

1. E. J. Bickerman, *Chronology of the Ancient World*, revised edition (London: Thames and Hudson, 1980), p. 24.
2. Sacha Stern, *Calendar and Community: A History of the Jewish Calendar 2nd Century* BCE *– 10th Century* CE (Oxford: Oxford University Press, 2001), p. 28.
3. Marshall Clagett, *Ancient Egyptian Science*, 3 vols. (Philadelphia: American Philosophical Society, 1995), vol. II: *Calendars, Clocks and Astronomy*, pp. 7–22.
4. Nahum Sarna, *Exploring Exodus* (New York: Schocken, 1996), p. 82.
5. Jack Finegan, *Handbook of Biblical Chronology*, revised edition (Peabody, MA: Hendrickson, 1998), p. 7.
6. Jan Wagenaar, 'Passover and the First Day of the Festival of Unleavened Bread in the Priestly Festival Calendar', *Vetus Testamentum* 54 (2004), 250–68, at 263.
7. Nina L. Collins, 'The Start of the Pre-Exilic Calendar Day of David and the Amalekites: A Note on 1 Samuel XXX 17', *Vetus Testamentum* 41 (1991), 203–10. The correct interpretation of 1 Samuel 30:17 has been the subject of considerable debate among scholars. Nina Collins says that the text makes perfect sense as it stands if the calendar day of David started at dawn and that of the Amalekites started in the evening. The passage then may thus be understood: 'And David fought them [the Amalekites], from twilight just before dawn, until soon after sunset in the evening, following the start of their [i.e., the Amalekites'] new calendar day.'
8. Roland de Vaux, *Les institutions de l'Ancient Testament* (Paris: Les Editions du Cerf, 1958), pp. 275–8, trans. John McHugh *Ancient Israel: Its Life and Institutions* (London: Darton, Longman and Todd, 1961 and

Grand Rapids: Eerdmans, 1997), pp. 180–3. De Vaux writes: 'When they [the pre-exilic Israelites] wanted to indicate the whole day of twenty-four hours, they said "day and night", putting the day first: scores of references could be quoted (Deuteronomy 28:66–67; 1 Samuel 30:12; Isaiah 28:19; Jeremiah 32:20, etc.). This suggests that they reckoned their day starting from the morning ... [However], in the latest books in the Old Testament the expression "day and night" is reversed: Judith praises God "night and day" (Judith 11:17); Esther asks for a fast of three days "night and day" (Esther 4:16); Daniel speaks of 2,300 "evenings and mornings" (Daniel 8:14).'

9. Scholars give various interpretations of 'between the two evenings' (see Houtman, *Exodus*, vol. II, p. 175). It may mean the late afternoon, between the decline of the sun and sunset, but it probably means between sunset and the first stars appearing. Confirmation, in Old Testament times, that the killing of the lambs commenced at sunset (a clear boundary) may be indicated in Deuteronomy: 'There you must sacrifice the Passover in the evening, when the sun goes down' (Deuteronomy 16:6). The coming of darkness is of course a gradual event. Jewish rabbis held that the evening could be extended until the first stars appeared (another clear boundary). They cited Nehemiah 4:21: 'So we continued the work with half the men holding spears, from the first light of dawn [in the morning] till the stars came out [in the evening]' as evidence that the day could be taken to end either at sunset or when the first stars came out. The phrase 'between the two evenings' then refers to the time between sunset and the first stars appearing (two clear boundaries), typically about eighty minutes for Jerusalem. The new crescent moon is only visible in this period between the two evenings (see Chapter 4), and hence the start of the *first* day of each new month in the Jewish calendar was when the first stars appeared, rather than at sunset (however, the other days in the month started at sunset). Interestingly, 'twilight' is defined by modern astronomers to be the same period of time between sunset and the first stars appearing.

   As we have seen, at the time of Christ, Josephus writes that the first Passover lambs were killed at 3 p.m., so if originally the sacrifice of the lambs started at sunset then at some point in Jewish history the slaughtering of the first lambs was brought forward from sunset to 3 p.m., almost certainly because of the large numbers of lambs to be killed. Josephus states (*Jewish Wars* 6.425) that at Passover time in the first century AD the temporary population of Jerusalem could swell to almost 3 million people. Jeremias reduces this figure to a more realistic 180,000 (*Jerusalem in the Time of Jesus* (London: SCM Press, 1969), pp. 83f). If we assume that about ten people could share the meat of one lamb then about 18,000 lambs would have to be slain in the temple at Passover time. This would have been a huge logistical problem (see Mishnah *Pesahim*) and the eighty minutes of twilight is unlikely to have been long enough to kill this number of lambs, for the priests to catch their blood in basins, etc. (see *Pesahim*). Hence it is easy to see why, by the first century AD, the slaughtering of the lambs had been brought forward to 3 p.m. in order to provide more time to sacrifice the large numbers of lambs involved.

10. Wagenaar, 'Passover and the First Day of the Festival of Unleavened Bread', p. 250. Wagenaar appreciates that the Israelites had a sunrise-to-sunrise day before the exile, and a sunset-to-sunset day after. He also suggests that the pre-exilic calendar of Israel was based upon the Egyptian lunar calendar (Wagenaar, 'Passover and the First Day of the Festival of Unleavened Bread', 262–6).
11. Parker, *The Calendars of Ancient Egypt*, pp. 58–9.
12. It is difficult to date very precisely the Hebrew in the book of Exodus because we have too little ancient Hebrew outside of the Bible. However, experts in ancient Hebrew are agreed that the Hebrew in the book of Exodus as we have it today corresponds to its being in its final form hundreds of years after the time of Moses. The actual date is the subject of considerable debate. For example Professor Alan Millard, the Emeritus Professor of Hebrew and Ancient Semitic Languages at the University of Liverpool, suggests that the date of the present book of Exodus is likely to be before the Exile because the Hebrew language used in it shows no traces of Aramaic influence. On the other hand, the language is not so archaic as to date from the time of Moses (probably in the thirteenth century BC). Millard believes an older text was 'modernised', probably in the eighth to seventh centuries BC (Alan R. Millard, 'How Reliable Is Exodus?', *Biblical Archaeology Review* 26.4 (2000), 51–7).

    Kenneth Kitchen states: 'Thus we should consider a Moses or a Joshua writing on papyrus, skins, or even waxed tablets ... Copies [of originals] would be recopied, modernising outdated grammatical forms and spellings, a process universal in the ancient Near East during the period from 2500 BC to Greco-Roman times ... literary recopying was an art practiced throughout the ancient Near East for three thousand years ... Experienced scribes at their best were able to transmit very accurate copies of works for centuries, and to modernise archaic usage if called upon. Egyptian, Mesopotamian ... and other texts exemplify all this' (K. A. Kitchen, *On the Reliability of the Old Testament* (Grand Rapids: Eerdmans, 2003), p. 305).

I am aware that, to some readers, to suggest that the Pentateuch (the first five books of the Bible) reached their final form long after the death of Moses may seem to challenge their authenticity. I would like to assure such readers that this is not the case. The events described in the Pentateuch cover many centuries and so inevitably some of these events must have been finally written down many centuries after they occurred. What I am saying is that the evidence suggests that *all* the reports in the Pentateuch were edited in their final form many centuries after the events occurred. The important question is not *when* this final editing occurred, but whether the events described in the Pentateuch have been faithfully transmitted over many centuries, down to the final editing. Many scholars believe the Pentateuch was put together from four major literary sources. This approach is known as the Documentary Hypothesis. Several of my conclusions fit well with the usual view of P (the Priestly writer).

13. Bo Reicke, *The New Testament Era: The World of the Bible from 500 BC to AD 100*, trans. David E. Green (London: A. & C. Black, 1968), p. 179. I interpret 'The Lord's Passover begins at twilight on the fourteenth day of the first month' (Leviticus 23:5) as referring to the Passover sacrifice which begins at twilight on the fourteenth day. The Passover meal is then eaten on the fifteenth day, coinciding with the first day of the Feast of Unleavened Bread (Leviticus 23:6), using an evening-to-evening day. Similarly, Numbers 28:16, 'On the fourteenth day of the first month the Lord's Passover is to be held,' refers to the Passover sacrifice. The Passover meal is eaten on the fifteenth day (Numbers 28:17), the first day of the Festival of Unleavened Bread.
14. For example, Keil writes: 'The Passover [in Ezekiel] is to be celebrated in the manner appointed in Exodus 12, with the paschal meal in the evening of the 14th Abib [Nisan]' (C. F. Keil, *Biblical Commentary on the Prophecies of Ezekiel*, 2 vols. (Edinburgh: T&T Clark, 1876), vol. II, p. 336). Cooke writes: 'Many [biblical scholars] think that *fourteenth* [in Ezekiel] has been altered to agree with P [the Priestly source of Exodus 12], and that the original reading was *fifteenth* ... but this is to remove a feature of interest, which shows that the *fourteenth* was too firmly fixed in tradition to be altered' (G. A. Cooke, *The Book of Ezekiel* (Edinburgh: T&T Clark, 1936), p. 503). Cooke is saying here that it is unlikely that the text of Ezekiel was revised to agree with the Priestly source; rather, celebrating the Passover Feast on the fourteenth day was firmly fixed in tradition despite the instructions in Numbers and Leviticus to hold this feast on the fifteenth day.
15. Carl G. Howie, *Ezekiel, Daniel* (Westminster: John Knox, 1961), p. 84.
16. Walther Zimmerli writes: 'There is an obscurity in the reckoning of days [for the Passover in Ezekiel] ... Must one really acknowledge that

here, intentionally, a different reckoning is intended which advances the festival [Passover and the Feast of Unleavened Bread] by a day?' Walther Zimmerli, *A Commentary on the Book of the Prophet Ezekiel Chapters 25–48*, trans. James D. Martin (Philadelphia: Fortress Press, 1983), p. 485.

17. Ezekiel 37:24–28 refers to a rebuilt sanctuary and a future David (taken to be the Messiah) leading God's people to follow his laws. See E. P. Sanders, *Jesus and Judaism* (London: SCM Press, 1985), pp. 77–90, and R. T. France, *The Gospel of Mark* (Grand Rapids: Eerdmans; Carlisle: Paternoster, 2002), p. 438.

10 WAS THE LOST ANCIENT JEWISH CALENDAR USED IN ISRAEL AT THE TIME OF JESUS?

1. Menachem Mor, 'The Persian, Hellenistic and Hasmonaean Period', in *The Samaritans*, ed. Alan D. Crown (Tübingen: Mohr Siebeck, 1989), p. 1.
2. *The Anchor Bible Dictionary*, 1992, vol. v, p. 941. The Samaritans claim that many of them survived the destruction of the northern kingdom of Israel by the Assyrians in 722 BC. The inscription of the Assyrian king Sargon II records the deportation of a relatively small proportion of the Israelites, 27,290, so it is likely that a significant population remained in Samaria, and hence the Samaritans regard themselves as true Israelites.
3. Josephus, *Antiquities*, 9.277–91.
4. Mor, 'Samaritan History', p. 2.
5. G. W. Ahlström, 'The Origin of Israel in Palestine', *Scandinavian Journal of the Old Testament* 2 (1991), 19–34.
6. Sylvia Powels, 'The Samaritan Calendar and the Roots of Samaritan Chronology', in *The Samaritans*, ed. Crown, pp. 691–742.
7. Powels, 'The Samaritan Calendar', p. 693.
8. *Taulida* 2:2–6. The *Taulida* also contains genealogical lists from Adam until the entry of the Israelites into Canaan, and of subsequent Samaritan families of high priests.
9. Powels, 'The Samaritan Calendar', p. 700.
10. Powels, 'The Samaritan Calendar', p. 700.
11. Abu'l-Hasan as-Suri, 'Kitab al-Tabbakh, Rylands Samaritan Codex IX', *Bulletin of the John Rylands Library* 30 (1946/47), 144–56. In about the twelfth century AD, the Samaritan scholar Abu'l-Hasan as-Suri explained that 'fixing the first of each month according to the conjunction is the only way of arriving at the true beginning of each month, as the conjunction signifies the real, new moon, whereas the

later new lunar crescent differs only in degree from the moon's later phases (half-moon, full-moon, etc) during the month'.

12. Heinrich Brugsch, *Matériaux pour servir à la reconstruction du calendrier des anciens égyptiens* (Leipzig: J. C. Hinrichs, 1864). See also Marshall Clagett, *Ancient Egyptian Science*, 3 vols. (Philadelphia: American Philosophical Society, 1995), vol. II, pp. 280–1 and 285–6.
13. Powels, 'The Samaritan Calendar', p. 721.
14. Powels, 'The Samaritan Calendar', p. 723.
15. Powels, 'The Samaritan Calendar', p. 705, reproduces part of the Samaritan calendar for AD 1971–72 and shows that mostly the Samaritan calendar was one day ahead of the official Jewish calendar, but in the month corresponding to July it was two days ahead.
16. Bruce Hall, 'From John Hyrcanus to Baba Rabbah', in *The Samaritans*, ed. Crown, pp. 36–7.
17. *The Anchor Bible Dictionary*, vol. V, p. 941.
18. *The Anchor Bible Dictionary*, vol. V, pp. 941–2; Josephus, *Antiquities* 13.254–6.
19. Joachim Jeremias, *Die Passahfeier der Samaritanar* (Giessen: Töpelmann, 1932), p. 56.
20. Reinhard Pummer, 'Samaritan Rituals and Customs', in *The Samaritans*, ed. Crown, p. 679.
21. John Wilson, *The Lands of the Bible*, 2 vols. (Edinburgh: William Whyte, 1847), p. 66.
22. Amnon K'fir, *Israel Travel*, 05.02.07.
23. Sacha Stern, *Calendar and Community: A History of the Jewish Calendar 2nd Century* BCE *– 10th Century* CE (Oxford: Oxford University Press, 2001), p. 13.
24. S. Talmon and I. Knohl, 'A Calendrical Scroll from a Qumran Cave: Mismarot Ba, 4Q321', in *Pomegranates and Golden Bells: Studies in Biblical, Jewish and Near Eastern Ritual, Law and Literature in Honour of Jacob Milgrom*, ed. D. P. Wright, D. N. Freedman and A. Hurvitz (Winona Lake: Eisenbrauns, 1995), pp. 297–8.
25. *The Anchor Bible Dictionary*, vol. VI, pp. 1045–50.
26. I. Howard Marshall, *The Gospel of Luke: A Commentary on the Greek Text* (Exeter: Paternoster Press, 1978), p. 240. F. F. Bruce, *The Acts of the Apostles* (Leicester: Inter-Varsity Press, 1952), p. 73.
27. Josephus, *War* 5.99 states: 'When the day of unleavened bread came round on the fourteenth of the month Xanthicus, the reputed anniversary of the Jews' first liberation from Egypt, Eleazar and his men partly opened the gates and admitted citizens desiring to worship within the building [the Jerusalem temple].' The context of this statement is that in the spring of AD 70 three different Jewish groups were fighting

to control the Jerusalem temple. The Eleazar mentioned here was Eleazar ben Simon, the leader of the Jewish group called the Zealots. Xanthicus is the name of the month in the Macedonian calendar that is equivalent to Nisan in the Hebrew calendar. Josephus states: 'Moses, however, appointed Nisan, that is to say Xanthicus, as the first month for the festivals, because it was in this month that he brought the Hebrews out of Egypt' (*Antiquities* 1.81).

The statement of Josephus in *War* 5.99, that the day the Jews left Egypt was on the *fourteenth* of Xanthicus [Nisan], is curious because elsewhere Josephus states: 'They left Egypt in the month of Xanthicus, on the *fifteenth* by lunar reckoning' (*Antiquities* 2.318). Similarly the statement in *War* 5.99 that the day of unleavened bread was on the *fourteenth* of Xanthicus [Nisan] is curious because elsewhere Josephus states: 'On the *fifteenth* the Passover is followed up by the Feast of Unleavened Bread' (*Antiquities* 3.249).

Josephus was a Pharisee and he would have been taught from birth that in the official Jewish calendar the Jews left Egypt on Nisan 15, and hence that the first day of the Feast of Unleavened Bread, which commemorated this, was on Nisan 15. Why then did Josephus state in *War* 5.99 that the Jews left Egypt on Xanthicus [Nisan] 14, the 'reputed anniversary' of the Jews' first liberation from Egypt? Reputed by whom? Clearly from the context it was the reputed date believed in by Eleazar and the Zealots, who opened the temple gates on the fourteenth of Xanthicus so that those citizens who desired could worship in the temple on that day. Josephus is explaining that the Zealots believed the fourteenth of Xanthicus was the anniversary of the Jews' first liberation from Egypt. The two dates given by Josephus for the first day of the Feast of Unleavened Bread therefore result from the use of two different calendars.

It is interesting to note that, for different reasons, the Jewish historian Cecil Roth suggested that the Zealots used a different calendar from the official one. He writes: 'On Passover 68, for example, they [the Zealots] made an attack on Engedi, midway between Masadah and Qumran. Josephus denounces their impiety in taking military action on the holy day: but, if it is true that the Zealots followed a different religious calendar from that of normative Judaism, it may well be that they themselves observed the feast on some other date' ('The Zealots in the War of 66–73', *J. Semitic Studies* 4 (1959), 347–8). Roth is making the very good point that a Jewish group would never launch an attack on Passover day, a day of rest, a special Sabbath. Hence if they did launch an attack on this day then it could not have been *their* Passover day: they must have been using a different calendar. Later in the same article (p. 351), and referring to the Jewish groups fighting over the temple in

AD 70, Roth states: 'As Jews at this time would have refrained from offensive hostilities especially against fellow-Jews on a holy day, there may have been on this occasion, too, a difference of calendar between the two factions.'

28. *Anchor Bible Dictionary*, vol. II, p. 899 states: 'Galilee does not feature prominently in the Jewish sources ... In the Mishnah it functions for the most part as a separate region from Judea.'
29. Mishnah Pesahim 4.5.
30. Darrell C. Bock and Gregory J. Herrick, *Jesus in Context* (Grand Rapids: Baker Academic, 2005), p. 238.
31. Harold W. Hoehner, *Chronological Aspects of the Life of Christ* (Grand Rapids: Zondervan, 1977), p. 88.
32. If some Galilean Jews used a different lunar calendar from Judean Jews to celebrate Passover, they would have had to determine when their lunar month started. The only plausible option was to look for the last visibility of the old lunar crescent, and to take the next day, the day of first invisibility of the moon, to be the first day of the month (the true new moon: the day of conjunction). This results in the pre-exilic calendar, and not the simple twelve-hour shift suggested by Hoehner. In addition, Galilean Jews may have used the pre-exilic calendar since the time of Joshua. If so, observing the first invisibility of the old lunar crescent would have been well established in their tradition.

11 THE DATE OF THE LAST SUPPER: THE HIDDEN CLUES IN THE GOSPELS

1. Rudolf Bultmann, *History of the Synoptic Tradition*, revised edition (New York: Harper and Row, 1976), p. 265.
2. Joachim Jeremias, *The Eucharistic Words of Jesus*, trans. Norman Perrin (London: SCM Press, 1966), p. 18.
3. Mishnah *Pesahim* 1: 1–3.
4. R. T. France, *The Gospel of Mark* (Grand Rapids: Eerdmans, 2002), pp. 563–4.
5. Harold W. Hoehner, *Chronological Aspects of the Life of Christ* (Grand Rapids: Zondervan, 1977), pp. 85–90. It seems to be a widespread belief that a lunar calendar based on observing the new moon is compatible with a sunrise-to-sunrise day. For example, Kenneth Doig writes: 'The Exodus calendar was a lunar calendar with the months beginning with the sunrise following the first observation of the new crescent moon' (*New Testament Chronology* (Lewiston: Edwin Mellen Press, 1990), p. 5). This is fundamentally wrong. As we have seen, the new crescent moon is

only visible in the *evening* sky shortly after sunset and therefore the day starts in the evening.

Howard Marshall, *Last Supper and Lord's Supper* (Exeter: Paternoster Press, 1980), pp. 71–5, describes different calendar theories by Hoehner and others. Hoehner recognises that Mark 14:12 implies that Jesus must have used a calendar having a sunrise-to-sunrise day. However Hoehner assumes Jesus used a new-crescent-moon calendar. Some other scholars (including Calvin, Pickl, Chwolson and Billerbeck) have related theories (see references in *Last Supper and Lord's Supper* by Marshall).

Hoehner, and those with similar theories, I believe correctly argue that Jesus used a calendar with a sunrise-to-sunrise day for his last supper, but they then assume he used a lunar calendar based on observing the new crescent moon. Astronomical considerations rule out all such theories. There is no known calendar in the ancient world based on observing the new crescent moon which has a sunrise-to-sunrise day.

6. I. Howard Marshall, *The Gospel of Luke: A Commentary on the Greek Text* (Exeter: Paternoster Press, 1978), p. 792.
7. B. Pixner, *Wege des Messias und Stätten der Urkirche*, ed. R. Riesner (Giesen and Basel: Brunnen Verlag, 1991), pp. 219–21. See further B. J. Capper, '"With the Oldest Monks . . ." Light from Essene History on the Career of the Beloved Disciple?', *Journal of Theological Studies* 49 (1998), 1–55.
8. Joseph Ratzinger, Pope Benedict XVI, *Jesus of Nazareth*, trans. Adrian J. Walker (London: Bloomsbury, 2007), pp. 3–6. The Pope writes powerfully here on Jesus as the new Moses.
9. The calculations of Waddington show that for an observer in Jerusalem for the period 500 BC to AD 100, the period of lunar invisibility was 36 hours in 1 per cent of cases, 60 hours in 51 per cent, 84 hours in 47 per cent and 108 hours in 1 per cent. (I asked Waddington to perform these calculations for an observer in *Jerusalem*. The previous similar calculations by Parker mentioned in Chapter 8 were for an observer in Egypt. Differences between the two locations can be significant.) The period of invisibility runs from the last sighting of the morning lunar crescent prior to conjunction (last visibility) to the first sighting of the lunar crescent in the evening after conjunction (first visibility). It is important to note that this is not the same as the difference between an Egyptian-style lunar calendar and the official Jewish calendar, since the first day of the month in the Egyptian calendar is the day of the first morning when the moon could not be seen, and so a day (twenty-four hours) after the day of last visibility. Hence the period between the morning of first invisibility and the evening of first visibility is twenty-four hours shorter than the period of invisibility itself.

10. It is possible that John intended 'the Passover' in John 12:1 to refer to the Passover sacrifice. If so, the Triumphal Entry would have been on Sunday and the withering of the fig-tree on Tuesday. This would still rule out a last supper on Monday.
11. The Tosefta *Pesahim* supplements the teaching in the Mishnah about the Passover and it contains a section concerning Passover sacrifices performed at the wrong time which states: 'The Passover which is slaughtered on the morning of the 14th [of Nisan] not under its [proper] designation ["under some other name"]: Rabbi Joshua validates [it], *like those [offered by people who say that Passover can] be slaughtered on the 13th*' (Tosefta *Pesahim* 4.8). This passage seems to indicate that some people presented Passover lambs before the official time under different names (Maurice Casey, 'The Date of the Passover Sacrifices and Mark 14:12', *Tyndale Bulletin* 48 (1997), 245). David Instone-Brewer writes of this passage: 'Some people were bringing Passover offerings before the normal time on the assumption that this was allowed by Torah' (David Instone-Brewer, to be published as *Traditions of the Rabbis from the Era of the New Testament*, vol. IIA, Grand Rapids: Eerdmans). Who were these people? Presumably not orthodox Jews, who would have sacrificed their lambs on Nisan 14. If Passover lambs were sacrificed by people using the pre-exilic calendar, this would have occurred on Nisan 14 in that calendar, which was on Nisan 13 in the official calendar in the majority of years, as our reconstructed pre-exilic calendar shows. I therefore suggest that it may have been those using the pre-exilic calendar that gave rise to the rabbinical discussions of whether it was permissible to sacrifice Passover lambs in the temple on Nisan 13.

12 FROM THE LAST SUPPER TO THE CRUCIFIXION: A NEW ANALYSIS OF THE GOSPEL ACCOUNTS

1. *Anchor Bible Dictionary*, vol. IV, p. 871.
2. John A. T. Robinson, *The Priority of John* (London: SCM Press, 1985), p. 251.
3. Geza Vermes, *The Passion* (London: Penguin, 2005), pp. 20, 21, 24, 111.
4. J. B. Segal, *The Hebrew Passover: From the Earliest Times to AD 70* (Oxford: Oxford University Press, 1963), pp. 37–9.

5. Emil G. Hirsch in *The Jewish Encyclopedia*, ed. Isidore Singer, 12 vols. (New York: Funk and Wagnalls, 1901–5), vol. IX, p. 553, states that the Sadducees and the Samaritans slaughtered the lamb between sunset and darkness. *Targum Onkelos* is rendered 'between the two evenings' and in Exodus 12:6 as 'between the two suns', and this was then explained as meaning the time between sunset and the coming out of the stars (see Jack Finegan, *Handbook of Biblical Chronology*, revised edition (Peabody, MA: Hendrickson, 1998), p. 12; S. R. Driver, *The Book of the Exodus* (Cambridge: Cambridge University Press, 1911), p. 89n).
6. I am grateful to Graeme Waddington for this calculation.
7. Cornelis Houtman, *Exodus*, 2 vols. (Kampen: Kok Publishing, 1996), vol. II, p. 183. Earlier, on pp. 177–8, Houtman mentions a time of about three hours for the roasting itself.
8. Houtman, *Exodus*, vol. II, p. 181.
9. Joachim Jeremias, *The Eucharistic Words of Jesus*, trans. Norman Perrin (London: SCM Press, 1966), p. 46.
10. F. F. Bruce, *The Gospel of John* (Grand Rapids: Eerdmans, 1983), p. 339.
11. Bruce, *The Gospel of John*, p. 343.
12. Raymond E. Brown, *The Death of the Messiah*, 2 vols. (New York: Doubleday, 1994), vol. I, p. 405. Brown points out that Josephus still calls Annas high priest at the end of Caiaphas' reign. The power Annas had can be deduced from the fact that, in the fifty years following his deposition as high priest in AD 15, five of his sons became high priests, which Josephus states is something which had never happened before in Jewish history (*Antiquities* 20.198), as well as a son-in-law and a grandson. In addition, as Howard Marshall points out, the retired priest kept his title, rather like some retired professors (I. Howard Marshall, *The Gospel of Luke* (Exeter: Paternoster Press, 1978), p. 134).
13. Brown, *The Death of the Messiah*, vol. I, p. 405.
14. For example, France argues that the reference in Mark to two cock crows is genuine and that Mark is preserving the account in its fullest and most detailed form (R. T. France, *The Gospel of Mark* (Grand Rapids: Eerdmans, 2002), p. 579). Brown also argues that the reference in Mark to two cock crows is original (Brown, *The Death of the Messiah*, vol. I, p. 137).
15. All four gospels agree on the location of Peter when he denied Jesus three times: he was 'in the courtyard of the high priest' (Matthew 26:58; Mark 14:54; Luke 22:55; John 18:15). However, we have the ambiguity referred to earlier as to whether the high priest referred to here was the official high priest at the time, Caiaphas, or the effective high priest, Annas.

    Matthew writes: 'Those who had arrested Jesus took him to Caiaphas, the high priest … But Peter followed him at a distance, right up to the courtyard of the high priest' (Matthew 26:57–58). The natural reading of Matthew is that Peter was in the courtyard of Caiaphas. Mark and Luke do not name the high priest in their accounts. John writes: 'They brought him [Jesus] first to Annas, who was the father-in-law of Caiaphas, the high priest that year ... Simon Peter and another disciple were following Jesus. Because this disciple was known to the high priest, he went with Jesus into the high priest's courtyard ... spoke to the girl on duty there and brought Peter in' (John 18:13–16). The natural reading of John is that Peter was in the courtyard of the high priest Caiaphas, because John had just referred to Caiaphas as the high priest. If this is correct, then Matthew and John agree: the interrogation of Jesus by Annas was in the palace of Caiaphas and Peter was outside in the courtyard. Some commentators do not agree. For example, Bruce writes that the interrogation of Jesus was 'in the house of Annas' (Bruce, *The Gospel of John*, p. 344), yet John writes that Jesus was brought to Annas, not to the house of Annas. However, this is a minor detail compared with the rest of the story.

Josephus says that the house of the high priest was in the Upper City (*War* 2.427) on the west side of Jerusalem. There are several traditional sites and we do not know if any of them is correct. However, they are all large buildings with a central courtyard. I suggest that Jesus was taken to the palace of Caiaphas and that Annas used one of the rooms in this palace to interrogate Jesus. Whether or not Annas also lived in this palace, he would have been familiar with it because his daughter, who was married to Caiaphas, lived there. While Annas was interrogating Jesus in one wing of the palace, Caiaphas was assembling the Sanhedrin and witnesses in the other wing, ready for the daytime trial by the Sanhedrin, which Annas would no doubt have attended. It therefore made sense for Annas to be 'on site'. If my interpretation is correct, when Jesus was transferred bound from Annas to Caiaphas he would have been led from one wing of the palace, across the courtyard, where he looked at Peter (Luke 22:61), to the wing where Caiaphas was. If the interpretation of Bruce and some other scholars is correct, then Jesus was transferred from the house of Annas to the palace of Caiaphas.

16. The reason given is that cocks scratch the ground and pick up objects that are levitically unclean, and are thus likely to spread uncleanness (Baba Kam, 826).
17. Mishnah *Sukkah* 5.4 states: 'When the cock crowed they sounded a sustained, a quavering and a sustained note on the shofar.' Mishnah *Tamid* 1.2 states: 'Sometimes he [the superintendent] comes at cock crow.' Mishnah *Yoma* 1.8 has: 'Every day they take up the ashes from

the altar at the cock's crow or near it ... and never did the cock crow before the courtyard was filled with masses of Israelites.'

18. See France, *The Gospel of Mark*, p. 578 and Brown, *The Death of the Messiah*, vol. 1, p. 607.
19. For example, France, *The Gospel of Mark*, p. 579, and Brown, *The Death of the Messiah*, vol. 1, p. 606.
20. Jack Finegan, *The Archaeology of the New Testament* (Princeton: Princeton University Press, 1978), pp. 152–4.
21. The use of puns by Jesus is often not evident in English translations of the Bible. Perhaps the best-known pun is: 'You are Peter, and on this rock I will build my church' (Matthew 16:18). In Greek, Peter is *petros* and rock is *petra*. In Aramaic the pun is even clearer since the same word *kepha* is used for both. (For examples of other puns of Jesus see Robert H. Stein, *The Method and Message of Jesus' Teachings*, revised edition (Louisville: Westminster John Knox Press, 1995), pp. 12–14.)
22. Richard Bauckham, *Jesus and the Eyewitnesses* (Grand Rapids: Eerdmans, 2006), p. 342. Bauckman states: '*Vivid imagery*. Where it is found, this is particularly characteristic of Mark, and it is significant that in Matthew and Lukan parallels to this material the vivid imagery is usually not present (e.g. Mark 2:4; 4:37–38; 6:39–40; 7:33–34; 9:20; 10:32, 50; 11:4). The reason is that Matthew and Luke tell these stories much more concisely than Mark does (Matthew generally more so than Luke). Vivid detail is among the features that have to be dropped to make space for all the non-Markan material that both Matthew and Luke include in their Gospels. This is a simple matter of space, since both were attempting a much more comprehensive collection of Jesus traditions than Mark's, but needed to keep within the limit of the ordinary size of a papyrus scroll if their books were not to be prohibitively expensive to copy and use.'
23. In Luke, the three denials by Peter (Luke 22:54–62) precede the main daytime trial of Jesus before Caiaphas and the Sanhedrin (Luke 22:66–71). John interweaves his account of the interrogation by Annas with the denials: Jesus is taken to Annas (John 18:12–14), then Peter denies Jesus (John 18:15–18); meanwhile Jesus is interrogated by Annas, who then sends him to Caiaphas (John 18:19–24); John then returns to reporting the second and third denials of Peter and the cock crow (John 18:25–27). Luke pointedly states immediately following the final denial and cock crow that, 'The Lord turned and looked straight at Peter' (Luke 22:61). It would seem that this must have been when Annas had finished his interrogation, and Jesus was being led from Annas across the courtyard to Caiaphas. Hence I conclude that John 18:25–27 is not meant to be read later in time than John 18:19–24, but

is a continuation of relating the three denials of Peter during the interrogation by Annas.

24. Bauckham (*Jesus and the Eyewitnesses*, pp. 12–14) writes that Papias, the Bishop of Hierapolis, was collecting oral reports about Jesus in about 80 AD, which was after the time when Mark was written but probably around the time that Matthew, Luke and John were being written. Papias then wrote a major five-volume history of Jesus some time near the beginning of the second century, which unfortunately has not survived, but from which later writers have quoted. The church historian Eusebius quotes Papias as follows: 'Mark, in his capacity as Peter's interpreter, wrote down accurately as many things as he [Peter?] recalled from memory – *though not in an ordered form* [my italics] – of the things either said or done by the Lord' (Bauckham, *Jesus and the Eyewitnesses*, p. 203). As Bauckham says (p. 217), according to Papias, Mark transcribed the words of Peter about the life and sayings of Jesus accurately, but not in order, and by order Papias meant chronological order (p. 221).
25. Vermes, *The Passion*, p. 46.
26. A. E. J. Rawlinson, *The Gospel According to St Mark*, sixth edition (London: Methuen, 1947), p. 223.
27. France, *The Gospel of Mark*, p. 626.
28. Some scholars may object to my analysis, arguing that there was only one Sanhedrin trial and not two. Such scholars would argue that Luke 22:66–71, my first Sanhedrin trial at daybreak, is in parallel with Matthew 27:1 and Mark 15:1, my second trial at daybreak, and that all three gospels are reporting one and the same trial. I disagree for the following reasons. Luke 22:67 reports the Sanhedrin asking Jesus if he was the Christ, which is in parallel with Matthew 26:63 and Mark 14:61. Luke 22:68 then reports Jesus replying that he will be seated at the right hand of God, in parallel with Matthew 26:64 and Mark 14:62. Luke 22:71 further reports the Sanhedrin asking 'Why do we need any more testimony?' This is in parallel with Matthew 26:65 and Mark 14:63. Hence Luke 22:66–71 is in parallel with Matthew 26:57–66 and Mark 14:53–64, and not with Matthew 27:1 and Mark 15:1.

    Matthew 26:57–66 and the parallel Mark 14:53–64 describe a trial by the Sanhedrin which comes to a clear end. Mark 14:64 states: 'They all condemned him as worthy of death', and Matthew 26:66 repeats this. The trial has finished and the death sentence has been passed. Immediately following sentencing, Jesus is handed over to the guards, who beat him (Mark 14:65). Matthew and Mark then separate this trial from a second Sanhedrin trial by placing the denials by Peter between the two trials (Matthew 26:69–75; Mark 14:66–72). Although I have argued that these denials by Peter are not narrated in their strict chronological position by Matthew and Mark, nevertheless in Matthew and Mark they serve to separate the two trials by the Sanhedrin, and Matthew and Mark use them in this way.

Mark 15:1 and Matthew 27:1 then describe how the Sanhedrin met very early in the morning and reached a decision. R. T. France states that they met 'to ratify formally the result of the night's proceedings' (France, *The Gospel of Mark*, p. 627). However, according to Luke, the first trial had started at daybreak and was not at night (Luke 22:66). Mark and Matthew are describing here, in only one sentence, a short Sanhedrin trial, at daybreak, confirming the decision of the main Sanhedrin trial, which also started at daybreak. Since both trials started at daybreak, the two trials were necessarily on successive days.

29. Talmud Jerusalem *Sanhedrin* 180 and 246 (related to Mishnah *Sanhedrin* 1.1 and 7.2), see Brown, *The Death of the Messiah*, vol. 1, p. 365.
30. Bruce, *The Gospel of John*, p. 349.
31. Bruce W. Winter, 'Official Proceedings and the Forensic Speeches in Acts 24–26', in *The Book of Acts in its First Century Setting*, vol. 1: *Ancient Literature Setting*, ed. Bruce W. Winter and Andrew D. Clarke (Grand Rapids: Eerdmans, 1993), pp. 305–37.
32. Bruce, *The Gospel of John*, p. 364 states: 'As for the time of day, it was getting on towards noon ... No evidence is forthcoming that at this time, whether among Romans, Greeks or Jews, hours were ever reckoned otherwise than from sunrise.' Although in daily life hours were counted from sunrise, for legal purposes Romans counted from midnight. Pliny, *Natural History*, 2.79.188 states: 'The Roman priests and the authorities who fixed the official day [reckon the hours of the day from] the period from midnight to midnight.' The appropriate form of time reckoning for Romans to use when pronouncing a legal sentence would have been official Roman time starting at midnight, hence this would have been the time system Pilate used when sentencing Jesus at the about sixth hour, i.e. at about 6 a.m.

13 A NEW RECONSTRUCTION OF THE FINAL DAYS OF JESUS

1. Judith C. S. Redman, 'How Accurate Are Eyewitnesses? Bauckham and the Eyewitnesses in the Light of Psychological Research', *Journal of Biblical Literature* 129 (2010), 177–97, at 177.
2. Geza Vermes, *The Passion* (London: Penguin, 2005), p. 2.

Bibliography

Abegg, Martin G., 'Does Anyone Really Know What Time It Is: A Reexamination of 4Q503 in Light of 4Q317', in *The Provo International Conference on the Dead Sea Scrolls*, ed. D. W. Parry and E. Ulrich, Leiden: Brill, 1999, 396–406.

Ahlström, G. W., 'The Origin of Israel in Palestine', *Scandinavian Journal of the Old Testament* 2 (1991), 19–34.

The Anchor Bible Dictionary, ed. D. N. Freedman, 6 vols. New York: Doubleday, 1992.

Anderson, Paul N., Just, Felix and Thatcher, Tom (eds.), *John, Jesus and History*, vol. II: *Aspects of Historicity in the Fourth Gospel*, Atlanta: Society of Biblical Literature, 2009.

Barrett, C. K., *The Acts of the Apostles: A Shorter Commentary*, London and New York: T&T Clark, 2002.

The Gospel According to John: An Introduction with Commentary and Notes on the Greek Text, second edition, Philadelphia: Westminster, 1978.

Bauckham, Richard, *Jesus and the Eyewitnesses*, Grand Rapids: Eerdmans, 2006.

Beckwith, Roger T., *Calendar and Chronology, Jewish and Christian: Biblical, Intertestamental and Patristic Studies*, Leiden: Brill, 2001.

Bickerman, E. J., *Chronology of the Ancient World*, revised edition London: Thames and Hudson, 1980.

Black, M., VanderKam, J. C. and Neugebauer, O., *The Book of Enoch: A New English Edition*, Leiden: Brill, 1985.

Blinzler, Josef, *Der Prozess Jesu*, fourth edition, Regensburg: Pustet, 1969.

Blomberg, Craig L., *The Historical Reliability of John's Gospel*, Leicester: Inter-Varsity Press, 2001.

Bock, Darrell L. and Herrick, Gregory J., *Jesus in Context*, Grand Rapids: Baker Academic, 2005.

Bockmuehl, Marcus (ed.), *The Cambridge Companion to Jesus*, Cambridge: Cambridge University Press, 2001.

Borg, Marcus J. and Crossan, John Dominic, *The Last Week: What the Gospels Really Teach about Jesus's Final Days in Jerusalem*, San Francisco: Harper San Francisco, 2006.

Brown, Raymond E., *The Death of the Messiah*, 2 vols. New York: Doubleday, 1994.

Brown, Robert Hanbury, *The Land of Goshen and the Exodus*, London: E. Stanford, 1919.

Bruce, F. F., *The Acts of the Apostles*, Leicester: Inter-Varsity Press, 1952.

The Book of the Acts, revised edition, Grand Rapids: Eerdmans, 1988.

The Gospel of John, Grand Rapids: Eerdmans, 1983.

Brugsch, Heinrich, *Matériaux pour servir à la reconstruction du calendrier des anciens égyptiens*, Leipzig: J. C. Hinrichs, 1864.

Bultmann, Rudolf, *History of the Synoptic Tradition*, revised edition, New York: Harper and Row, 1976.

Burnett, A., Amandry, M. and Ripollès, P. P., *Roman Provincial Coinage*, vol. I: *From the Death of Caesar to the Death of Vitellius (44 BC–AD 69)*, London: British Museum Press, 1992.

Capper, B. J., '"With the Oldest Monks . . ." Light from Essene History on the Career of the Beloved Disciple?', *Journal of Theological Studies* 49 (1998), 1–55.

Carson, D. A., *The Gospel According to John*, Leicester: Inter-Varsity Press; Grand Rapids: Eerdmans, 1991.

Casey, Maurice, 'The Date of the Passover Sacrifices and Mark 14:12', *Tyndale Bulletin* 48 (1997), 245–7.

Charlesworth, J. H. (ed.), *The Old Testament Pseudepigrapha*, 2 vols., London: Darton, Longman and Todd, 1983.

Clagett, Marshall, *Ancient Egyptian Science*, 3 vols. Philadelphia: American Philosophical Society, 1995, vol. II: *Calendars, Clocks and Astronomy*.

Cohen, Mark E., *The Cultic Calendars of the Ancient Near East*, Bethesda, MD: CDL Press, 1993.

Collins, Nina L., 'The Start of the Pre-Exilic Calendar Day of David and the Amalekites: A Note on 1 Samuel xxx 17', *Vetus Testamentum* 41 (1991), 203–10.

Cooke, G. A., *The Book of Ezekiel*, Edinburgh: T&T Clark, 1936.

Davidson, Norman, *Astronomy and the Imagination: A New Approach to Man's Experience of the Stars*, London and New York: Routledge and Kegan Paul, 1985.

Dawkins, Richard, *The God Delusion*, London: Transworld Publishers, 2006.

Depuydt, Leo, *Civil Calendar and Lunar Calendar in Ancient Egypt*, Leuven: Peeters, 1997.

Doig, Kenneth, *New Testament Chronology*, Lewiston: Edwin Mellen Press, 1990.

Driver, S. R., *The Book of the Exodus*, Cambridge: Cambridge University Press, 1911.

Edwards, Ormond, *The Time of Christ: A Chronology of the Incarnation*, Edinburgh: Floris Books, 1986.

Faulkner, R. O., *The Ancient Egyptian Coffin Texts*, 3 vols., Oxford: Aris and Phillips, 1973.

Finegan, Jack, *The Archaeology of the New Testament*, Princeton: Princeton University Press, 1978.

Handbook of Biblical Chronology, revised edition, Peabody, MA: Hendrickson, 1998.

Fotheringham, J. K., 'The Evidence of Astronomy and Technical Chronology for the Date of the Crucifixion', *Journal of Theological Studies* 34 (1934), 146–62.

France, R. T., *The Gospel of Mark*, Grand Rapids: Eerdmans; Carlisle: Paternoster, 2002.

Freyne, Sean, *Galilee*, Edinburgh: T&T Clark, 1980.

Gibson, Shimon, *The Final Days of Jesus: The Archaeological Evidence*, New York: HarperOne, 2009.

Hall, Bruce, 'From John Hyrcanus to Baba Rabbah', in *The Samaritans*, ed. Alan D. Crown, Tübingen: Mohr Siebeck, 1989, 32–54.

Hirsch, Emil G., in *The Jewish Encyclopedia*, ed. Isidore Singer, 12 vols., New York: Funk and Wagnalls, 1901–5, vol. IX, 553.

Hoehner, Harold W., *Chronological Aspects of the Life of Christ*, Grand Rapids: Zondervan, 1977.

Horowitz, Wayne, 'The 360 and 364 Day Year in Ancient Mesopotamia', *Journal of the Ancient Near Eastern Society* 24 (1996), 35–42.

Houtman, Cornelis, *Exodus*, 2 vols. Kampen: Kok Publishing, 1996.

Howie, Carl G., *Ezekiel, Daniel*, Westminster: John Knox, 1961.

Humphreys, Colin J., *The Miracles of Exodus*, San Francisco: Harper San Francisco; London: Continuum, 2003.

'The Star of Bethlehem – a Comet in 5 BC – and the Date of the Birth of Christ', *Quarterly Journal of the Royal Astronomical Society* 32 (1991), 389–407.

'The Star of Bethlehem, a Comet in 5 BC and the Date of Christ's Birth', *Tyndale Bulletin* 43.1 (1992), 31–56.

Humphreys, Colin J. and Waddington, W. G., 'Astronomy and the Date of the Crucifixion', in *Chronos, Kairos, Christos: Nativity and Chronological Studies Presented to Jack Finegan*, ed. Jerry Vardaman and Edwin Yamauchi, Winona Lake: Eisenbrauns, 1989, 165–81.

'Dating the Crucifixion', *Nature* 306 (1983), 743–6.

Hyatt, J. Philip, *Commentary on Exodus*, Grand Rapids: Eerdmans, 1980.

Instone-Brewer, David, *Traditions of the Rabbis from the Era of the New Testament*, vol. IIA, Grand Rapids: Eerdmans, forthcoming.

Isaac, E., '1 Enoch: A New Translation and Introduction', in *The Old Testament Pseudepigrapha*, ed. J. H. Charlesworth, London: Darton, Longman and Todd, 1983, vol. I, 5–89.

James, M. R., *The Apocryphal New Testament*, Oxford: Oxford University Press, 1924.

Jaubert, Annie, *La date de la cène*, EBib; Paris: Gabalda, 1957. Trans. Isaac Rafferty, *The Date of the Last Supper*, Staten Island, NY: Alba House, 1965.

Jeremias, Joachim, *The Eucharistic Words of Jesus*, trans. Norman Perrin, London: SCM Press, 1966.

Jerusalem in the Time of Jesus, London: SCM Press, 1969.

Die Passahfeier der Samaritanar, Giessen: Töpelmann, 1932.

Jewett, Robert, *Dating Paul's Life*, London: SCM Press, 1979.

Josephus, *Jewish Antiquities*, trans. Louis H. Feldman, Loeb Classical Library, Cambridge, MA: Harvard University Press, 1965.

The Jewish War, trans. H. St. J. Thackeray, Loeb Classical Library, Cambridge, MA: Harvard University Press, 1927.

Keil, C. F., *Biblical Commentary on the Prophecies of Ezekiel*, 2 vols., Edinburgh: T&T Clark, 1876.

Kitchen, K. A., *On the Reliability of the Old Testament*, Grand Rapids: Eerdmans, 2003.

Kokkinos, Nikos, 'Crucifixion in AD 36', in *Chronos, Kairos, Christos: Nativity and Chronological Studies Presented to Jack Finegan*, ed. Jerry Vardaman and Edwin Yamauchi, Winona Lake: Eisenbrauns, 1989, 133–63.

Lane Fox, Robin, *The Unauthorised Version: Truth, and Fiction in the Bible*, London: Viking, 1991.

Magness, Jodi, *The Archaeology of Qumran and the Dead Sea Scrolls*, Grand Rapids: Eerdmans, 2002.

Maier, Paul L., 'The Date of the Nativity and the Chronology of Jesus' Life', in *Chronos, Kairos, Christos: Nativity and Chronological Studies Presented to Jack Finegan*, ed. Jerry Vardaman and Edwin Yamauchi, Winona Lake: Eisenbrauns, 1989, 113–30.

Marshall, I. Howard, *The Gospel of Luke: A Commentary on the Greek Text*, Exeter: Paternoster Press, 1978.

'The Last Supper', in *Key Events in the Life of the Historical Jesus: A Collaborative Exploration of Context and Coherence*, ed. D. L. Bock and R. L. Webb, Tübingen: Mohr Siebeck, 2009, 481–588.

Last Supper and Lord's Supper, Exeter: Paternoster Press, 1980.

Meier, John P., *A Marginal Jew: Rethinking the Historical Jesus*, vol. I: *The Roots of the Problem and the Person*, New York: Doubleday, 1991.

Millard, Alan R., 'How Reliable Is Exodus?', *Biblical Archaeology Review* 26.4 (2000), 51–7.

Mor, Menachem, 'The Persian, Hellenistic and Hasmonaean Period', in *The Samaritans*, ed. Alan D. Crown, Tübingen: Mohr Siebeck, 1989, 1–18.

'The Samaritans and the Bar-Kokhbah Revolt', in *The Samaritans*, ed. Alan D. Crown, Tübingen: Mohr Siebeck, 1989, 19–31.

Neil, William, *The Acts of the Apostles*, London: Oliphants, 1973.

Neugebauer, Otto, *A History of Ancient Mathematical Astronomy*, 3 vols., Berlin: Springer, 1975.

NIV (New International Version) Study Bible, London: Hodder and Stoughton, 1987.

Parker, Richard A., *The Calendars of Ancient Egypt*, Chicago: University of Chicago Press, 1950.

Pearce, E. A. and Smith, C. G., *The Hutchison World Weather Guide*, Oxford: Helicon, 2000.

Pixner, B., *Wege des Messias und Statten der Urkirche*, ed. R. Riesner, Giesen and Basle: Brunnen Verlag, 1991.

Pliny, *Natural History*, trans. H. Rackham, Loeb Classical Library, Cambridge, MA: Harvard University Press, 1940.

Powels, Sylvia, 'The Samaritan Calendar and the Roots of Samaritan Chronology', in *The Samaritans*, ed. Alan D. Crown, Tübingen: Mohr Siebeck, 1989, 691–742.

Pritchard, J. B. (ed.), *Ancient Near Eastern Texts Relating to the Old Testament*, third edition, Princeton: Princeton University Press, 1969.

Pummer, Reinhard, 'Samaritan Rituals and Customs', in *The Samaritans*, ed. Alan D. Crown, Tübingen: Mohr Siebeck, 1989, 650–90.

Pusey, P. E., *Cyrilli Archiepiscopi Alexandrini In XII Prophetas* (1868), cited by G. R. Driver, 'Two Problems in the New Testament', *Journal of Theological Studies* 16 (1965), 334–5.

Ratzinger, Joseph (Pope Benedict XVI), *Jesus of Nazareth*, trans. Adrian J. Walker, London: Bloomsbury, 2007.

Rawlinson, A. E. J., *The Gospel According to St Mark*, sixth edition, London: Methuen, 1947.

Redman, Judith C. S., 'How Accurate Are Eyewitnesses? Bauckham and the Eyewitnesses in the Light of Psychological Research', *Journal of Biblical Literature* 129 (2010), 177–97.

Reicke, Bo, *The New Testament Era: The World of the Bible from 500 BC to AD 100*, trans. David E. Green, London: A. & C. Black, 1968.

Riesner, Rainer, *Paul's Early Period: Chronology, Mission Strategy, Theology*, Grand Rapids: Eerdmans, 1998.

Robinson, John A. T., *The Priority of John*, London: SCM Press, 1985.

Roth, Cecil, 'The Zealots in the War of 66–73', *Journal of Semitic Studies* 4 (1959), 343–54.

Sacks, Jonathan, *The Chief Rabbi's Haggadah: Hebrew and English Text with New Essays and Commentary*, London: HarperCollins, 2003.

Sanders, E. P., *The Historical Figure of Jesus*, London: Penguin, 1993.

Jesus and Judaism, London: SCM Press, 1985.

Sarna, Nahum, *Exploring Exodus*, New York: Schocken, 1996.

Schürer, Emil, *The History of the Jewish People in the Age of Jesus Christ: 175 BC – AD 135*, revised edition; vols. I–II, ed. G. Vermes and F. G. B. Millar, with M. Black; and vol. III, ed. with M. Goodman, Edinburgh: T&T Clark, 1973 and 1987.

Segal, J. B., *The Hebrew Passover: From the Earliest Times to AD 70*, London: Oxford University Press, 1963.

Simons, J. J., *Handbook for the Study of Egyptian Topographical Lists Relating to Western Asia*, Leiden: Brill, 1937.

Stein, Robert H., *The Method and Message of Jesus' Teachings*, revised edition, Louisville: Westminster John Knox Press, 1995.

Stephenson, F. Richard, *Historical Eclipses and Earth's Rotation*, Cambridge: Cambridge University Press, 1997.

Stephenson, F. Richard and Clark, David H., *Applications of Early Astronomical Records*, London: Adam Hilger, 1978.

Stern, Sacha, *Calendar and Community: A History of the Jewish Calendar 2nd Century BCE – 10th century CE*, Oxford: Oxford University Press, 2001.

as-Suri, Abu'l-Hasan, 'Kitab al-Tabbakh, Rylands Samaritan Codex IX', *Bulletin of the John Rylands Library* 30 (1946/47), 144–56.

Talmon, Shemaryahu, 'Calendar Controversy in Ancient Judaism: The Case of the Community of the Renewed Covenant', in *The Provo International Conference on the Dead Sea Scrolls*, ed. D. W. Parry and E. Ulrich, Leiden: Brill, 1999, 379–95.

'Divergences in Calendar-Reckoning in Ephraim and Judah', *Vetus Testamentum* 8 (1958), 46–74.

Talmon, S. and Knohl, I., 'A Calendrical Scroll from a Qumran Cave: Mismarot Ba, 4Q321', in *Pomegranates and Golden Bells: Studies in Biblical, Jewish and Near Eastern Ritual, Law and Literature in Honor of Jacob Milgrom*, ed. D. P. Wright, D. N. Freedman and A. Hurvitz, Winona Lake: Eisenbrauns, 1995, 267–302.

Trevor, John C., *The Untold Story of Qumran*, Westwood, NJ: Revell, 1965.

VanderKam, James C. 'Ancient Israelite and Early Jewish Calendars', in *The Anchor Bible Dictionary*, ed. D. N. Freedman, New York: Doubleday (1992), vol. I, 814–20.

VanderKam, James C. and Flint, Peter, *The Meaning of the Dead Sea Scrolls: Their Significance for Understanding the Bible, Judaism, Jesus and Christianity*, London: T&T Clark International, 2002.

Vardaman, Jerry, 'Jesus' Life: A New Chronology', in *Chronos, Kairos, Christos: Nativity and Chronological Studies Presented to Jack Finegan*, ed. Jerry Vardaman and Edwin Yamauchi, Winona Lake: Eisenbrauns, 1989, 55–84.

Vaux, Roland de, *Ancient Israel: Its Life and Institutions*, trans. John McHugh, London: Darton, Longman and Todd, 1961.

Vermes, Geza, *The Passion*, London: Penguin, 2005.

Wacholder, Ben Zion and Weisberg, David B., 'Visibility of the New Moon in Cuneiform and Rabbinic Sources', *Hebrew Union College Annual* 42 (1971), 227–42.

Wagenaar, Jan, 'Passover and the First Day of the Festival of Unleavened Bread in the Priestly Festival Calendar', *Vetus Testamentum* 54 (2004), 250–68.

Wilkinson, John, *Jerusalem as Jesus Knew It*, London: Thames and Hudson, 1978.

Wilson, John, *The Lands of the Bible*, 2 vols., Edinburgh: William Whyte, 1847.

Winter, Bruce, 'Official Proceedings and the Forensic Speeches in Acts 24–26', in *The Book of the Acts in its First Century Setting*, vol. I, ed. Bruce W. Winter and Andrew D. Clarke, Grand Rapids: Eerdmans, 1993, 305–37.

Wintermute, O. S., 'Jubilees: A New Translation and Introduction', in J. H. Charlesworth (ed.), *The Old Testament Pseudepigrapha*, 2 vols., London: Darton, Longman and Todd, 1983, vol. II, 35–142.

Wright, J. Edward, *The Early History of Heaven*, Oxford: Oxford University Press, 2000.

Wright, N. T., *Jesus and the Victory of God*, Minneapolis: Fortress, 1996.

What Saint Paul Really Said, Oxford: Lion, 1997.

Yadin, Y., *The Temple Scroll*, 4 vols., Jerusalem: Israel Exploration Society, 1983.

Zimmerli, Walther, *A Commentary on the Book of the Prophet Ezekiel Chapters 25–48*, trans. James D. Martin, Philadelphia: Fortress Press, 1983.

Index of biblical and other ancient sources

General index

Made in the USA
Lexington, KY
23 April 2011